Combat Studies Institute

Research Survey No. 5

Standing Fast: German Defensive Doctrine on the Russian Front During World War II

Prewar to March 1943

by Major Timothy A. Wray

U.S. Army
Command and General
Staff College
Fort Leavenworth, Kansas 66027-6900

Library of Congress Cataloging-in-Publication Data

Wray, Timothy A. (Timothy Allen), 1949-
  Standing fast.

  (Research survey/Combat Studies Institute; no. 5)
  "September 1986."
  Bibliography: p.
  Contents: Prewar to March 1943.
  1. World War, 1939-1945—Campaigns—Russian
S.F.S.R. 2. Russian S.F.S.R.—History. 3. Germany.
Heer—History—World War, 1939-1945. 4. Defensive
(Military strategy). I. U.S. Army Command and General
Staff College. Combat Studies Institute. II. Title.
III. Series: Research survey (U.S. Army Command and
General Staff College. Combat Studies Institute);
no. 5, etc.
  D764.7.R85W73   1986   940.54'21   86-21554

For sale by the Superintendent of Documents, U.S. Government Printing Office, Washington, D.C. 20402

CONTENTS

Illustrations v
Introduction vii

Chapter

1. The Origins of German Defensive Doctrine 1
   Elastic Defense: Legacy of the Great War 1
   The Final Collapse: Unanswered Questions 6
   German Defensive Doctrine in the Interwar Years 9
   Antitank Defense 16
   Defensive Use of German Tanks 18
   Early Trials: Poland and France 18
   Overview: German Doctrine on the Eve of Barbarossa 20

2. Barbarossa—The German Initiative 23
   The Defensive Aspects of Blitzkrieg 25
   German Strategy Reconsidered 33
   Defense by Army Group Center, July—September 1941 39
   Prelude to Winter 48

3. Winter Battles, 1941—42 57
   Standing Fast 57
   Strongpoint Defense: Origins 68
   Strongpoint Defense: Conduct 76
   The Winter Campaign: Overview and Analysis 89
   German Doctrinal Assessments 98

4. New Victories, New Defeats 109
   Problems on the Defensive Front 111
   The Führer Defense Order of 8 September 1942 118
   Bolstering Combat Manpower 123
   Winter Battles on the Defensive Front 128
   The Offensive Front 135
   German Doctrinal Assessments 166

5. Observations and Conclusions 173

Notes 179

Bibliography 211

ILLUSTRATIONS

Figures

1. The Elastic Defense, 1917–18 4
2. Defense in stabilized and open situations, 1921 11
3. German Elastic Defense, 1933 15
4. German antitank concept 17
5. German *Keil und Kessel* tactics, 1941 26
6. Extended strongpoint 79
7. German squad fighting positions and living bunker 80
8. German strongpoint defense tactics, winter 1941–42 86

Maps

1. Operation Barbarossa German offensive operations, 22 June–25 August 1941 24
2. Soviet counteroffensive against open flank of Army Group North and counterattack by Manstein's panzer corps, 12–22 August 1941 36
3. Situation and revised German strategy, 22 August 1941 (Army Group Center defends in place while flank offensives proceed) ... 38
4. Soviet attacks on Army Group Center, August–September 1941 43
5. Soviet winter counteroffensives, December 1941–March 1942 58
6. Soviet attacks against Army Group Center, December 1941 60
7. Second phase of the Soviet winter counteroffensive, January–March 1942 94
8. Plan Blau and German offensive operations, May–November 1942 110
9. Soviet attacks on Army Groups Center and North, winter 1942–43 133
10. Southern portion of Russian Front, 1 November 1942 141
11. Soviet winter counteroffensive, 19 November–12 December 1942 143

12. German attack to relieve Stalingrad and defensive battles of the XLVIII Panzer Corps on the Chir River, 7—24 December 1942 149

13. Widening Soviet offensive and threat to German southern wing, 16 December 1942—18 January 1943 153

14. Manstein withdraws First and Fourth Panzer Armies from southern wing and counterattacks to recapture Kharkov, January—March 1943 157

15. Situation, spring 1943 165

INTRODUCTION

Correctly foreseeing the nature of a future war is the most critical problem confronting military leaders in peacetime. Effective investments in training, equipment, and weaponry depend on the accuracy with which leaders can, in effect, predict the future. To aid them in their predictions, strategists often attempt to isolate relevant lessons from recent wars to guide them in their decision making.

Within the past several years, Western military analysts have paid new attention to the German Army's defensive battles in Russia during World War II. Much of this interest has had a strongly utilitarian flavor, with writers brandishing Eastern Front examples in support of various doctrinal theories. Unfortunately, however, the general historical understanding of the German war against the Soviet Union is rather limited, and the use of examples from German operations in Russia too often shows a lack of perception either for specific situations or for the "big picture."[1] This lack of insight into German experiences on the Russian Front stems from two historiographical problems.

First, although the Russo-German War was, in fact, the greatest land campaign in World War II, it has remained very much "the forgotten war" to most Western historians and military leaders. In contrast to the rich literature covering the actions of the Western Allies during World War II, few good English-language histories of the war between Russia and Germany exist. Consequently, the existing general histories of this conflict are frequently anecdotal and lack the depth of understanding necessary to allow meaningful analysis.[2]

Second, the shallow knowledge of Western analysts is often based as much on myth as on fact. A major reason for this is that Western knowledge of the Russo-German War has been unduly influenced by the popular memoirs of several prominent German military leaders. While interesting and even instructive to a point, these memoirs suffer from the prejudices, lapses, and wishful remembering common to all memoirs and, therefore, form a precarious foundation on which to build a useful analysis. For example, even though Heinz Guderian's *Panzer Leader* and F. W. von Mellenthin's *Panzer Battles* regularly appear on U.S. Army professional reading lists and contain interesting insights into German military operations, each book paints a somewhat distorted picture of the German war against Russia. These distortions are the result of outright exaggeration and misrepresentation (as is common in Guderian's work) or the omission of important qualifying data and contextual background (as is more often the case in Mellenthin's book).

Particularly misunderstood are the general methods by which the German Army conducted defensive operations against the Soviets. Various Western writers have mistakenly generalized the German defensive system as being a "strongpoint line" backed by powerful mobile reserves or occasionally even a "mobile defense."[3] Likewise, the myth persists that "on a tactical level . . . the Germans consistently stopped the Red Army's local offensive[s]."[4] The strategic defeat of Hitler's armies in Russia is commonly regarded as having been done in spite of this permanent German tactical ascendancy and accomplished by a Red Army that remained throughout the war "a sluggish instrument that depended on numbers of men and tanks to achieve victories."[5] The widespread belief in these myths hampers contemporary analysts in their search for historical lessons and fails to do justice either to the Germans' complex and difficult defensive problems or to the Soviets' tactical skill and adaptability.

This research survey attempts to avoid the common myths about German defensive battles in Russia by relying extensively on primary sources—German after-action reports, unit war diaries, doctrinal manuals, training pamphlets, and various other military memoranda—to reconstruct the actual doctrinal basis for German operations. As will be seen, this archival material, which goes beyond that previously available, provides additional important information about German methods and, in some cases, amends or qualifies the postwar remembrances of German military memoirists. Such memoirs are, of course, invaluable for establishing the state of mind of some of the actors in those historical events and have been used where necessary.

In tracing the development of German defensive doctrine used against the Soviet Red Army, this research survey spans the period from Germany's prewar doctrinal development, which established the initial framework for the defensive battles against the Soviets, through the spring of 1943, when tremendous changes in the overall strategic picture altered the basic nature of the German war against Russia.

In addition to discussing doctrinal methods, this research survey also probes the constraints and circumstances that shaped German battlefield practices. It shows how the evolution of German defensive doctrine was greatly affected by considerations other than mere tactical efficiency. The weather and terrain in Russia, as well as the changes in the strength, leadership, training proficiency, and steadfastness of German units, influenced German defensive methods. Also, battlefield methods were warped by Adolf Hitler's personal interference, as the German dictator periodically ordered the application of his own tactical nostrums.

During the first two years of combat in Russia, the Germans implemented substantial changes to the doctrinal defensive methods described in their prewar manuals. Although these improvisations changed details of the German defensive technique, they remained generally true to the fundamental principles of their doctrine. Therefore, the German experiences on the Eastern Front reveal the detailed evolution of their tactical system and the simplicity and adaptability of the basic German defensive concepts.

Of particular interest to modern readers is the fact that so many of the problems faced by German armies are analogous to problems confronting NATO forces today. In the defense, the German Army on the Eastern Front was hamstrung by a number of political and territorial imperatives that restricted strategic flexibility. German defensive operations were hobbled not only by allies of varying style and ability, but also by large differences in the training, mobility, composition, and combat power of German units as well. The Red Army battled by the Germans in World War II bears a strong resemblance to the current Soviet Army (and its Warsaw Pact siblings) in doctrine, command style, and strategic philosophy. Finally, of course, the German Army fought against an adversary whose preponderance in men and materiel was absolute. While it did not "fight outnumbered and win" by achieving final victory, the German Army waged its defensive battles in Russia with sufficient skill, tenacity, and resourcefulness to merit close scrutiny.

Chapter 1

The Origins of German Defensive Doctrine

In 1941, the German Army's doctrine for defensive operations was nearly identical to that used by the old Imperial German Army in the final years of World War I. The doctrinal practice of German units on the Western Front in 1917 and 1918—the doctrine of elastic defense in depth—had been only slightly amended and updated by the beginning of Operation Barbarossa. In contrast to German offensive doctrine, which from 1919 to 1939 moved toward radical innovation, German defensive doctrine followed a conservative course of cautious adaptation and reaffirmation. Consequently, although the German Army in 1941 embraced an offensive doctrine suited for a war of maneuver, it still hewed to a defensive doctrine derived from the positional warfare (*Stellungskrieg*) of an earlier generation.

Elastic Defense: Legacy of the Great War

The Imperial German Army adopted the elastic defense in depth during the winter of 1916–17 for compelling strategic and tactical reasons. At that time, Germany was locked in a war of attrition against an Allied coalition whose combined resources exceeded those of the Central Powers. The German command team of Field Marshal Paul von Hindenburg and General Erich Ludendorff hoped to break the strategic deadlock by conducting a major offensive on the Russian Front in 1917. Therefore, they needed to economize Germany's strength on the Western Front in France and Belgium, minimizing casualties while repelling expected Allied offensives. To accomplish this, they sanctioned a strategic withdrawal in certain sectors to newly prepared defensive positions. This Hindenburg Line shortened the front and more effectively exploited the defensive advantages of terrain than did earlier positions. This withdrawal was a major departure from prevailing defensive philosophy, which hitherto had measured success in the trench war solely on the basis of seizing and holding terrain. In effect, Ludendorff* adopted a new policy that

---

*Hindenburg and Ludendorff nominally operated according to the dual-responsibilty principle of the German General Staff, whereby the commander and his chief of staff shared responsibility and authority on a nearly equal basis. In practice, Ludendorff's energies were so great that Hindenburg regularly deferred to his judgment. Ludendorff also routinely involved himself in matters of technical detail far beneath the Olympian gaze of Hindenburg. In the matters being discussed, Ludendorff thus played the dominant role at both the strategic and tactical levels.

emphasized conserving German manpower over blindly retaining ground—a strategic philosophy whose tactical component was an elastic defense in depth.

To complement his strategic designs, Ludendorff directed the implementation of the Elastic Defense doctrine.[1] This new doctrine supported the overall strategic goal of minimizing German casualties and also corresponded better than previous methods to the tactical realities of attack and defense in trench warfare.

Through the war's first two years, German (and Allied) doctrinal practice had been to defend every meter of front by concentrating infantry in forward trenches. This prevented any enemy incursion into the German defensive zone but inevitably resulted in heavy losses to defending troops due to Allied artillery fire. Such artillery fire was administered in increasingly massive doses by the Allies, who regarded artillery as absolutely essential for any successful offensive advance. (For example, even the stoutest German trenches had been almost entirely eradicated by the six-day artillery preparation conducted by the British prior to their Somme offensive in 1916.) Consequently, the Germans sought a defensive deployment that would immunize the bulk of their defending forces from the annihilating Allied cannonade.

The simple solution to this problem was to construct the German main defensive line some distance to the rear of a forward security line. Although still within range of Allied guns, the main defensive positions would be masked from direct observation. Fired blindly, most of the Allied preparatory fires would thus be wasted.

General Erich Ludendorff. Ludendorff's sponsorship caused the Elastic Defense to be adopted by the Imperial German Army during the winter of 1916—17

In developing the Elastic Defense doctrine, the Germans analyzed other lessons of trench warfare as well. The German Army had realized that concentrated firepower, rather than a concentration of personnel, was the most effective means of dealing with waves of Allied infantry. Too, the Germans had learned that the ability of attacking forces to sustain their offensive vigor was seriously circumscribed. Casualties, fatigue, and confusion debilitated assaulting infantry, causing the combat power of the attacker steadily to wane as his advance proceeded. This erosion of offensive strength was so certain and predictable that penetrating forces were fatally vulnerable to counterattack—provided, of course, that defensive reserves were available to that end. Finally, the Allied artillery, so devasting when laying prepared fires on observed targets, was far less effective in providing continuous support for advancing infantry because of the difficulty in coordinating such fires in the days before portable wireless communications. Indeed, because the ravaged terrain hindered the timely forward displacement of guns, any successful attack normally forfeited its fire support once it advanced beyond the initial range of friendly artillery.[2]

Between September 1916 and April 1917, the Germans distilled these tactical lessons into a novel defensive doctrine, the Elastic Defense.[3] This doctrine focused on defeating enemy attacks at a minimum loss to defending forces rather than on retaining terrain for the sake of prestige. The Elastic Defense was meant to exhaust Allied offensive energies in a system of fortified trenches arrayed in depth. By fighting the defensive battle within, as well as forward of, the German defensive zone, the Germans could exploit the inherent limitations and vulnerabilities of the attacker while conserving their own forces. Only minimal security forces would occupy exposed forward trenches, and thus, most of the defending troops would be safe from the worst effects of the fulsome Allied artillery preparation. Furthermore, German firepower would continuously weaken the enemy's attacking infantry forces. If faced with overwhelming combat power at any point, German units would be free to maneuver within the defensive network to develop more favorable conditions. When the Allied attack faltered, German units (including carefully husbanded reserves) would counterattack fiercely. Together, these tactics would create a condition of tactical "elasticity": advancing Allied forces would steadily lose strength in inverse proportion to growing German resistance. Finally, German counterattacks would overrun the prostrate Allied infantry and "snap" the defense back into its original positions.

The Germans accomplished this by designating three separate defensive zones—an outpost zone, a battle zone, and a rearward zone (see figure 1). Each zone would consist of a series of interconnected trenches manned by designated units. However, in contrast to the old rigid linear defense that had trenches laid out in parade-ground precision, these zones would be established with a cunning sensitivity to terrain, available forces, and likely enemy action.

The outpost zone was to be manned only in sufficient strength to intercept Allied patrols and to provide continuous observation of Allied positions. When heavy artillery fire announced a major Allied attack, the forces in the outpost zone would move to avoid local artillery concentrations. When Allied infantry approached, the surviving outpost forces would disrupt and delay the enemy advance insofar as possible.

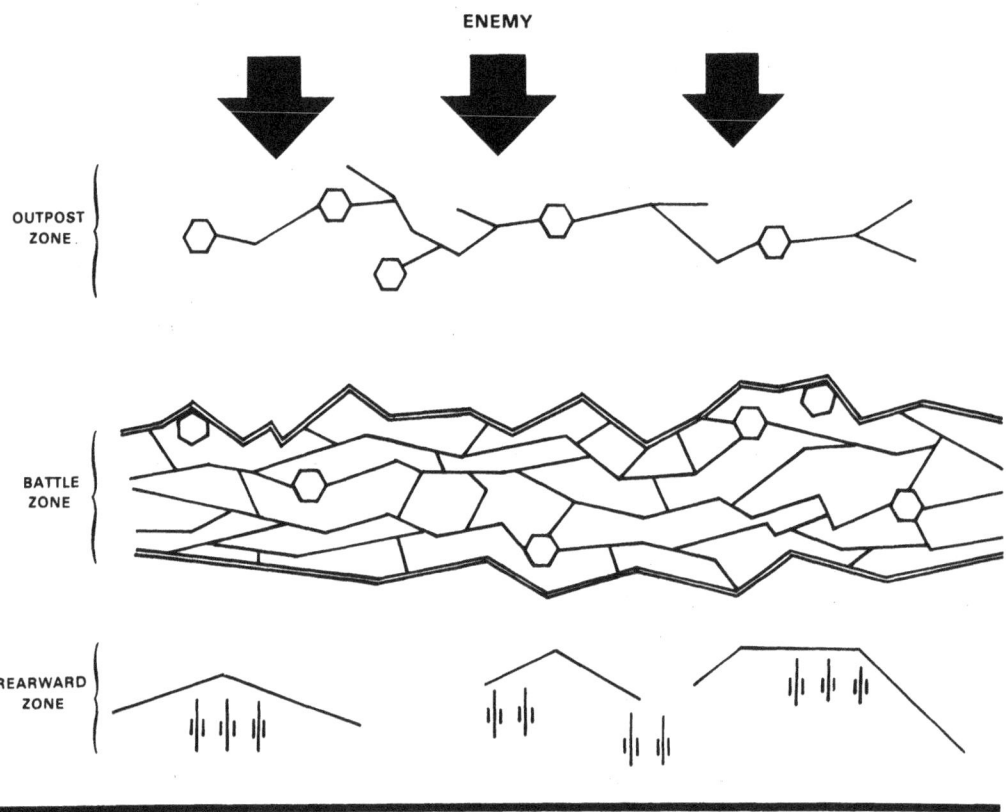

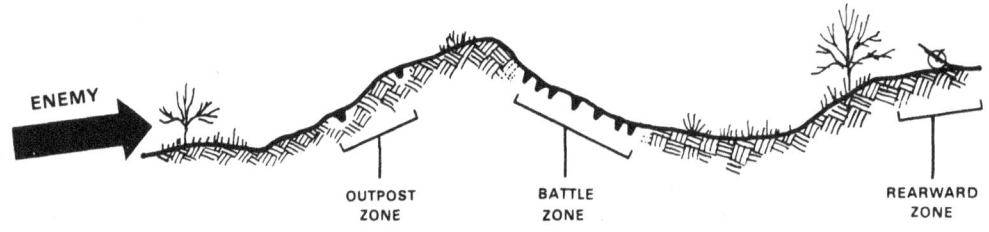

Figure 1. The Elastic Defense, 1917—18

If a determined Allied force advanced through the outpost zone, it was to be arrested and defeated in the battle zone, which was normally 1,500 to 3,000 meters deep. The forward portion of the battle zone, or the main line of resistance, was generally the most heavily garrisoned and, ideally, was masked from enemy ground artillery observation on the reverse slope of hills and ridges. In addition to the normal trenches and dugouts, the battle zone was infested with machine guns and studded with squad-size redoubts capable of all-around defense.

When Allied forces penetrated into the battle zone, they would become bogged down in a series of local engagements against detachments of German troops. These German detachments were free to fight a "mobile defense" within the battle zone, maneuvering as necessary to bring their firepower to bear.[4] When the Allied advance began to founder, these same small detachments, together with tactical reserves held deep in the battle zone, would initiate local counterattacks. If the situation warranted, fresh reserves from beyond the battle zone also would launch immediate counterattacks to prevent Allied troops from rallying. If Allied forces were able to withstand these hasty counterattacks, the Germans would then prepare a deliberate, coordinated counterattack to eject the enemy from this zone. In this coordinated counterattack, the engaged forces would be reinforced by specially designated assault divisions previously held in reserve. If delivered with sufficient skill and determination, these German counterattacks would alter the entire complexion of the defensive battle. In effect, the German defenders intended to fight an "offensive defensive" by seizing the tactical initiative from the assaulting forces.[5]

The rearward zone was located beyond the reach of all but the heaviest Allied guns. This zone held the bulk of the German artillery and also provided covered positions into which forward units could be rotated for rest. Additionally, the German counterattack divisions assembled in the rearward zone when an Allied offensive was imminent or underway.

In summary, in late 1916, the Imperial German Army adopted a tactical defensive doctrine built on the principles of depth, firepower, maneuver, and counterattack. The Germans used the depth of their position, together with their firepower, to absorb any Allied offensive blow. During attacks, small German units fought a "mobile defense" within their defensive zones, relying on maneuver to sustain their own strength while pouring fire into the Allied infantry. Finally, aggressive counterattacks at all levels wrested the tactical initiative from the stymied Allies, allowing the Germans finally to recover their original positions.

Using the new defensive techniques, the Imperial German Army performed well in the 1917 battles on the Western Front. In April, the massive French Nivelle offensive was stopped cold, with relatively few German losses. The British also tested the German defenses with attacks in Flanders at Arras and Passchendaele. Although the British enjoyed some local successes, no serious rupture of the German defensive system occurred.

Throughout the 1917 battles, the Germans modified and refined the Elastic Defense: among other changes, the battle zone was deepened, heavy machine guns were removed from the static redoubts to provide suppressive fire for the local counterattacks, and German artillery was encouraged to displace rapidly to evade counterbattery fire.[6] On the whole, however, the novel system of elastic defense in depth was thoroughly vindicated. As the German Crown Prince Friedrich Wilhelm remarked in his memoirs, "Had we held to the stiff defense which had hitherto been the case [rather than the Elastic Defense system], I am firmly convinced that we would not have come victoriously through the great defensive battles of 1917."[7]

One ominous development that seemed to challenge the continued effectiveness of the Elastic Defense was the British tank attack at Cambrai in November 1917. There, massed British tanks broke through the entire German defensive system, and only the combined effects of German counterattacks and British irresolution restored the German lines. This wholesale use of tanks to sustain the forward advance of an Allied attack seemingly upset the logic on which the German defensive concept was based.

Although insightful in other aspects of battlefield lore, the Germans mistakenly discounted the combat value of tanks despite the Cambrai incident. While the Germans were impressed by the "moral effect" that tanks could produce against unprepared troops, they also felt that local defensive countermeasures (antitank obstacles, special antiarmor ammunition for rifles and machine guns, direct-fire artillery, and thorough soldier training) virtually neutralized the offensive value of the tank.[8] In the German assessment, tanks were similar to poison gas and flamethrowers as technological nuisances without decisive potential.[9] The Germans minimized the British success at Cambrai by stating that it was the result of tactical surprise, achieved by the absence of the customary ponderous artillery preparation, rather than from the tank attack itself. In consequence, no reassessment of the Elastic Defense was deemed necessary, and none was undertaken. For example, the updated version of the German doctrinal manual for defensive operations published in 1918 made no special reference to tank defense.[10]

The Final Collapse: Unanswered Questions

In 1918, the Imperial German Army launched a series of offensive drives on the Western Front. Between March and August, the Germans surged forward in a desperate attempt to achieve a decisive military victory before infusions of American manpower could resuscitate the groggy Allies. Although successful at the tactical level, these attacks were not well conceived strategically.[11] As a result, these "Ludendorff offensives" achieved only a meaningless advance of the German lines and fatally depleted the last reservoirs of German strength. In fact, they so exhausted the German Army that it was incapable even of consolidating its gains against Allied counterattacks from August onward. The Germans attributed the rapid collapse of their defense after August 1918 primarily to demoralization and inadequate resources rather than to faulty doctrinal methods. As one German general later wrote, "Under such conditions, there could be no longer any mention of tactics" due to the chaotic state of the German armies.[12]

The Ludendorff offensives consumed the most combat-worthy divisions in the German Army. The German attacks were carried forward by specially designated "assault divisions." When the German offensives faltered, feeble "trench divisions," whose personnel and equipment were inferior to the assault units, assumed the burden of defensive operations. These trench divisions, which had been purposely starved of replacements to flesh out the shock divisions, turned out not to be merely second-rate but to be flatly "listless and unfit."[13] Without support from the burned-out assault divisions, the trench divisions were unable to hold their own against the Allied counteroffensives. As the Allied counterblows gathered momentum, German morale plummeted, and German troops began to surrender in unprecedented numbers. Under these circumstances, German small units could not be relied on to demonstrate the determination and aggressiveness essential to the Elastic Defense.[14]

The tottering German forces were especially vulnerable to the shock effect of Allied tanks, particularly when used with chemical smoke. Looming out of the murk at close range, tanks often touched off epidemics of "tank fright." Ludendorff belatedly conceded that tank attacks "remained hereafter our most dangerous enemies. The danger increased in proportion as the morale of our troops deteriorated and as our divisions grew weaker and more exhausted."[15] Since the Germans had discounted the value of tanks, they had virtually none of their own with which to bolster the morale of their beleaguered infantry.[16]

The increasingly general use of tanks by the Allies prompted expedient modifications to the Elastic Defense in the latter months of the war. When used by the Allies en masse, tanks could overrun single lines or even belts of antitank weapons. Consequently, the Germans distributed all types of antitank weapons in greater numbers throughout the depth of the battle zone, transforming it into a tank defense zone wherein enemy armor and infantry could both be destroyed.[17] These techniques successfully halted even heavy tank attacks, provided that the defending German infantry remained steadfast. As one German commander insisted, "The infantry must again and again be made to realize that the tanks hardly deserve a battle-value at all and that their threatening danger is overcome when the infantry does not permit itself to become frightened by them."[18] German commanders exhorted their men to steel their nerves and to stand bravely as had the "Teutons of old against the Romans."[19] Brave words could not compensate for a lack of brave soldiers, however, and the "surrender bacillus" continued to rage through the German ranks.[20]

Lack of sufficient manpower hurt the Germans as much as the lack of combat will. Because of losses in the Ludendorff offensives, the German

Tank of the U.S. 27th Division destroyed by a German mine, September 1918

armies no longer disposed of sufficient reserves to deliver the timely counterattacks that the Elastic Defense required. Time and again, Allied penetrations prompted large-scale German withdrawals lest neighboring frontline units be encircled or enveloped from the enemy salients.[21] Too, the Allies (particularly the British) had refined their own offensive techniques, eschewing elephantine artillery preparations in favor of short, sharp barrages. Without the customary long artillery pounding that signaled Allied intentions, the Germans were less able to shuttle their few reserves to threatened sectors.

The German High Command finally bowed to the inevitable, and an armistice was enacted on 11 November 1918. In later years, many Germans allowed bitterness to cloud the memory of their defeat in the last months of World War I. Many high-ranking military officers blamed Germany's demise on a "stab in the back" by defeatist elements at home.[22] In reality, the Imperial German Army was in serious disarray from August 1918 onward and could not have prevented a complete Allied military victory. Frustration and Nazi demagoguery gave the stab-in-the-back story a certain currency during the interwar years, but the popular memory simply did not conform to historical reality.

The distorted memories of World War I left behind an uncertain and even contradictory military legacy. Through four grim years, the conflict had been dominated by positional warfare. Consequently, the overriding recollection of the war on the Western Front was of entrenched stalemate, in which the first doctrinal priority was to assure a strong tactical defense.

In the German view, the war as a whole had been an attritional contest, ultimately decided by the superior weight of Allied manpower and resources. Unable to match the Allied coalition in either of these categories, the Germans had sought to maximize their own fighting power by doctrinal means. The Elastic Defense stood alone as the best system for conducting an effective positional defense at minimal cost. (Even the Allies testified to the superiority of the German techniques. The British, for example, attempted to incorporate the German defensive methods into their own postwar field service regulations.[23]) Consequently, a generation of German officers emerged from the Great War steeped in the tactical precepts of the Elastic Defense. To these, the value of the Elastic Defense had been repeatedly assayed by tests in France and Flanders. On many fields, the Germans had successfully pitted defensive depth, firepower, maneuver, and aggressive counterattack against the brutish weight of Allied artillery, infantry, and even tanks. It was a tactical creed that was not to be forgotten.

Less clear, however, were the tactical lessons learned from the war's final months. Then, positional warfare had briefly given way to battles of movement. The Ludendorff offensives demonstrated the possibility of penetrating Allied trench defenses through attacks by infiltration. The successful Allied counteroffensives from August 1918 onward showed that perhaps even the Elastic Defense was not a perfect talisman against renewed maneuver warfare, since weak and demoralized German forces could not turn away overwhelming tank and infantry assaults through doctrinal charms alone. However, most Germans excused the final Allied victories as being due to the prostration of German armies rather than to any failure of defensive doctrine. Indeed,

American infantrymen escort German prisoners to the rear, 1918

isolated examples of German defensive success right up until the armistice seemed to indicate that the Elastic Defense would have prevailed if determined troops had practiced it correctly.

German Defensive Doctrine in the Interwar Years

In the years following 1918, all major armies sought to divine from the Great War's confusing impressions the nature of future wars. Would future battlefields resemble the entrenched *Stellungskrieg* of the 1914—17 Western Front? Or would new tactics, together with the new technology of armored vehicles and motorized movement, produce fluid battles of maneuver? The development of the German blitzkrieg offensive techniques foresaw the latter scenario, a leap of faith not shared by the French or the British.

The clarity of German doctrinal vision in defensive matters was less certain, however. By their very nature, defensive operations generally imply surrendering the initiative to the enemy. As a consequence, defensive measures must be able to accommodate the attacker's tactic of choice, a circumstance that breeds caution and redundancy. For the purposes of defining defensive doctrine, the Germans were unable to predict for certain whether future wars would be of a positional or of a maneuver nature. Therefore, the German Army pursued a doctrinal compromise that would operate effectively in either environment.

The Elastic Defense became the German Army's all-purpose defensive doctrine. As the familiar, proven method of World War I, the Elastic Defense was the obvious theoretical starting point for interwar doctrinal development. With minor alterations, it remained the essence of German defensive practice until the beginning of World War II. However, the retention of the basic

Elastic Defense concept was not a simple, straightforward process. To many German officers, the Elastic Defense seemed too trench oriented, and they argued that the retention of a doctrine designed for positional warfare would invite disaster in future wars. At the very least, the Elastic Defense needed to have its antitank properties upgraded in order to confirm its continuing validity in an armored warfare environment. Therefore, these and other considerations weighed on the interwar development of German defensive doctrine.

The building of a new German Army began in 1919. Since wholesale desertions had caused the old Imperial German Army to evaporate within weeks of the 1918 armistice, the new *Reichswehr** was created virtually from scratch.[24] Among the many immediate problems pressing the *Reichswehr* and its acting chief of staff, General Hans von Seeckt, was the publication of new field manuals to guide postwar training.

Seeckt sought to compile the most practical and effective combat procedures from the Great War into a single doctrinal manual. First published in 1921, *Führung und Gefecht der verbundenen Waffen* (Leadership and Combat of the Combined Arms) remained the standard operations manual for the *Reichswehr* until 1933.

The German postwar uncertainty about the positional versus the maneuver visions of future war was evident in the new manual. Although Seeckt was an ardent advocate of maneuver warfare, his early influence was counterbalanced by other senior officers of the "trench school."[25] To these, the harsh catechism of *Stellungskrieg* demanded the retention of a trench-oriented defense doctrine. *Führung und Gefecht* compromised by conceding that either form of warfare was possible and showed how the Elastic Defense could be adapted to either circumstance (see figure 2).

For stabilized situations, *Führung und Gefecht* prescribed an elastic defense in depth that was identical in every major detail to the Elastic Defense described in the 1917 and 1918 Imperial German Army pamphlets. The defense was to be organized in three principal defensive zones as before, within which the defending forces would "exhaust [the enemy's] power of attack by resistance in depth."[26] Attacking enemy forces were to be subjected to a withering combination of small-arms and artillery fire throughout the depth of the battle area. Defending units would "seek timely and unnoticed evasion of hostile superiority at one point, while offering resistance elsewhere (mobile defense)."[27] Finally, fierce counterattacks by engaged units as well as by reserve forces held in readiness to the rear would be "of decisive importance."[28] *Führung und Gefecht* thus endorsed the same defensive formula of depth, firepower, maneuver, and counterattack as had been developed during World War I.

The only departures from World War I usage were minor. Defensive zones were increased in depth, and the distance between them was extended to ensure that, "in the event of a breakthrough, a displacement by the enemy artillery [would] be necessary before the attack [could] be continued against

---

*Technically, the new German Army was the *Reichsheer*. However, except in offical documents, the term *Reichswehr* was used indiscriminately to describe both the German armed forces in general and the land army in particular. The *Reichswehr* went through a series of provisional incarnations immediately after the war before assuming its "final" form in 1920.

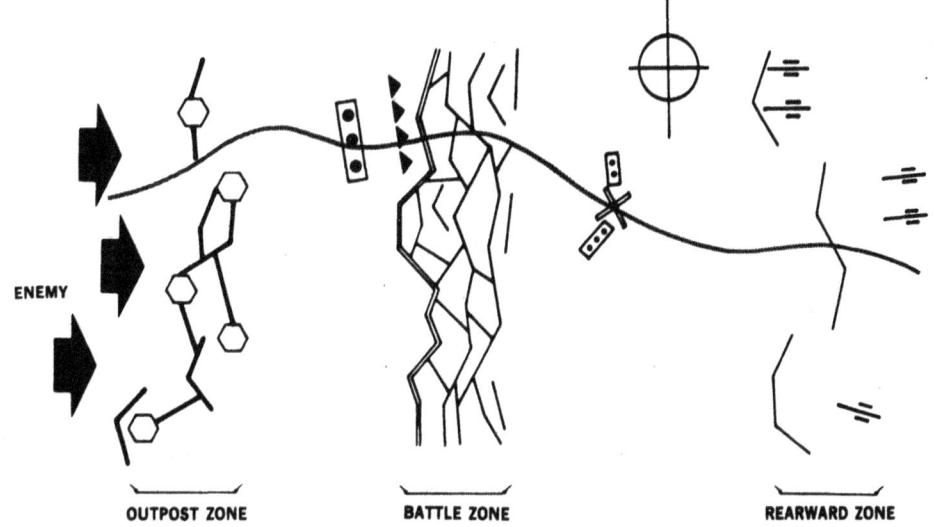

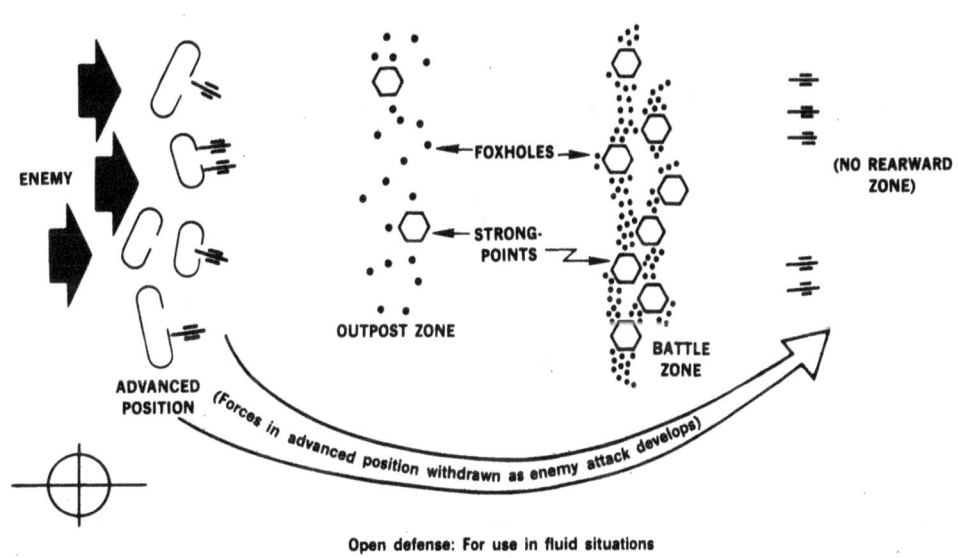

Figure 2. Defense in stabilized and open situations, 1921

the next position."[29] Furthermore, the 1921 manual finally deigned to discuss measures for defense against tanks, although the measures consisted mainly of local obstacles and artillery concentrations along tank avenues of approach.[30]

When forces were defending in open situations during battles of maneuver, *Führung und Gefecht* simply advised a somewhat looser application of the Elastic Defense. Since the presumed pace of operations would prevent the construction of fully fortified trenchworks, both the outpost zone and the battle zone would normally consist of a system of "foxholes and weapons pits" with-

Senior German officers observe *Reichswehr* maneuvers, circa 1928

out connecting trenches.³¹ A rearward zone would not even be constructed. To provide greater operational depth and warning, an advanced position would be created where possible. This position would be held by covering forces whose missions were to provide early warning of the enemy's approach, confuse the enemy as to the location of the actual defensive zones, and in general, constitute an additional defensive buffer when the armies were not in close contact.³² Despite these slight alterations to the defensive posture, the "defense in open situations" still conformed to the Elastic Defense. Depth and maneuver were emphasized in order to strengthen the combat power of the defending forces, and integrated firepower and counterattack would still be used to destroy the enemy.³³

The *Reichswehr*'s principal doctrinal publication thus steered an equivocal course between the positional and the maneuver scenarios, prescribing a form of Elastic Defense for each. However, in practice, the willful General von Seeckt temporarily suspended the Elastic Defense instructions in *Führung und Gefecht*.

Seeckt, whose wartime experience had been mostly on the more fluid Russian and Balkan Fronts, retained an enthusiasm for maneuver undampened by the gory disappointments of France and Flanders. Seeckt was convinced that a renewed emphasis on bold offensive maneuver could, in the future, result in rapid battlefield victories. A man of strong convictions, Seeckt was intolerant of subordinates who did not endorse his ideas. Those officers of the trench school who were unwilling to adapt themselves to Seeckt's theories were either silenced or dismissed.[34] Therefore, Seeckt was able to bend the *Reichswehr*'s training sharply in the direction of mobility and maneuver. Although the Elastic Defense remained on the books as official *Reichswehr* doctrine, Seeckt whipped the German Army into a fervid pursuit of mobility and offensive action that caused the Elastic Defense to be all but ignored in practice.

Seeckt wrote in a 1921 training directive that the strongest defense lay in mobile attack, a policy that cultivated offensive action at the tactical level for even defensive purposes.[35] Seeckt insisted that skillful maneuver could reduce virtually all battlefield actions to a form of meeting engagement in which aggressive actions would prevail.[36] Where overwhelming enemy strength precluded the possibility of attack, Seeckt advocated a mobile delaying action to preserve freedom of maneuver by friendly forces.[37] The use of initiative and speed of movement to create opportunities for offensive thrusts was emphasized in *Reichswehr* field exercises. Also, as early as 1921, military maneuvers examined the feasibility of using motor vehicles to enhance mobility and offensive striking power in nominally "defensive" scenarios.[38]

Seeckt's emphasis on swift offensive action suited the temper and means of the German Army. German military studies conducted after World War I were virtually unanimous in blaming Germany's defeat on the exhausting *Stellungskrieg*.[39] Thus, Seeckt's theories pointed a way out of that attritional wilderness. By means of rapid offensive blows against even superior rivals, Germany hoped to avoid the attritional quicksand of the Great War and return instead to the battles of maneuver and annihilation at which German armies had traditionally excelled.

Too, the pitifully small resources allowed the *Reichswehr* by the Treaty of Versailles precluded positional defense. Restricted to an army of only 100,000 men, the Germans were prohibited from possessing antitank or antiaircraft guns and from erecting defensive fortifications along their western frontiers.[40] These stipulations meant that, for the foreseeable future, the *Reichswehr* would be only the shadow of an army, patently incapable of serious defensive operations save those related to internal security. The *Reichswehr*'s defensive impotence was revealed in 1920 and 1921 when incursions by Polish and Soviet irregulars along Germany's eastern borders had to be opposed by hastily assembled *Freikorps* units rather than by the inconsequential *Reichswehr*.[41] When French forces occupied the Ruhr in 1923, German studies assessing the possibility of resistance by the *Reichswehr* concluded that any such action was militarily impossible.[42]

Theory and reality thus converged to enforce a reliance on maneuver and offensive initiative within the new German Army since no other type of defensive action seemed desirable or practicable. Remembering the attritional slaughter of the Great War, many German officers were eager to embrace any tactical system that promised to avoid such battles. Too, the Versailles constraints guaranteed that the *Reichswehr* could not resort to the Elastic Defense that had stymied the Allies in 1917 since the *Reichswehr* was forbidden to have the materiel to do so.

German offensive and defensive tactics were based on Seeckt's theories of maneuver and aggressive action and were in effect until the early 1930s. Then, German offensive and defensive doctrines diverged: offensive practice continued on the road to mobility that led finally to blitzkrieg, while defensive doctrine reverted to more conservative practices reminiscent of the Great War. Accordingly, the Elastic Defense was revived for three major reasons.

First, a gradual broadening of German military perspective began following General Seeckt's 1926 resignation. Although Seeckt's ideas—and Seeckt himself—continued to be influential for some time, his successors were more tolerant of traditional doctrinal theories.

Second, the German Army began quietly to ignore some of the more onerous provisions of the Versailles Treaty, thereby increasing German military strength. This therefore allowed German military leaders to consider a wider variety of strategic options than the desperate, all-purpose formula of offensive maneuver championed by Seeckt.[43]

Finally, a rapprochement between the French and German governments in the late 1920s lessened French hostility and, with it, the likelihood of renewed French military intervention. The looming threat of the French Army—its potential for strategic mischief painfully demonstrated by the 1923 occupation of the Ruhr—was greatly diminished by the emerging French reliance on the Maginot Line. With French military resources so strongly committed to the passive Maginot doctrine of *couverture* from 1930 onward, Germany's overall military security was better than it had been at any time since 1918.[44]

In this atmosphere of greater strength and security, the *Reichswehr* took a more well-rounded view of military strategy. The Seecktian emphasis on aggressive maneuver was relaxed, and the German Army once again acknowledged that traditional defensive operations—including, in certain circumstances, positional warfare—would probably be necessary in future conflicts. Consequently, the Elastic Defense was revived as the fundamental German defensive technique.

The German field manuals published in the 1930s revealed the renaissance of the Elastic Defense and, with a few changes in later editions, were still in effect at the beginning of World War II. The most important of these publications, entitled *Truppenführung* (Troop Command), appeared in 1933 and replaced *Führung und Gefecht* as the basic German operations manual. Prepared under the supervision of General Ludwig Beck, chief of the German General Staff from 1933 to 1938, *Truppenführung* endorsed the traditional German method of elastic defense in depth.[45]

In fact, the doctrine in *Truppenführung* ended the distinction between positional defense and maneuver defense that had been created in *Führung und Gefecht* and specifically declared that "the defense of a hastily prepared, unreinforced position [such as would occur in open warfare] and that of a fully completed position is conducted on the same principles."[46] Also, the advanced position that *Führung und Gefecht* had placed in front of the defensive zones in open situations was made standard. Consequently, the 1933 version of the Elastic Defense consisted of the same three defensive zones as had appeared in Ludendorff's original concept, but with an additional advanced position posted in front[47] (see figure 3).

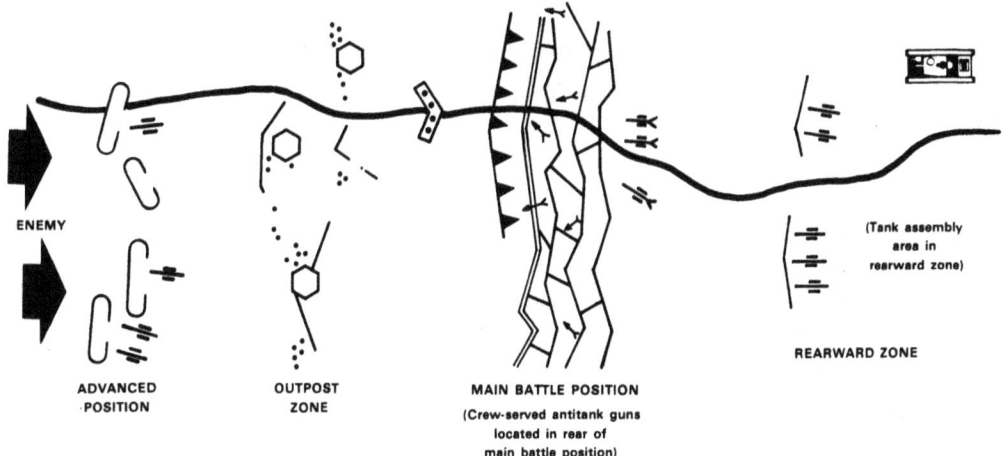

Figure 3. German Elastic Defense, 1933

In addition to *Truppenführung*, other specialized manuals such as the 1938 *Der Stellungskrieg* and the 1940 *Die Ständige Front* elaborated on the problems of positional warfare in greater tactical detail.[48] These manuals were supplemented by instructional material in professional journals. For example, from 1936 onward, *Militär-Wochenblatt* periodically published tactical problems hypothesizing static defensive operations. Significantly, the solutions to these exercises discussed the experiences of 1917 and 1918 as illustrative examples of proper technique.[49] Together, these field manuals and journal articles breathed new life into the Elastic Defense doctrine and fully revived the defensive system that the German Army had developed during World War I.

Other German military authors addressed the strategic ramifications of the Elastic Defense, assuring their readers that this new interest in defensive tactics did not signal a full return to the disastrous strategy of attrition. General Wilhelm Ritter von Leeb (later to command Army Group North during Operation Barbarossa in 1941) wrote a series of historical articles on defensive operations in *Militärwissenschaftliche Rundschau* in 1936 and 1937. Although predicting that future wars would still be decided by offensive maneuver, he argued that strategic defensive operations could not be discounted: "We Germans have to look to defensive operations as an important, essential method of conduct of war and conduct of combat, since we are in a central position, surrounded by highly equipped nations. Defensive should not be kept in the background as before the last war."[50] Leeb further stressed that the tried defensive principles of the Great War—depth and counterattack—could still be effective in modern battles of maneuver.[51] Echoing Leeb, a Major General Klingbeil warned readers of *Militär-Wochenblatt* in 1938 not to discredit positional defensive operations on principle since they could create circumstances favorable for decisive offensive action.[52]

The new manuals and spate of journal articles demonstrated the remarkable extent to which German military thinkers had reaccommodated themselves to the possibility of positional warfare. While most professed a preference for offensive maneuver, German theorists conceded that *Stellungskrieg* was likely to be present, at least to a limited extent, on future battlefields.[53] Within this intellectual climate, Beck's revival of the orthodox doctrine of the Elastic Defense seemed not only prudent, but even virtually indispensable.

The problem of armored warfare, however, prevented a simple return to Great War tactics. World War I had provided brief glimpses of the potential combat value of tanks and motor vehicles, and from 1919 to 1939, all armies puzzled over how best to exploit these new machines.

In terms of German defensive doctrine, the tank problem posed two distinct questions. First, how could German defenses be made attack-proof against enemy tank and tank-infantry forces? Second, what was the best defensive use of the new German panzer units? The Germans framed their answers to both of these questions within the Elastic Defense schema.

Antitank Defense

Because the Allies used tanks impressively in 1918, German officers gave serious consideration to antitank defense methods. Rooted in their memories of the 1918 collapse was the nagging fear that—as Ludendorff had finally conceded—tanks had become the single most effective tool for prying open the German Elastic Defense. However, General Beck confined this interest to traditional channels.

Beck, who in *Truppenführung* returned the German Army to the Elastic Defense, held profoundly orthodox views. One symptom of this orthodoxy was Beck's reluctance to embrace new ideas about tank warfare. Beck's logic recalled the emphatic pronouncements of German officers in 1918 that tanks were merely nuisances to a properly organized elastic defense in depth. Beck saw the traditional combat arms—infantry, artillery, and even cavalry—as being decisive, and he resisted the notion that armored formations could have a pivotal battlefield impact.[54] Given such a conception, Beck deemed antitank defense measures as secondary to the central problem of halting artillery-supported attacks by enemy infantry.

According to the new German field manuals, the key to defeating enemy combined arms attacks thus lay in separating the enemy's tank and infantry forces. German soldiers were trained to concentrate their small-arms fire on the enemy infantrymen in order to separate them from any supporting tanks. While shredding the attacking infantry forces, German defenders were supposed to dodge enemy tanks, leaving the destruction of these metal monsters to specially designated antitank teams.[55] Once the opposing infantry attack had been smashed, any surviving tanks were considered both vulnerable and relatively inconsequential. Those tanks, rampaging through the German defensive zones like rogue elephants, could be dispatched almost at leisure by antitank weapons located to the rear.

Specific measures prescribed for antitank defense were mostly codifications of 1918 practices. Tanks were to be neutralized by a combination of obstacles, minefields, and antitank weapons. Although antitank rifles would be available in all parts of the German defensive zones, the crew-served antitank guns (*Panzerabwehr Kanonen,* or *Paks*) and direct-fire artillery would generally be located to the rear of the main line of resistance.[56] (The rearmed German

Army of 1939 had a seven-man antitank section armed with three antitank rifles in each rifle company. Each infantry regiment also contained a *Pak* antitank company, and each infantry division had a divisional antitank battalion of three additional *Pak* companies.[57]

Although *Pak* sections could be attached to forward elements in certain circumstances, the Germans thought these guns could be used more effectively as a "backstop" for the main infantry trench systems. They reasoned that these rearward antitank weapons would be relatively safe from any preliminary artillery bombardment, would be free to mass opposite tank penetrations as necessary, and would be able to engage those tanks without embarrassment from enemy infantry (see figure 4). German doctrine also allowed for the creation of special antitank assault groups composed of small teams of infantrymen who would try to destroy enemy tanks with mines and explosive charges from close range. As always, all German units were expected to counterattack vigorously in order to regain any position, even if it had been temporarily overrun by hostile tanks.

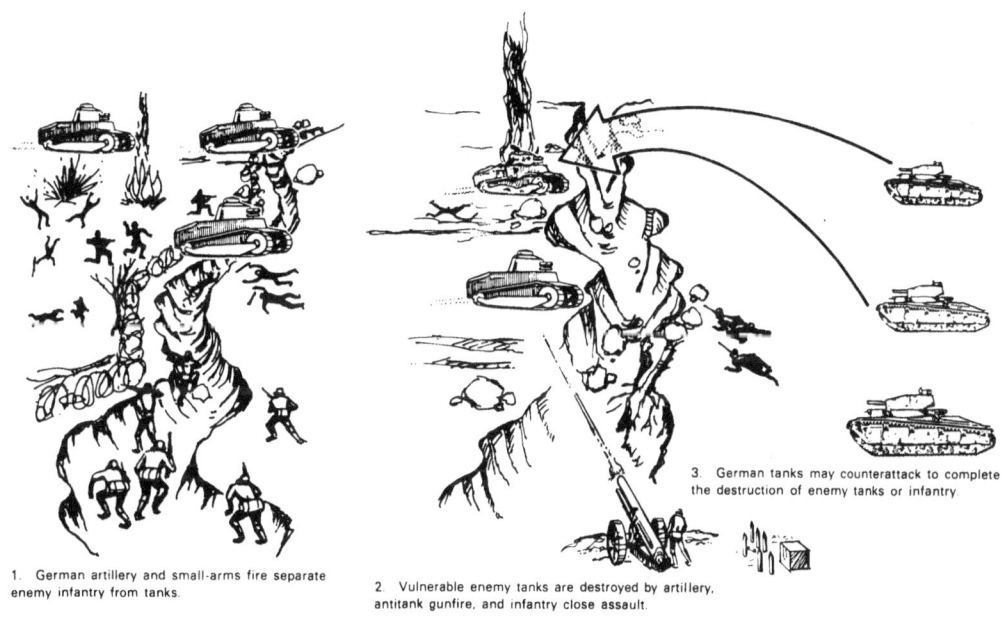

1. German artillery and small-arms fire separate enemy infantry from tanks.
2. Vulnerable enemy tanks are destroyed by artillery, antitank gunfire, and infantry close assault.
3. German tanks may counterattack to complete the destruction of enemy tanks or infantry.

Figure 4. German antitank concept

Through the 1930s, German antitank doctrine thus corresponded to the techniques first hammered out in 1917 and 1918. The first task of the defending forces was to halt the enemy infantry; that done, the isolated enemy tanks would then be at the mercy of German antitank weapons and close assault.[58] Virtually all German writings about antitank warfare in the interwar period were based on the assumption that tanks without infantry were pitifully vulnerable to antitank weapons, an article of faith reaching back to the difficult last days of the Great War. One retired general praised the ability of "nearly invisible" antitank riflemen to prey on enemy tanks.[59] Another

German officer spoke for many when he asserted that experience in the Spanish Civil War confirmed that "the defense is superior" to tanks since every tank-antitank duel in Spain had allegedly ended with victory for the antitank gunners.[60]

Defensive Use of German Tanks

One remarkable omission from the list of German antitank weapons was the tank itself. General Ludwig Ritter von Eimannsberger, a prolific writer on antitank matters, characterized most German officers when he wrote in 1934 that "the principle claiming the tank to be the best antitank weapon has already been outlived and rendered untrue."[61] Like other facets of German doctrine, this belief stemmed from remembrances of the Great War, in which German tanks had played no such role. German tank design in the 1930s provided physical evidence of this prejudice, since few German tanks in production prior to September 1939 mounted a truly effective antitank gun.[62] Furthermore, during World War I, the German Army had become convinced that tanks were "expressly weapons of attack." This opinion was elevated to dogma in interwar German manuals and was frequently reiterated by Heinz Guderian and other German tank enthusiasts.[63]

Although panzers were not considered antitank weapons themselves, the Germans did develop a doctrinal role for their armored forces that exploited the tank's offensive nature and conformed neatly to the Elastic Defense format. In defensive battles, panzer units were to be held in reserve for delivering the counterattacks vital to the elastic defense in depth. The shock and mobility of the panzers would lend weight to German counterblows, thus assuring the annihilation of enemy infantry or armor mired in the German defensive zones.[64]

Some German officers saw in this system a clear-cut division of labor between tanks and infantry. Panzer units would be used exclusively in offensive roles, even within defensive scenarios. Infantry forces, presumably unable to keep up with the offensive battles of maneuver envisioned by the panzer generals, would be indispensable for defensive purposes due to their ability to occupy and hold terrain. That panzer forces might have to conduct defensive operations unrelieved by German infantry divisions was almost totally discounted.[65]

Early Trials: Poland and France

The campaigns in Poland and France provoked no changes to German defensive doctrine. If anything, operations during these spectacularly successful German offensives seemed to diminish the importance of defensive precautions. Skewered by German panzer thrusts, the Polish and French Armies succumbed without seriously testing German defensive measures in return. In each campaign, the Germans fought a small number of defensive engagements. Although the Germans learned some valuable tactical lessons, they were insufficient to spur a reevaluation of German defensive techniques.

After-action reports from the Polish campaign revealed a general dissatisfaction with training and small-unit leadership within the German Army.[66] Singled out for criticism were a number of reservist units that in their training and cohesion were not prepared for the rigors of the Elastic Defense.[67] In October 1939, in an Army High Command memorandum detailing deficiencies uncovered in Poland, defensive operations was listed as an area in need of immediate improvement. This complaint, however, emphasized performance rather than doctrine.[68]

The campaign in France likewise was not without its defensive lessons. Most disquieting was the British tank attack at Arras on 21 May 1940. There, the rapidly advancing German panzers had become separated from their following infantry. Falling on the unsupported German infantry forces, the British armored attack illustrated not only the danger inherent in the de facto German policy of giving separate offensive and defensive roles to their tanks and infantry, but also the inadequacy of German antitank weaponry. Only the timely fire of German 88-mm flak guns and 105-mm field guns prevented the German infantry from being entirely overrun, as shells from the German 37-mm *Paks* and the even lighter antitank rifles rattled off the British Matildas without apparent effect. German tanks, hurriedly retracing their steps and returning to the scene, were also outgunned by both the British tanks and antitank guns.

The close call at Arras caused some ripples of concern within the German Army; however, this concern did not mature into reform. Although the German panzer and infantry forces had become perilously divided during the advance to the Channel—a situation to be repeated on an even grander scale in Russia—neither the French nor the British had been able to exploit this vulnerability decisively. The Germans, therefore, shrugged off the potential danger. A few new motorized infantry divisions were activated in the year

German light tanks capture Polish supply column, 18 September 1939

German troops load a 37-mm antitank gun onto a pneumatic raft during a pre-Barbarossa exercise, May 1941

between the fall of France and the invasion of Russia, but not nearly enough to provide defensive security for the panzers or to take up the slack between the mobile units and the trudging infantry forces. Indeed, the Germans shortly reaffirmed the exclusively offensive role of their panzer divisions: a new panzer operations manual published in December 1940 devoted twenty-six pages to discussing attack techniques, but only two paragraphs discussed defense.[69]

More immediately disquieting was the woeful German antitank weaponry. Hitler ordered the punchless Panzer IIIs upgunned, an overhaul that was completed within the next year.[70] The German *Paks*, however, could not be so easily replaced or repaired. Although some captured French 47-mm guns and a few new 50-mm *Paks* were introduced to augment the 37-mm antitank guns, the smaller (and virtually ineffective) weapons remained the primary dedicated crew-served antitank weapons of German infantry divisions at the beginning of Barbarossa.[71] As an interim precautionary measure, German field artillery units placed greater emphasis on close-range antitank engagements during training in the spring of 1941.[72]

Overview: German Doctrine on the Eve of Barbarossa

Before the beginning of Operation Barbarossa in 1941, the German Army adhered to a defensive doctrine originally developed to address battlefield conditions of World War I. Although temporarily shunted aside in the 1920s during a faddish pursuit of offensive maneuver, the conservative defensive practices of 1918 had been reinstated in the German Army by the mid-1930s. This defensive doctrine concentrated on halting enemy infantry attacks by means of a defense in depth consisting of a series of defensive zones. Within these zones, enemy infantry forces were to be defeated by firepower, tactical maneuver, and vigorous counterattack. In the 1918 tradition, tanks were regarded as a lesser threat than enemy infantry. German antitank measures followed the 1918 outlines: enemy tanks would have their accompanying infantry stripped away; their advance would be obstructed by mines and obstacles; and a mixture of direct-fire artillery, antitank gunfire, and individual close assault would destroy those tanks that actually penetrated the German defensive positions. German tank units had no defensive role other than to deliver counterattacks where necessary to help crush enemy penetrations.

Whatever its potential faults, this doctrine suited the structure of the 1941 German armies. Its few panzer units aside, the *Wehrmacht* was as overwhelmingly pedestrian as had been the Imperial German Army of 1918. The Elastic Defense fit the skills, capabilities, and disposition of this preponderantly infantry-based force. On the eve of World War II, foreign military observers correctly concluded that, with regard to defensive doctrine, the "German training manuals [showed] that the new German Army accepted the legacy of war-experience of its predecessors unreservedly."[73]

The German Elastic Defense doctrine made the following assumptions about modern warfare, and they would be severely tested in the campaign against Russia.

• The burden of any sustained defensive fighting would be borne by infantry divisions, supported only as necessary by panzers held in reserve for counterattack.

• Sufficient quantities of German infantrymen would be available in defensive situations to organize a cohesive defense in depth.

• The principal threat would be posed by the enemy's infantry forces, and therefore, any German defense should be disposed primarily with an eye to defeating a dismounted attack.

• German commanders in defensive operations would be allowed the flexibility to select positions and conduct the defense in an "elastic" fashion as had been the 1918 custom.

None of these assumptions had been disproved in the 1939 or 1940 campaigns. However, within the first two years of the Russian campaign, the German Army conducted major defensive operations under circumstances that invalidated them all.

Chapter 2

Barbarossa—The German Initiative

The greatest land campaign of World War II began on 22 June 1941 when Adolf Hitler ordered German armies eastward against the Soviet Union. Confident that Operation Barbarossa would result in a rapid offensive victory over the Russians, the Germans were unprepared for the prolonged, savage conflict that followed. Germany's unpreparedness showed in a variety of ways. Strategic planning was haphazard, logistical support was insufficient, and given the magnitude of both the theater and the enemy, the number of committed German divisions was wholly inadequate.

The first year of the Russo-German War consisted of two separate phases. The first phase—the German initiative—lasted from 22 June until the first week of December 1941. During that period, three German army groups, numbering more than 3 million men, marched toward Leningrad, Moscow, and Rostov. The second phase—the Soviet initiative—began at the end of 1941, as the final German attacks ground to a halt short of Moscow. From early December until the following spring, the Soviets lashed back at the Germans with a series of furious counteroffensives.

German defensive operations played a major role in each phase. The accounts of the spectacular early successes of Barbarossa tend to obscure the fact that those offensive victories frequently required hard defensive fighting by German units. Once the Soviet winter counteroffensives began, German military operations were, of course, almost entirely defensive.

In both phases, the German Army was largely unable to execute the defensive techniques prescribed by German doctrine. As the German armies advanced from June to December 1941, the deployment posture of German divisions was governed by offensive rather than defensive considerations. Consequently, German units seldom had the time or the inclination to organize the sort of careful defense in depth described in their training manuals. Likewise, German defensive operations during the Soviet winter counteroffensives seldom conformed to the procedures in *Truppenführung*. Limitations imposed by terrain and weather; critical frontline shortages of men, supplies, and equipment; and Hitler's reluctance to allow any withdrawals by forward elements prevented a general implementation of the Elastic Defense. Instead, embattled German divisions resorted to expedient defensive methods dictated by the exceptional conditions in which they found themselves.

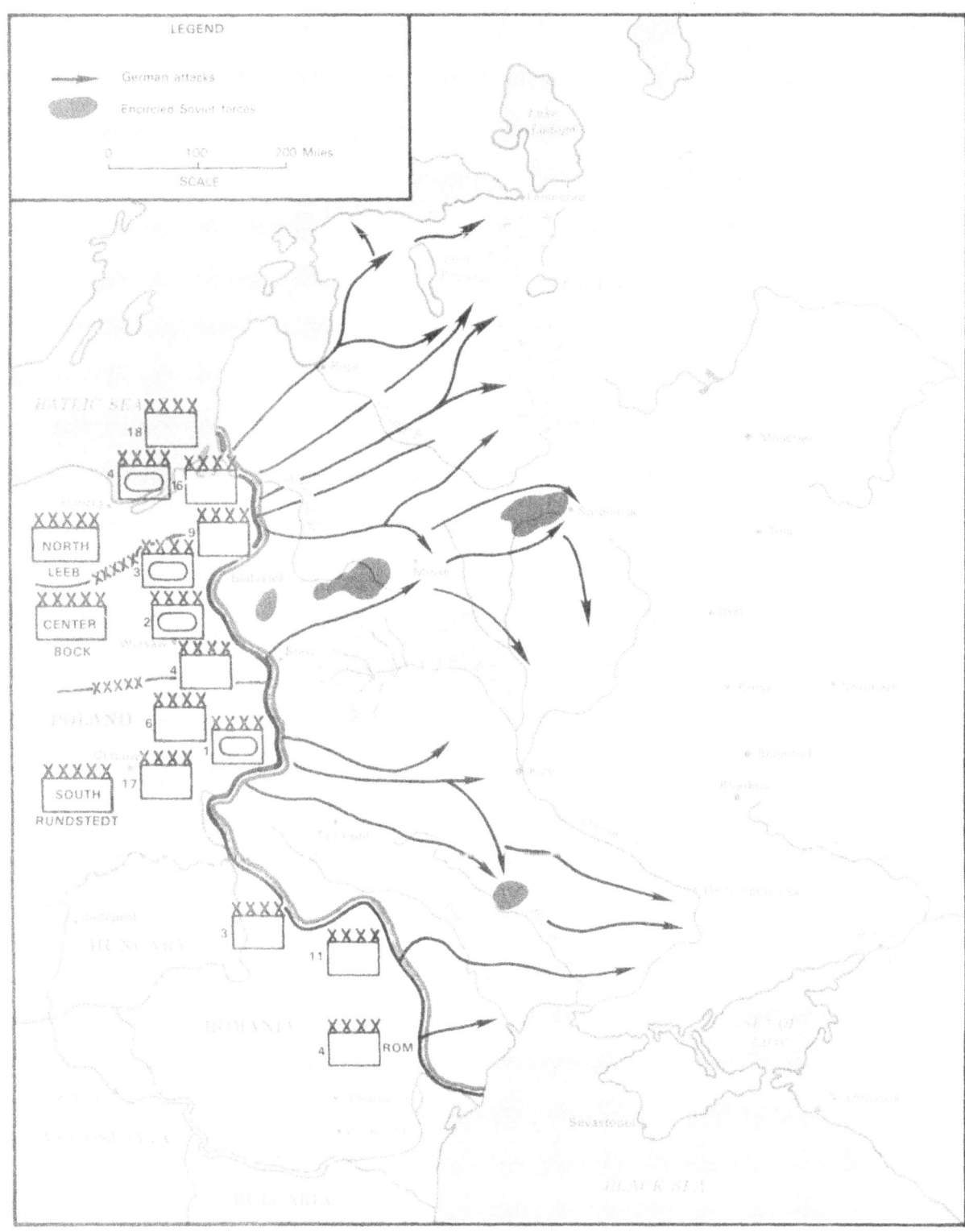

Map 1. Operation Barbarossa German offensive operations, 22 June—25 August 1941

The Defensive Aspects of Blitzkrieg

To avoid the dissipation of a two-front war, the German High Command expected to "crush Soviet Russia in a lightning campaign" during the summer of 1941 (see map 1). The key to this rapid victory lay in destroying "the bulk of the Russian Army stationed in Western Russia... by daring operations led by deeply penetrating armored spearheads." To achieve this goal, the Germans planned to trap the Soviet armies in a series of encircled "pockets."[1] Not only would this strategy chop the numerically superior Soviet forces into manageable morsels, but it also would prevent the Soviets from prolonging hostilities by executing a strategic withdrawal into the vast Russian interior.

In the campaign's opening battles, the Germans used *Keil und Kessel* (wedge and caldron) tactics to effect the encirclement and destruction of the Red Army in western Russia (see figure 5). After penetrating Soviet defenses, rapidly advancing German forces—their *Keil* spearheads formed by four independent panzer groups—would enclose the enemy within two concentric rings. The first ring would be closed by the leading panzer forces and would isolate the enemy. Following closely on the heels of the motorized elements, hard-marching infantry divisions would form a second inner ring around the trapped Soviet units. Facing inward, these German infantry forces would seal in the struggling Russians, containing any attempted breakouts until the caldron, or pocket, could be liquidated. Meanwhile, the mobile forces in the wider ring faced outward, simultaneously parrying any enemy relief attacks while preparing for a new offensive lunge once the pocket's annihilation was complete.[2]

Generally, in offensive maneuvers, the Germans sought to place their units in a position from which they could conduct tactical defensive operations.[3] This way, the Germans could enjoy both the advantages of *strategic* or *operational* initiative and the benefits of *tactical* defense. True to this principle, the encirclement operations conducted during Barbarossa contained major defensive components. Once a *Kessel* was formed, the temporary mission of both the panzer and the infantry rings was defensive: the inner (infantry) ring blocked enemy escape, while the outer (armored) one barred enemy rescue. The defensive fighting that attended the formation and liquidation of these pockets revealed serious problems in applying German defensive doctrine, however.

Fearsome in the attack, German panzer divisions were ill-suited for static defensive missions due to their relative lack of infantry.[4] Prewar German defensive doctrine had envisioned using infantry for defensive combat and reserving panzer units for counterattacks, a role commensurate with their supposedly offensive nature. Panzer divisions were neither trained nor organized to fight defensively without infantry support. However, during the deep, rapid advances of Barbarossa, the German panzers routinely ranged far ahead of the marching infantry and were therefore on their own in defensive fighting.

During their deep encirclements, panzer divisions found even their own self-defense to be a problem. Field Marshal Erich von Manstein, when describing his experiences as a panzer corps commander in Russia during the

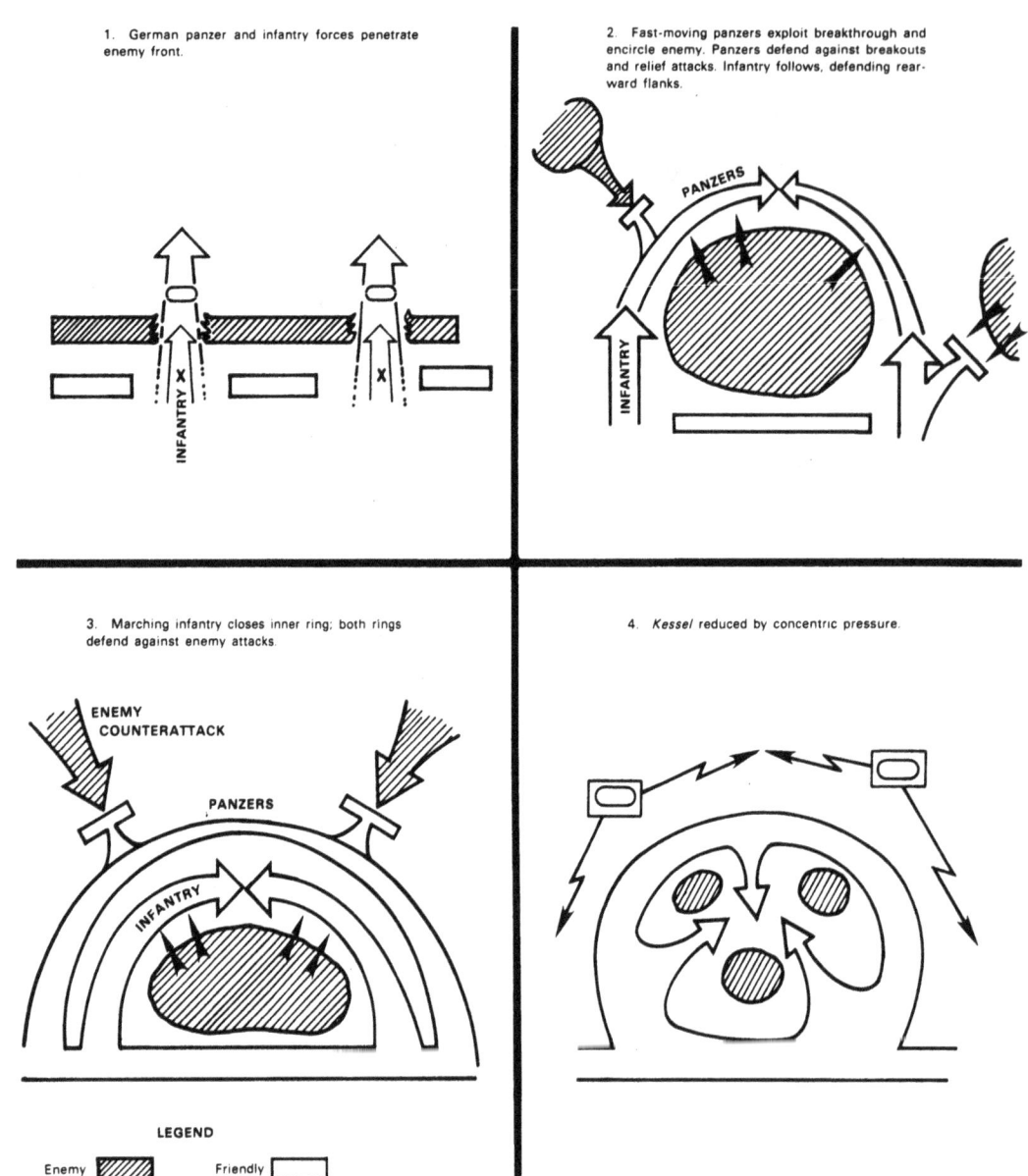

Figure 5. German *Keil und Kessel* tactics, 1941

summer of 1941, observed that "the security of a tank formation operating in the enemy's rear largely [depended] on its ability to keep moving. Once it [came] to a halt, it [would] be immediately assailed from all sides by the enemy's reserves." The position of such a stationary panzer unit, Manstein added, could best be described as "hazardous."[5] To defend itself, a halted panzer unit would curl up into a defensive laager called a hedgehog. These hedgehogs provided all-around security for the stationary panzers and were used for night defensive positions as well as for resupply halts.[6]

The panzer hedgehogs solved the problem of self-defense but were not suitable for controlling wide stretches of territory. The German *Keil und*

Kessel offensive tactics, however, required that enveloping panzer divisions control terrain from a defensive posture: first, until the following infantry could throw a tighter noose around the encircled enemy and then as a barrier against relief attacks by enemy reserves. Not surprisingly, the panzer divisions often had difficulty in performing these two tasks. On at least one occasion, for example, an encircling German panzer unit actually had to defend itself from simultaneous attacks on both its inner and outer fronts. The 7th Panzer Division, having just closed the initial ring around the Smolensk pocket, faced such a crisis on 1 August 1941. General Franz Halder, the chief of staff of the Army High Command, glumly wrote in his personal diary that "we need hardly be surprised if 7th Panzer Division eventually gets badly hurt."[7] Ideally, German motorized infantry divisions should have assisted the panzers in defensive situations. However, in 1941, the number of motorized divisions was too few and the scope of operations too great for this to occur in practice.[8]

Until relieved by infantry, German panzer divisions were hard-pressed to contain encircled enemy forces. As Red Army units tried to escape from a pocket, the German panzers continually had to adjust their lines to maintain concentric pressure on the Soviet rear guards and to block major breakout efforts. Containment of such a "wandering pocket" required nearly constant movement by the panzer divisions, a process that prevented even the divisional infantry units from forming more than hasty defensive positions.[9] Even so, until the following infantry divisions closed up, the panzer ring around a *Kessel* remained extremely porous.[10] As a result, many Soviet troops avoided German prisoner-of-war cages by simply filtering through the hedgehog picket line. Although the panzer divisions did their best to disrupt this egress with artillery fire and occasional tank forays, German commanders conceded that large numbers of Russians managed to melt through the German lines.[11]

Soviet relief attacks posed problems of a different sort for the German panzer units. While the Germans devoted themselves to forming and digesting a particular *Kessel*, Soviet units outside the pocket often had time to gather their operational wits and organize a coordinated counterblow. When delivered, these counterattacks fell heavily on the outer ring of the German armor. The panzer units fared better in these circumstances, since they could often use their own mobility and shock effect to strike at the approaching Soviets. However, the German defensive problem was greatly compounded when the Soviet counterattacks included T-34 or KV model tanks, both of which were virtually invulnerable to fire from German tanks.[12] The predicament of the German armor in these circumstances might have been truly desperate had it not been for the support that attached *Luftwaffe* antiaircraft batteries provided to most of the panzer divisions. Originally assigned to the spearhead divisions to protect them against Soviet air attack, these *Luftwaffe* batteries—and especially the 88-mm high-velocity flak guns—had their primary mission gradually altered from air defense to ground support.[13] Although German armored units were thus generally successful in repelling counterattacks, the sheer weight of these coordinated relief attempts—especially when supported by the heavier Soviet tanks—hammered the panzer divisions as no other fighting in the war had yet done.

German infantrymen march forward along a dusty Russian road, July 1941

The German infantry divisions, tramping forward in the wake of the motorized vanguards, had the double responsibility of providing timely support for the armored spearheads and of concurrently guarding the flanks of the German advance against Soviet counterattacks. General Halder described the marching infantry as a "conveyor belt" defensive screen along which successive units passed en route to the *Kessel* battles at the front.[14] The German infantry advanced at a forced-march pace in order to catch up with the mobile forces as quickly as possible. (Those infantry divisions marching immediately to the rear of the panzer groups were especially abused by being shunted onto secondary roads in order to avoid congesting the supply arteries of the far-ranging panzers.[15])

Like the panzer forces, the German infantry units had defensive difficulties of their own. The lathered haste of the infantry advance reduced defensive efficiency, since there was little time for organizing defensive positions. In accordance with published German doctrine, infantry units tried to site their emplacements on the reverse slopes of hills and ridges and stood poised to eject penetrating enemy forces with immediate counterattacks.[16] As a rule, however, only hasty defensive positions could be prepared during halts, and even then, infantry units remained deployed more in a marching posture than in the alignments specified by the Elastic Defense.[17]

Even though the infantry advance was rapid, infantry units did not receive the same kind of protection from Soviet counterattacks that mobility provided for motorized units. From the beginning of the campaign, Soviet counterblows were almost a daily occurrence for German infantry units. An early Soviet High Command directive ordered Red Army counterattacks at every opportunity. This directive continued to animate Soviet tactics throughout the summer and autumn of 1941.[18]

To supply additional protective fire for German infantry units on the march, artillery batteries of various calibers were spaced throughout the march columns. By providing responsive fire support to nearby units, these batteries simplified the otherwise complex problem of fire control for scattered, moving, and occasionally intermixed infantry forces.[19] In some units, improvised flak combat squads, consisting of two 88-mm and three 20-mm antiaircraft guns, were also distributed among the ground infantry forces to bolster defensive firepower.[20] Moreover, the dispersal of artillery and antiaircraft units throughout the divisional columns reduced the vulnerability of the guns to ground attack—an important consideration in the chaos of June and July 1941 when bypassed or overlooked Red Army units often appeared unexpectedly along the march route.

The posting of artillery and flak units in the infantry march columns also lent additional antitank firepower to the foot soldiers. As with the panzers elsewhere, the infantry found its *Pak* antitank guns and antitank rifles ineffective against any but the lightest Soviet tanks. The result, as one German commander wrote, was that "the defense against enemy tanks had to be left to the few available 88mm Flaks, the 105mm medium guns, and the division artillery."[21] Although the use of artillery in a direct-fire, antitank role was consistent with German doctrine in *Truppenführung*—and was, for that matter, in keeping with the German practices of 1917 and 1918—the antitank experience was unpleasant for German gunners. The German artillery pieces and their caissons were cumbersome, had high silhouettes, and were too valuable to be risked in routine duels with Soviet tanks.[22]

Given the anemic firepower of the German *Paks* and the reluctance of the artillerists, the German infantryman often became the antitank weapon of last resort. German combat reports frequently spoke of Soviet tanks being knocked out in close combat by German infantrymen using mines and grenade clusters.[23] Such heroism exacted a high price, and heavy infantry casualties often resulted when Soviet tanks actually overran German positions. On 10 July, for example, the German Eleventh Army reported that elements of its 198th Infantry Division had been caught without antitank support and mauled badly by a heavy tank attack.[24] Not surprisingly, such incidents caused some German infantry units to be skittish in the face of tank assaults. Experience proved to be the best tonic for this condition: German division commanders reported that any lingering tank fear disappeared following the first successful defeat of a Russian tank onslaught.[25]

One of the first set-piece antitank actions fought by German infantry in World War II occurred on 25—26 June near Magierov. There, the German 97th Light Infantry Division hastily deployed its own infantry and artillery forces in depth to defeat a division-strength Soviet tank attack. In this engagement, the Russian tank and infantry contingents were separated and then annihilated in a textbook application of the German antitank technique.[26]

During the first months of Barbarossa, German infantry waged some of its heaviest defensive combat while containing encircled Soviet units. *Keil und Kessel* tactics required that the German infantry divisions reduce pocketed Russian forces by offensive pressure and also block the frenzied Russian attempts to break out.

One of the campaign's first defensive engagements to be widely reported by the German press illustrated the tactical difficulty of these battles. While

A German newspaper sketch showing German troops destroying a Soviet tank with grenades and gasoline

German infantrymen in hasty defensive positions face encircled Soviet forces, June 1941

barring the eastward escape of Red Army units from the Bialystok *Kessel* during the night of 29—30 June, the 82d Infantry Regiment (31st Infantry Division) was subjected to successive attacks by Russian infantry, cavalry, and tank forces. This German regiment had been unable to establish a defense in depth or even a continuous defensive line due to the extreme width—more than ten kilometers—of the regimental sector. Furious Soviet assaults conducted throughout the night penetrated the German line at several points, and some German units found themselves attacked simultaneously from front, flanks, and rear. In fact, the situation became so critical that regimental headquarters staff and communications personnel had to fight as infantry to prevent the German lines from being completely overrun. Although the Germans managed to prevent a large-scale rupture of their defensive front, they could not block the escape of small bands of Soviet troops who, abandoning their heavier weapons and equipment, stole through the German lines during the chaos of combat.[27]

Luckily for the Germans, Russian counterattacks during the early weeks of Barbarossa were frequently uncoordinated and lacked tactical sophistication. The surprise German onslaught had caught the Red Army in a state of disarray, and the speed and depth of the German advance prevented the Russians from regaining their operational equilibrium.[28] As a result, Soviet

A German antitank gun crew faces Soviet counterattack, 1941

counterattacks often lurched forward in piecemeal fashion, with little effective cooperation between supporting arms or adjacent units. Units attacking in the first week of July against the infantry-held flanks of German Army Group South, for example, used tactics that were "singularly poor. Riflemen in trucks abreast with tanks [drove] against our firing line, and the inevitable result [was] very heavy losses to the enemy."[29] One German general, in reporting his frontline observations to General Halder, described the Russian attack method as "a three minute artillery barrage, then pause, then infantry attacking as much as twelve ranks deep, without heavy weapon support. The [Russian] men [started] hurrahing from far off. [There were] incredibly high Russian losses."[30]

By the end of July, the German Army had triumphantly concluded the encirclement battles designed to destroy Soviet forces in western Russia. While shredding the Soviets with blitzkrieg offensive operations, German units had fought a large number of tactical defensive engagements. The German forces had generally been successful in these actions, although combat conditions had rarely allowed them the full use of standard German doctrine.

Instead of being decisively smashed, however, Soviet military resistance continued unabated. Despite the destruction of several Russian armies in encirclements at Bialystok, Minsk, and Smolensk, as well as in lesser pockets elsewhere, Halder conceded that "the whole situation makes it increasingly plain that we have underestimated the Russian Colossus.... At the outset of the war we reckoned with about 200 enemy divisions. Now we have already counted 360. These divisions indeed are not armed and equipped according to our standards, and their tactical leadership is often poor. But there they are, and if we smash a dozen of them, the Russians simply put up another dozen."[31] As the entire German strategy for Barbarossa had gambled on shattering Soviet resistance in a few battles of encirclement, continued Soviet pugnacity confounded German planning and provoked a strategic reassessment by the German High Command. This strategic reassessment shaped the next series of defensive battles fought by German soldiers in Russia.

German Strategy Reconsidered

In late July 1941, the German leadership was perplexed at the strategic situation on the ground. Barely five weeks into the campaign, the German armies were beginning to flounder in the vastness of Russian space. The Russian theater was so immense—and ever widening as the Germans pushed eastward—that concentrated German force could only be applied in a few areas. The overall ratio of German force to Russian space was so low, in fact, that a continuous German front line could not be maintained. Instead, sizable gaps routinely yawned between major German units. Too, substantial geographic obstacles divided the German army groups: the Pripyat Marsh region lay between Army Groups Center and South, while forests, streams, and poor roads reduced lateral movement within and between Army Groups North and Center.

German units became dangerously separated in depth as well as in width. The mobility differences between the motorized and nonmotorized elements of the *Wehrmacht* caused the Germans to advance, in effect, in two distinct echelons. During the frontier battles of encirclement, the Germans had managed this disparity through their *Keil und Kessel* tactics. However, the extended distances over which the Germans now operated aggravated this problem, opening larger gulfs between the advanced panzers and the following infantry. Increasingly, the German forces not only advanced separately but fought separately as well.[32]

The open areas between German units were, of course, populated by bypassed Red Army units, and these gaps constituted weak points that could easily be exploited by Soviet counterattacks. Already in the campaign, bypassed Red Army forces had waylaid the German 268th Infantry Division, stampeding the German troops. This incident had resulted in the capture of some of the division's artillery and had caused consternation within the German High Command.[33]

The awkwardness of the German position was not lost on the Soviets. On 19 July, Army Group Center reported the capture of a Russian order "indicating that the Russian High Command [is] aiming at separating the German armor from supporting infantry by driving attacks between them." Halder dismissed this as "a very pretty scheme, but in practice it [is] something that [can] be carried out only by an opponent superior in number and generalship." Halder could not picture the Russians applying such a technique against the Germans.[34]

General Heinz Guderian (second from right), commander of Panzer Group 2, discusses operations with officers of the 197th Infantry Division in late July 1941. German tanks and infantry became dangerously separated during the rapid advance into Russia.

Hitler was less sanguine than Halder in his evaluation of the vulnerable German position. In July, to the despair of General Halder and Field Marshal Walther von Brauchitsch, commander in chief of the German Army, Hitler began to renew the meddlesome interference in tactical operations that he had practiced in the French campaign. He directed the diversion of German units to "tidy up" and secure the German flanks against lurking Red Army contingents.[35] Hitler carried this idea further in mid-July, de-emphasizing large-scale operations in favor of smashing the enemy "piecemeal by small tactical operations."[36] Explaining the Führer's concept during a visit to Army Group Center headquarters on 25 July, Field Marshal Wilhelm Keitel of the German High Command announced that, for the time being, German operations would concentrate on small-scale mopping-up actions. These actions would complete the destruction of those Red Army elements that had escaped encirclement and destruction in the *Kessel* battles and would secure the German flanks for future operations. Furthermore, Keitel explained that the smaller scope of these operations would reduce the distance between the German tanks and infantry, thereby reducing the heavy combat losses inflicted on unsupported panzers by Soviet counterattacks.[37]

Brauchitsch, Halder, and other senior officers vehemently disagreed with Hitler's designs, arguing that such policies violated the principles of concentration and decisive maneuver. They urged, instead, an immediate march on Moscow, which they regarded as the military, political, and economic jugular of the Soviet Union. Such strong and nearly unanimous opposition caused Hitler to waver temporarily, and as a result, he issued a series of conflicting strategic directives between 30 July and the latter part of August.[38]

While the Germans argued strategy, the Soviets demonstrated that they could, in fact, exploit the fissures in the German front. During the second week of August, strong Russian forces (the Thirty-Fourth Army and parts of the Eleventh Army) thrust into a gap between the German X and II Corps south of Lake Ilmen (see map 2). Driving north and west from the area south of Staraya Russa, the Russians advanced nearly sixty kilometers by 14 August and threatened not only the flank of the German X Corps but the entire rearward communications of the Sixteenth Army and Army Group North.[39] Locked in desperate defensive combat, the divisions of the German X Corps were unable to establish an elastic defense in depth due to extended frontages and a severe shortage of reserves.[40] Furthermore, since Army Group North's motorized elements were concentrated in the Panzer Group 4 area north of Lake Ilmen, no panzers were available to counterattack enemy penetrations as had been envisioned in *Truppenführung*. Field Marshal von Leeb, commander of Army Group North and author of prewar articles on defensive operations, gave a grim situation report to the Army General Staff on 18 August. Halder wrote in his diary: "Very gloomy picture of the situation in X Corps. The last man has been thrown into the fighting; the troops are exhausted. The enemy keeps on pushing north of Staraya Russa. Only the engineer companies are left for commitment. The Commanding General, X Corps, and Commander-in-Chief, Army Group [North], think they are lucky if this front holds another day."[41]

Hitler was extremely agitated by this Soviet blow and created a stir within the German High Command by frantically ordering mobile units stripped from other sectors to deal with this new emergency.[42] Manstein's XLVI Panzer Corps (the 3d Motorized Infantry Division and the *Waffen SS Totenkopf* Motorized Division) was detached from Panzer Group 4 and brought on a circuitous rearward march to strike the enemy's western flank on 19 August. This surprise counterstroke quickly caused the Soviet offensive to collapse.[43]

Although the Germans could thus claim victory in this battle—the first substantial defensive crisis on the Russian Front—it bore little resemblance to the neat Elastic Defense of German doctrine. The width of the front and the scarcity of forces had robbed the Germans of their desired defensive depth and ready reserves. Consequently, the German defensive line had stood in imminent danger of collapse until saved by the counterattack of Manstein's mechanized posse. Even this use of German mobile forces had more correctly been a counteroffensive rather than a counterattack, since it had been marshaled and delivered apart from the defensive battle per se.

On 21 August, Hitler clarified German strategy by ordering new offensive drives on both wings of the Eastern Front. In the Army Group North area, German forces would strike toward Leningrad to isolate that city and link up with the Finns east of Lake Ladoga. Farther south, even stronger elements would advance southward from the right flank of Army Group Center to encircle and annihilate the Soviet armies facing Army Group South in the Kiev salient. This latter action would open the way to the Crimea, the Don

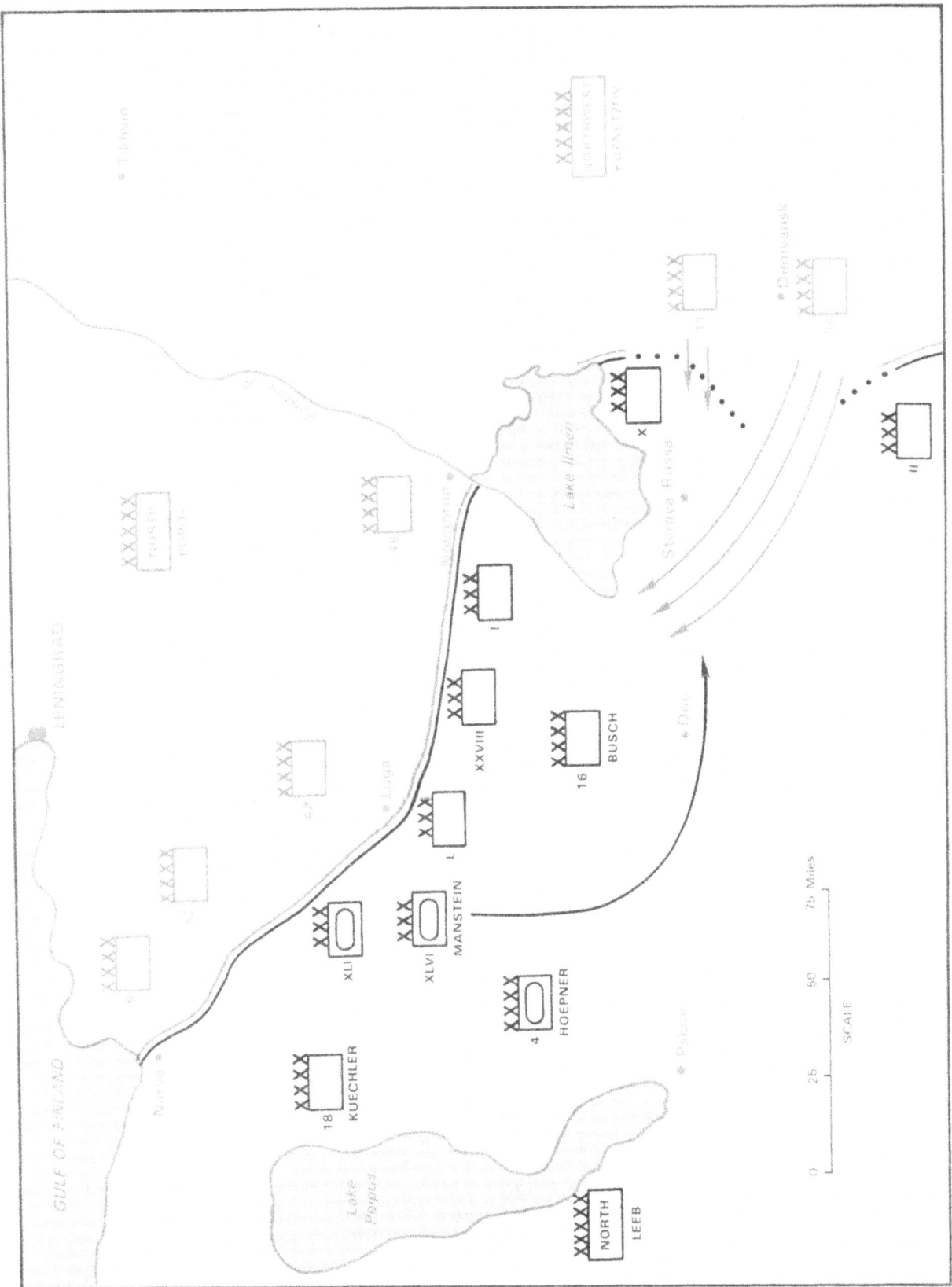

Map 2. Soviet counteroffensive against open flank of Army Group North and counterattack by Manstein's panzer corps, 12–22 August 1941

Basin industrial area, and the Caucasian oil-producing regions. Army Group Center, which since the second half of July had been primarily engaged in defensive fighting while attempting to consolidate and refit its divisions, would assume an outright defensive posture with the rump of its forces[44] (see map 3).

Hitler justified this controversial new strategy on dubious economic and political grounds, thereby overruling the purely military views of his senior officers. The recent Soviet offensive near Staraya Russa probably had helped Hitler make his decision by demonstrating the danger of leaving intact Soviet forces on either flank of Army Group Center. In this respect, Hitler's decided course of action—much criticized by German officers in later years as perhaps the decisive mistake of World War II—seemed militarily prudent since it eradicated, once and for all, the threats to the German flanks.[45]

Conducting offensives to the north and south meant that any drive on Moscow would have to be postponed indefinitely. Two months earlier at the beginning of Barbarossa, the concentration and power of the German forces had been sufficient to allow simultaneous offensives on all parts of the front. By late August, however, German units were too dispersed and their combat potential too diminished to repeat such a feat.

Since the beginning of the campaign, the line of contact with Russian forces had stretched by nearly 50 percent, yet few reinforcements had been added to the German order of battle. German combat units were fatigued from the combination of rapid advance and heavy combat experienced thus far. On 24 August, for example, Halder estimated that the combat strength of the German infantry divisions averaged 60 percent of full capacity and the panzer divisions only 50 percent.[46]

German combat power was adversely affected by logistical considerations as well. Available stocks of fuel, food, and ammunition had sunk to dangerously low levels in many units, and supply deliveries were becoming more erratic as distances increased. The execrable Russian roads were claiming a heavy toll on the mobile units so that German tanks and other motor vehicles desperately needed extensive maintenance. (Incredibly, through July, Hitler

German troops advance on foot, bicycle, and horse cart during the summer of 1941. Russia's poor roads and incompatible rail network disrupted German supply operations.

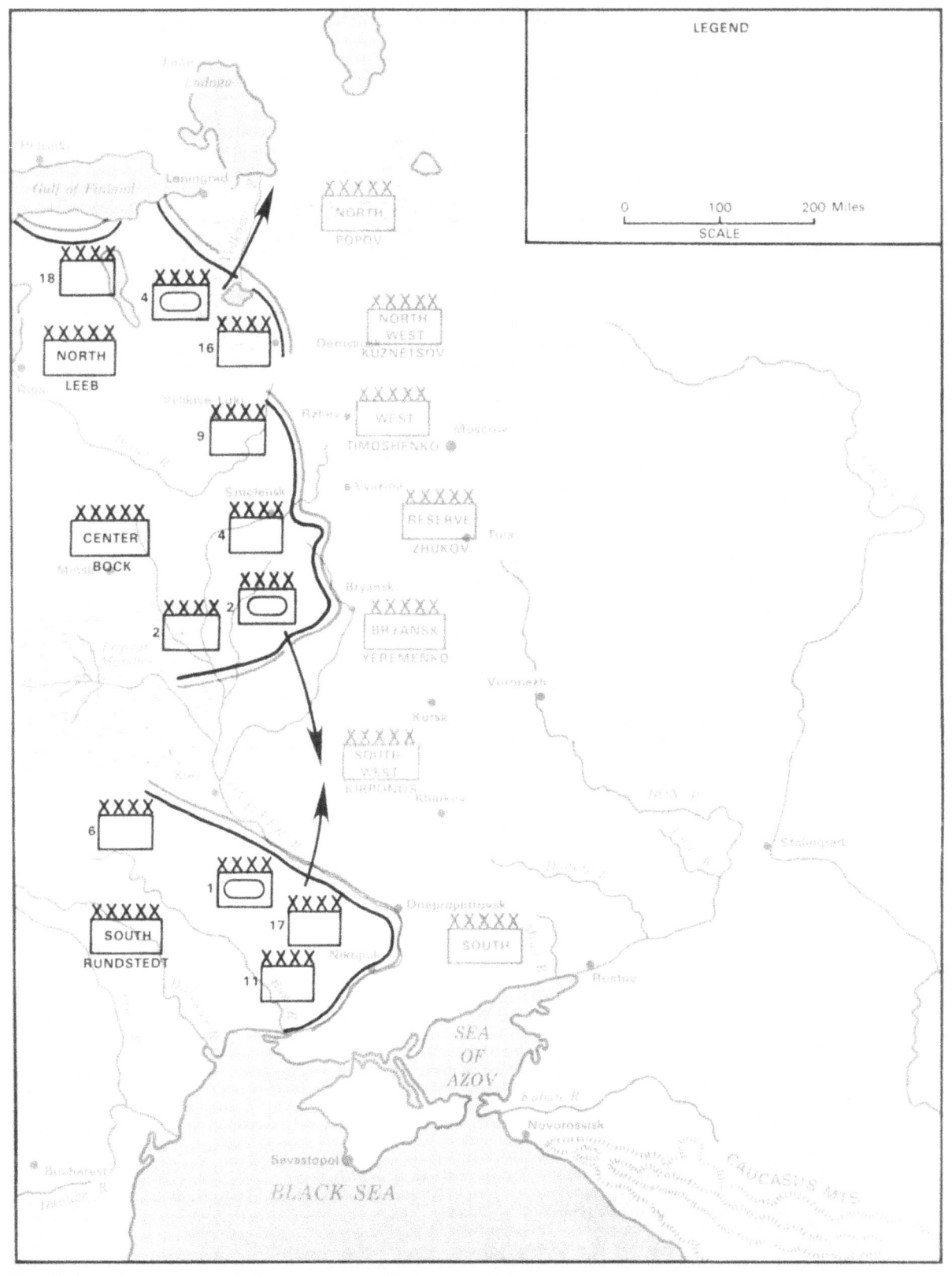

Map 3. Situation and revised German strategy, 22 August 1941 (Army Group Center defends in place while flank offensives proceed)

had ordered that replacement tanks be withheld from the east in order to build new divisions for later use elsewhere. This policy compounded the already difficult maintenance and equipment replacement problems of the panzer divisions.[47]) German personnel replacements—originally gauged for a short campaign—were running low.[48] Too, the replacement of lost weapons and other equipment was proceeding slowly: the German war economy had not been geared up for Barbarossa, and current production lagged behind consumption. Indeed, in anticipation of a rapid victory in Russia, German armaments production was already shifting emphasis away from army materiel. In fact, by December 1941, monthly weapons output had declined by 29 percent from earlier peak production.[49]

With German forces dissipated, the diverging operations that Hitler had ordered to the north and south dashed the Army High Command's hopes of a climactic advance on Moscow. To lend weight to the attack on Leningrad and the great envelopment at Kiev, Army Group Center had to relinquish most of its armor and a large share of its infantry. General Hermann Hoth's Panzer Group 3 had to hold a portion of Army Group Center's static front with nonmotorized infantry divisions inasmuch as both its XXXIX and LVII Panzer Corps were sent to assist Army Group North. General Heinz Guderian's Panzer Group 2 (less one corps) and General Freiherr von Weichs' Second Army were ordered south to fall on the rear of the Soviet Southwest *Front* guarding Kiev.

Shorn of its offensive cutting edge, Army Group Center thus had to remain on the defensive until the operations on its left and right concluded. The defensive battles waged by Army Group Center from the end of July through September 1941 are instructive for being the first German attempt in World War II to sustain a large-scale positional defense.

Defense by Army Group Center, July—September 1941

In late July, Army Group Center concluded a successful offensive by closing a large pocket at Smolensk. While this *Kessel* was being liquidated, the German forces endured the predictable Soviet assaults against their inner and outer encircling rings. Although hard-pressed at several points, the German lines remained generally intact.[50] Desperate to spring open the trap around Smolensk, the Soviet High Command released fresh Red Army forces to reinforce the counterattacks. Particularly ferocious were the relief attacks that Marshal Semën K. Timoshenko's Western *Front* hurled against the German lines north of Roslavl and near Yelnya.[51] The Soviet thrust from Roslavl misfired as forces of Panzer Group 2 deftly swallowed the attacking Russians into a new *Kessel* at the beginning of August. However, the Red Army attacks on the narrow, exposed German salient at Yelnya began a bitter six-week battle for that town.

Seized by the XLVI Panzer Corps of Guderian's panzer group on 20 July, the Yelnya salient enclosed a bridgehead over the Desna River and high ground valuable for the continuation of German offensive operations toward Moscow. If Yelnya had strategic value as a foothold from which future offensive operations might be launched, it also offered tactical liabilities: it was surrounded on three sides by powerful Soviet forces, its rearward communications were clogged with German units fighting to subdue the Smolensk *Kessel*, and it was also some 275 miles from the nearest German supply dumps.[52] Since other German forces were initially distracted by the Soviet attack from Roslavl, the motorized units (the 10th Panzer Division and the *SS Das Reich* Motorized Division) that had captured Yelnya had to hold it until Guderian could bring up marching infantry. As with the containment of surrounded pockets during encirclement battles, this sort of independent defensive action by panzer and motorized forces had not been envisioned in German prewar manuals on defense.

The two German mobile divisions fought at a severe disadvantage. Both units were fatigued and understrength from their earlier offensive efforts. Ammunition and fuel were in short supply, and the confining terrain within the salient nullified their mobility and shock effect. The 10th Panzer Division suffered from the shortage of infantrymen endemic to such units and therefore was poorly suited for positional defense.[53] To offset these handicaps, Guderian requested that the *Luftwaffe* concentrate close air support in the Yelnya area.[54] To Guderian's annoyance, German air support over Yelnya was abruptly withdrawn after only a brief appearance: its operating strength depleted by wear and a shortage of advanced airfields, the *Luftwaffe* began husbanding its resources for use in operations of "strategic" significance. In preference to the "tactical" defense at Yelnya, the *Luftwaffe* chose instead to concentrate its planes in the Second Army sector to protect the southern flank of Army Group Center.[55]

Timoshenko continued to concentrate forces opposite Yelnya and began a new series of attacks on 24 July. For two weeks thereafter, Soviet attacks battered the German lines at Yelna virtually without interruption. On 30 July, for example, the German defenders threw back thirteen separate attacks on their positions.[56] One measure of the growing German peril came on 3 August when Guderian ordered his last available reserve—the guard company for the panzer group headquarters—into the fighting at Yelnya.[57] In a telephonic report to General Halder on the same date, Field Marshal Fedor von Bock, the commander of Army Group Center, worried aloud about his lack of reserves against the costly Russian attacks. Bock further commented that, with present resources, he could not guarantee against a "catastrophe" at Yelnya.[58]

The catastrophe feared by Bock was averted through the timely arrival of infantry reinforcements, which became available as Russian resistance in the Smolensk *Kessel* died on 5 August. Guderian quickly moved infantry divisions into the Yelnya salient, hoping that their greater defensive capacities would repel the Russian assaults. Also, flak batteries of the *Luftwaffe*'s I Antiaircraft Artillery Corps were brought up to bolster the Yelnya defenses.[59] By 8 August, all Guderian's mobile units—including those previously holding Yelnya—had been withdrawn from combat and had commenced refitting.[60] This earliest phase of the Yelnya fighting had shown, however, that operational requirements would not allow the Germans the luxury of using their mobile panzer forces only in offensive roles. Moreover, this fighting had again demonstrated the unsuitability of using infantry-poor panzer units in static defensive operations.

Field Marshal Fedor von Bock, commander of Army Group Center during Barbarossa

As German infantrymen dug in along the Yelnya perimeter, the character of the fighting changed. Hitler, during a conference with Brauchitsch and Bock at Army Group Center headquarters on 4 August, confirmed the necessity of holding Yelnya.[61] Consequently, the German defense at Yelnya was no longer an expedient holding action awaiting offensive thrusts to be renewed. Instead, the newly arrived infantry deployed as best it could into a deliberate defensive posture. Acknowledging this, Halder noted on 6 August: "At Yelnya, we now have regular position warfare."[62] The Soviets, too, shifted their stance somewhat. With the capitulation of the trapped Red Army forces at Smolensk and Roslavl, a breakthrough by Timoshenko's forces no longer had any major strategic purpose. Therefore, on 8 August, Soviet attacks temporarily subsided as the Russians awaited the Germans' next move.[63]

When the Russians realized that the Germans were not going to follow their Smolensk triumph with an immediate drive on Moscow, Soviet attacks again flared up along the central front. The German passivity offered the Russians the unique opportunity of battering an entire German army group under conditions of Soviet choosing. Therefore, Marshal Timoshenko's Western *Front* pressed new attacks between Velikiye Luki and Toropets against the German Ninth Army, which was holding the northernmost portion of Army Group Center's sector. Meanwhile, General Georgi K. Zhukov's newly assembled Reserve *Front* was ordered to renew attacks on the inviting Yelnya salient. These assaults began during the second week of August and continued with unprecedented intensity for nearly a month.[64]

Field Marshal von Bock discerned the threat that these attacks posed to Army Group Center. Bock had no desire to see his units ground up piecemeal in battles of attrition and preferred instead to resume the fluid battles of maneuver that had earlier characterized the campaign. When the Soviet attack at Staraya Russa produced the mid-August crisis in the Army Group North area, Bock scorned Hitler's panicky orders to shift mobile forces there from Army Group Center. On 15 August, Bock argued to Halder that the best course of action against the numerically superior enemy facing his army group was an early return to the offensive. Any transfer of armored striking power away from Bock's command to support the offensives on the German wings would probably destroy the basis for such a general advance by Army Group Center. A prolonged defense, Bock continued, was "impossible in the present position. The front of Army Group [Center], with its forty divisions sprawled over the 130 kilometer front, is exceedingly overextended, and a changeover to determined defense entails far-reaching planning, to the details of which no prior thought has been given. The present disposition and line is in no way suited for sustained defense."[65] In doctrinal terms, Bock recognized that the width of the front held by the army group precluded the use of the Elastic Defense, since insufficient forces were available to create defensive depth and reserves ready for counterattack. Also, Army Group Center's front-line trace was defined by its recent offensive advances and therefore was unlikely to provide many terrain advantages for defense. Furthermore, Bock's warning that no logistical provisions had been made for a prolonged defense were shortly affirmed in battle: German forces lacked the stockpiles of supplies and ammunition necessary for sustained positional warfare.

Bock's worst fears came to pass on 21 August when Hitler stripped Army Group Center of most of its mobile divisions in order to support the attacks toward Leningrad and Kiev. While bulletins hailed new German victories on both flanks, Army Group Center manned a thin defensive dike against a tide of Red Army attacks. As Bock had warned, the weak forces and improvised defensive posture of his army group virtually invited disaster.

General Adolf Strauss' Ninth Army manned the northern half of Army Group Center's stationary front. Marshal Timoshenko's new attacks against Ninth Army benefited not only from heavy artillery and rocket bombardments, but from local Soviet air superiority as well.[66] The German divisions here were overextended and lacked depth: divisional frontages often exceeded twelve miles in width, and the German defenses normally consisted of a string of strongpoints rather than a continuous defense in depth[67] (see map 4).

From 11 August onward, Soviet attacks created local crises along the Ninth Army front on an almost daily basis. On Strauss' right, for example, heavy Russian attacks in the VIII Corps sector repeatedly punctured the front of the 161st Infantry Division. On 17 August, this German front was held only by counterattacks by the 161st Division's last few reserves. Renewed Russian assaults in the same sector broke open the front on succeeding days and captured some of the 161st Division's artillery on 19 August. Its line penetrated again on 21 August, the 161st Division was withdrawn from combat altogether on 24 August. At this time, it was reported to be at only 25 percent strength—a measure of the punishment that the entire VIII Corps had received during this period.[68]

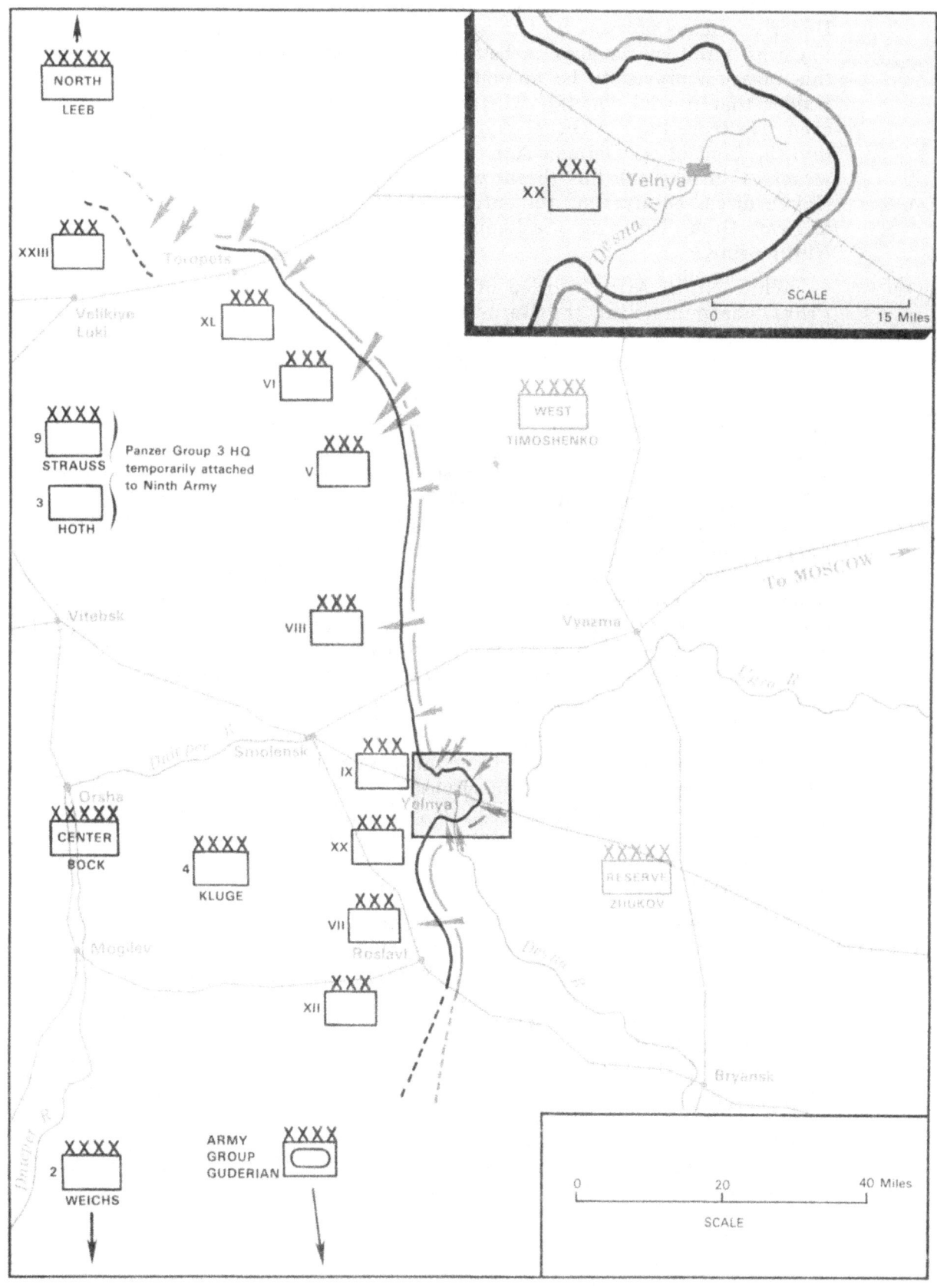

Map 4. Soviet attacks on Army Group Center, August—September 1941

Farther north, tank-supported attacks against the Ninth Army's V and VI Corps also endangered the German front, achieving many small break-ins. Under enormous pressure and in an attempt to tighten its defensive grip, the V Corps withdrew its lines to better defensive terrain on 25 August.[69] Even this measure proved to be unavailing, for on 28 August, Bock reported to Halder that it was doubtful whether the V Corps sector could be held for even five more days.[70] On 27 August, the Soviets made a deep penetration into the front of the German 26th Division (VI Corps).[71] The German counterattacks to drive back this threat were so narrowly successful that Bock and Halder discussed diverting the entire LVII Panzer Corps (which was en route to Army Group North for the Leningrad operation) to the threatened front of Ninth Army.[72]

While Ninth Army warded off these blows, General Zhukov's Reserve *Front* was pummeling the German salient at Yelnya. In spite of earlier German attempts to fortify the Yelnya position, that sector of the German front remained short of the Elastic Defense ideal.

As with Ninth Army, first among the German problems at Yelnya was the chronic shortage of men. Even after infantry divisions relieved the panzer forces in the salient in the first week of August, the German forces there were not sufficient to organize an elastic defense in depth. Two General Staff officers, reporting the results of a Yelnya fact-finding trip to General Halder, flatly described the German units there as "overextended."[73] When the German Fourth Army took control of the Yelnya sector from Guderian's headquarters on 22 August, conditions there appalled General Günther Blumentritt, Fourth Army's chief of staff. As he later wrote: "When I say that our lines are thin, this is an understatement. Divisions were assigned sectors almost twenty miles wide. Furthermore, in view of the heavy casualties already suffered in the course of the campaign, these divisions were usually understrength and tactical reserves were nonexistent."[74]

With manpower in such short supply, German defenses in the Yelnya area generally consisted of a single trenchline instead of the multizoned Elastic Defense. No advanced position or outpost zone stood in front of the main line of resistance, since troops for these posts could not be spared. Without adequate forward security, many units even had to abandon the reverse-slope defensive deployment that the Germans preferred for protection from enemy observation and fire.

An example is that of the 78th Infantry Division. During a forward reconnaissance on 19 August, while preparing to relieve another division at Yelnya, officers of the 78th discovered that the German front consisted mostly of a thin line of disconnected rifle pits. No rearward positions had been prepared, and due to a shortage of mines and barbed wire, only a handful of obstacles stood in the way of any Soviet attack. The German lines were poorly sited, being almost entirely exposed to enemy positions on higher ground. As a result, any daylight movement within the German lines invited a rain of enemy artillery and mortar shells. In fact, the Soviet fire was so dominant that German casualties had to remain in their foxholes until after dark before they could be evacuated.[75] Despite good intentions, leaders of the 78th Division found it virtually impossible to improve the defensive situation after occupying their sector on 22 August. A battalion commander in the 238th Infantry Regiment noted that the strength and accuracy of Soviet fire precluded all efforts to extend German entrenchments by day, while the necessity of guarding against Soviet infiltration at night prevented the formation of nocturnal work parties. Also, adequate reserves could not be found to reinforce threatened sectors; after manning its twelve-mile-wide sector, the entire 78th Division held less than one full battalion in reserve.[76]

Unable to rely to any great extent on the Elastic Defense principles of depth and local counterattack, the Germans were also hampered in their attempts to shrivel Russian attacks with firepower. German small-arms fire was diluted by the wide unit frontages, and an enduring shortage of artillery ammunition around Yelnya diminished large-caliber fire support.[77] With artillery rounds in short supply, the Germans could not afford to conduct counterbattery fire or even counterpreparations against suspected enemy attack concentrations. In sharp contrast, the Russians hammered the German lines unrelentingly. The Soviet bombardments included not only artillery and mortar shells of all calibers, but also the fearsome new Katyusha rockets and strikes by Russian planes.[78] German prisoners taken by the Soviets at Yelnya confessed that the heavy shelling—especially in comparison to the miserly German response—badly hurt German morale.[79] More directly, since bombardment always plays a major role in positional warfare, the greater weight of Soviet artillery fire probably caused a proportionately higher German daily casualty rate.

German troops defend captured Russian village, summer 1941

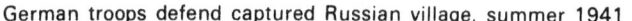

At the beginning of the renewed Yelnya battles, the German defense conformed to established doctrine in one important respect: panzer units were held in reserve to the rear of the German front. Although theoretically available for counterattack, these forces—the XLVI Panzer Corps, which had been relieved earlier on the Yelnya perimeter—with one exception did not intervene in the fighting. Through late August, the XLVI Panzer Corps (the *Grossdeutschland* Motorized Infantry Regiment, 10th Panzer Division, and *SS Das Reich* Motorized Division) was belatedly refitting and therefore was exempt from counterattack use. Even before these units had completed refitting, Guderian was badgering Bock to release them to reinforce the offensive drive on Kiev. After a series of heated arguments between Guderian and his superiors, *Grossdeutschland* and *Das Reich* were finally ordered south.[80] By that time, however, Bock judged that Fourth Army's deteriorating defensive front could only be salvaged by a major panzer counterattack and therefore detached the 10th Panzer Division from the XLVI Panzer Corps and assigned it to the Fourth Army. Thus it was that the 10th Panzer Division was the only one of the available mobile reserves that finally plunged into the fighting on 30 August.[81]

In its general outline, Fourth Army's battles for the Yelnya salient followed the same sequence as the fighting in the Ninth Army area. Prodigious Soviet bombardments and local attacks eroded the defending German divisions, and as German reserves were exhausted, the Russians exploited minor break-ins to pry open the German defensive front.[82] A major break occurred on 30 August when the Soviets drove a ten-kilometer wedge into the Fourth Army's 23d Infantry Division. (It was this serious penetration, which carried to a depth on line with the VII Corps headquarters, that prompted the commitment of the 10th Panzer Division.[83]) Although the panzer counterattack temporarily stabilized the situation, Brauchitsch, Bock, and

German infantrymen await Soviet counterattack, August 1941

Halder agreed on 2 September that Yelnya was no longer tenable in view of the strained condition of the Fourth Army. Consequently, on 5 September, German troops abandoned the Yelnya salient in a planned withdrawal.[84]

Russian attacks against Ninth Army broke off on 10 September, and the assaults against the Fourth Army ceased six days later. In both areas, the Soviets could point to limited territorial gains as the fruits of their efforts.[85] Indeed, the operational withdrawal from Yelnya was the first imposed on the German Army in World War II. However, the full significance of Army Group Center's defensive battles during August and early September could not be measured solely in real estate lost or won.

Like a great winded beast, Army Group Center had stood stolidly in place for more than six full weeks while the Russians stormed against its front. The Russians had been able to choose the times and places of attack and had possessed advantages in quantities of men and materiel. The Germans had waged an improvised defense on unfavorable ground, and because of the extended unit frontages and inadequate combat resources, a doctrinal Elastic Defense relying on depth, local maneuver, firepower, and counterattack had been impossible.

As a result of these conditions, Army Group Center paid an extraordinarily high price in blood. Whereas the Elastic Defense had been designed to minimize personnel losses in positional warfare even in the face of enemy superiority, the improvised methods that the German units were compelled to use in the central front battles resulted in heavy casualties. In the Ninth Army sector, the entire 161st Division had been temporarily disabled, while all of the divisions in the V and VIII Corps had their combat strength seriously diminished. For the Fourth Army, the hardest fighting had occurred in the Yelnya salient, where nine German divisions had seen combat since the end of July. In these divisions, infantry losses had been particularly high. The 263d Infantry Division, for example, had taken 1,200 casualties in only seven days of combat at Yelnya. The 78th Infantry Division reported the loss of 1,155 officers and men in just over two weeks, while the 137th Infantry Division lost nearly 2,000 in the same amount of time.[86] These losses probably represented 20 to 30 percent of the total infantry strength of these divisions at the time the defensive battles began.

These personnel losses permanently diminished the combat power of Army Group Center, and as General Halder had foreseen earlier, German personnel replacements were running out. The chief of the General Staff noted on 26 September that convalescents returning to duty constituted the only remaining short-term source of replacement manpower.[87] Although a few replacements trickled down to Bock's tired divisions during September, Army Group Center still reported a net shortage of 80,000 men on 1 October. Since most of these unreplaced losses were infantrymen, the German ability to seize and hold terrain was seriously eroded.[88] Furthermore, growing shortages of frontline officers and noncommissioned officers also affected the combat worthiness of German units. For example, the war diarist for Army Group Center noted that, two and one-half months after its near destruction by Timoshenko's forces in August, the luckless 161st Division continued to suffer needless casualties due to the division's lack of experienced junior leaders.[89]

The continuous defensive fighting also prevented Army Group Center from building up any appreciable stocks of ammunition. In fending off the attacks on the Ninth and Fourth Armies, the Germans had consumed ammunition almost as quickly as the overtaxed supply columns could deliver it. This meant that Army Group Center would either have to await the stocking of forward supply dumps before it resumed the offensive or continue to operate on an ever-lengthening logistical thread. As events turned out, Army Group Center eventually did a little of both.[90]

Army Group Center's positional battles left other less-visible scars. Timoshenko's attacks on Ninth Army disrupted the timetable for shifting mobile units northward to support Leeb's attack on Leningrad. A degree of command antagonism also developed between Bock and Leeb as the two field marshals, their nerves fraying, haggled over the availability of these forces. Also, the command relationship between Field Marshal von Bock and General Guderian was permanently soured by arguments over the control and use of mobile reserves in the Yelnya area. This growing friction between senior commanders would scarcely have mattered had it not been for the decline in health and influence of Field Marshal von Brauchitsch, the German Army's commander in chief. (Brauchitsch finally suffered a heart attack on 10 November.) Without Brauchitsch's firm and steady hand to adjudicate disputes, coordination between German armies increasingly fell to the dilettantish Hitler. Consequently, the strenuous defensive battles of August and September helped bring these problems to a boil.

Prelude to Winter

In the overall context of the Barbarossa campaign, the German thrust toward Leningrad and the Kiev encirclement overshadowed Army Group Center's defensive stand. The successful execution of these operations, which pulverized Russian concentrations on both flanks of the front, seemed at the time a reasonable return for Army Group Center's ordeal.

Reinforced by panzer elements stripped from Army Group Center, Leeb's Army Group North advanced to the Lake Ladoga-Volkhov River-Lake Ilmen-Valdai Hills-Demyansk line. This drive drained the German tank and motorized infantry forces, whose progress was slowed by marshy, forested terrain and desperate Soviet resistance. Relentless Soviet night counterattacks denied rest to the exhausted German assault troops, and even soldiers of the elite *Waffen SS Totenkopf* Division grumbled that the grueling routine of attacking by day and defending by night was becoming unendurable.[91] Nevertheless, by early September, the German advance had cut Leningrad's land communications, and Leeb's units stood poised to capture the city. At this point, however, Hitler again asserted his strategic prerogative by ordering that Leningrad not be stormed. Instead, the Führer ordered German troops merely to invest Leningrad and allow it to fall of its own weight.[92]

In the south, the encirclement of Soviet forces in the Kiev salient produced the most spectacular *Kessel* victory to date: 665,000 prisoners, 824 tanks, and 3,018 artillery pieces fell into German hands by 26 September.[93] Until the Kiev caldron could be liquidated by the infantry units of the German Second and Sixth Armies, the usual difficult defensive battles were fought by the panzer and infantry divisions forming the encircling rings. In describing Soviet breakout attempts, General Halder wrote on 17 September that "the encircled enemy units are ricocheting like billiard balls within the ring closed around Kiev."[94]

Even as the strangulation of Leningrad and the reduction of the Kiev pocket were underway, Hitler, flushed with success, on 6 September ordered German forces to reconcentrate in the Army Group Center sector for a belated attack on Moscow.

Adolf Hitler's turnabout decision to attack Moscow did not stem from any last-minute conversion to the strategic views of his military advisers. Rather, the impending victories at Leningrad and Kiev had fired Hitler's imagination, prompting him to envision a renewed grand advance into the Russian depths. The centerpiece of this effort was to be a new series of *Kessel* battles by Army Group Center that would destroy the Soviet armies ranged before Moscow. In the south, Field Marshal Gerd von Rundstedt's Army Group South would drive into the void created by the Kiev victory, aiming toward Kharkov, Rostov, and the Don Basin industrial area. Leeb's Army Group North would continue to throttle Leningrad while protecting the northern flank of Army Group Center.[95] In Hitler's mind, these strategic projections constituted the final, triumphal phase of Barbarossa: the crushing of the last Red Army field forces, the capture of the enemy capital, and the plundering of Russian economic wealth.

Most German commanders endorsed the concept of an attack on Moscow, though they regarded it to be a far more precarious operation than did the ebullient Führer. Their concern stemmed from the reduced combat and logistical capacity of German forces, the continuing resistance of the Red Army, and the approach of the autumnal rainy season, all of which lengthened the odds against a successful offensive. Weakened by the defensive battles against Timoshenko and Zhukov, Army Group Center, in particular, was incapable of early offensive action unless heavily reinforced. Since nearly all German divisions in Russia were already committed, reinforcements could only be mustered by disengaging units from other parts of the front and redeploying them into the Army Group Center area. Such a reshuffling of German forces would cause tremendous logistical and command difficulties and would fritter away most of the remaining good weather as well. Hitler, however, discounted these difficulties, remarking airily on 5 September that the Moscow attack "should if possible be launched within 8—10 days." (This estimate was so impossibly optimistic that Halder promptly dismissed it as "impossible.")[96]

As Hitler remained adamant in his demands for immediate action, the second half of September was spent moving German forces into position for Operation Taifun, the name of the Moscow attack. In all, more than twenty-five divisions joined, or rejoined, Army Group Center. This maneuvering further snarled German communications as units crisscrossed each other's supply lines. Not all units earmarked for the Moscow attack could even be concentrated by the 2 October start date: Guderian's Panzer Group 2 had to be given an independent, more southerly axis of advance in order to shorten its return march from the Kiev battles, while some panzers returning from

General Hermann Hoth (center) directs advance of Panzer Group 3 toward Moscow

Army Group North arrived too late to participate in the opening phases of the attack.[97] So confused was the shifting of units that Hoth's Panzer Group 3 and General Erich Hoepner's Panzer Group 4 actually swapped their entire commands during the month of September.[98]

Luckily for the Germans, the Soviets did little to interfere with these offensive preparations. Red Army forces facing Army Groups Center and South were themselves weakened from the battles of August and early September, and they used this time to restore their own strength.

Only on the Army Group North front did the Russians remain active, launching a series of sharp attacks in the hope of breaking the German grip on Leningrad. Between 18 and 28 September, for example, a flurry of Soviet attacks buckled the thin lines of the *Waffen SS Totenkopf* Division south of Lake Ilmen. German losses in this fighting were so heavy—one *SS* battalion lost 889 men, including all of its officers, between 24 and 29 September—that the division commander warned on 29 September that the continued combat worthiness of his unit was in doubt.[99] The 30th Infantry Division, dug in on the left of the *Totenkopf*, likewise defended itself against seemingly endless waves of Russian tanks and infantry. Effective defense was plagued by the same ailments as existed elsewhere: an excessively wide division frontage (over thirty kilometers for the 30th Infantry Division), defensive positions consisting of only a single trenchline without depth or obstacles, and no reserves. After German artillery successfully crushed several Russian breakthroughs, the Soviets switched their tactics to create shallow penetrations of great width.

This left the Germans no choice but to close these gaps by counterattack, suffering heavy casualties in doing so. In this way, the 30th Division lost 31 officers and 1,440 enlisted men in three weeks of nightmarish defensive fighting.[100]

The German drive on Moscow began on 2 October and immediately developed "on a truly classic pattern."[101] Three German panzer groups smashed through the Soviet defenses and enclosed more than six Soviet armies in two great caldrons at Vyazma and Bryansk. Though made purposely shallow in order to spare the panzer forces the agony of prolonged defensive fighting, these pockets yielded more than 550,000 prisoners by the third week of October.[102] As in previous *Kessel* battles, German units fought many extemporaneous defensive engagements in order to contain trapped Red Army divisions.[103] Soviet relief attacks from outside the pockets failed to materialize, however. The German pincers had enclosed the bulk of the combat-worthy Russian units guarding Moscow, and the few that remained outside of the pockets were busy forming a new defensive line in front of the Soviet

German troops enter Kharkov, October 1941

Autumn rains turned the Russian roads into quagmires, stalling the German attack on Moscow

capital.[104] These successes so heartened General Halder that the chief of the Army General Staff predicted in his diary on 8 October that "with reasonably good direction of battle [that is, no fatal interference by Hitler] and moderately good weather, we cannot but succeed in encircling Moscow." Halder's optimism was echoed by Otto Dietrich, the Reich press chief, who announced on 9 October that "for all military purposes, Soviet Russia is done with."[105]

The optimism following the battles of Vyazma and Bryansk was premature. Heavy rains began on 7 October and continued through the remainder of the month, turning the Russian countryside into a quagmire and stifling Army Group Center's offensive operations. German forces continued to slog ahead here and there, with tactical progress being made with great difficulty. However, the mud paralyzed the German logistical system, which depended entirely on motorized and horse-drawn vehicles to draw supplies overland from the rearward railheads. While the muddy season also dampened Soviet operations, the Russians enjoyed two important advantages over their enemies: a shorter line of communications and a nearly intact rail net. The rain-induced pause that suspended major operations for five crucial weeks in October and November thus worked greatly to the Soviets' advantage. When German attacks over frost-hardened ground resumed on 14 November, the way to Moscow was again barred by fresh Red Army forces and formidable defensive works.

On the southern portion of the front, Field Marshal von Rundstedt's Army Group South successfully sustained its offensive drive. General Ewald von Kleist's First Panzer Army* formed the cutting edge of the southern attack and advanced rapidly along the Azov coast toward Rostov. Rain, mud, and Soviet counterattacks slowed the advance of the Seventeenth Army and Sixth Army ranged on Kleist's northern flank, which resulted in the German armored spearhead virtually losing contact with the infantry forces echeloned to its rear. Despite his progress, Rundstedt doubted the German ability to crush the remaining Red Army forces facing him and to reach the far-flung

---

*1st and 2d Panzer Groups were redesignated panzer armies on 5 October 1941.

territorial objectives demanded by Hitler. Rundstedt unsuccessfully urged that German operations on the southern front be curtailed.[106]

The German III Panzer Corps seized Rostov on 20 November, capturing intact a bridge over the Don River leading to the Caucasian oil-producing regions coveted by Hitler.[107] Immediately, Russian counterattacks began to tear at the German salient at Rostov from three sides, while other Red Army forces swept down into the gap between the First Panzer Army and the Seventeenth Army. On 28 November, with Army Group South's offensive energies exhausted and with no strategic purpose to be served by holding Rostov in a risky defensive battle against superior Soviet forces, Rundstedt ordered First Panzer Army to withdraw to the Mius River where a winter defensive line could be consolidated.[108] This proposal was militarily prudent and conformed to the German defensive tradition of conserving combat power while not holding terrain for its own sake.

Hitler, however, did not regard strategic problems in traditional ways. In the German dictator's mind, the prestige value of holding Rostov outweighed any risk that German forces might have to endure in order to hold it. On 30 November, after a vitriolic conversation with Brauchitsch, Hitler countermanded Rundstedt's withdrawal order by directing that German forces stand and fight on the Don. Affronted at this interference in his command, Rundstedt asked to be relieved. Hitler promptly granted Rundstedt's request and named Field Marshal Walter von Reichenau as the new commander of Army Group South.[109]

The change in army group leadership, however, did not alter the tactical situation around Rostov. Russian pressure against First Panzer Army over-

Field Marshal Gerd von Rundstedt, commander of Army Group South

Soviet troops counterattack in the streets of Rostov, November 1941

whelmed Reichenau's attempts to hold forward defensive positions, and on 1 December, Hitler allowed Army Group South to fall back to the Mius defensive line, which was the position that had been advocated by Rundstedt earlier. Of Hitler's obstinacy and interference, Halder noted with grim satisfaction that "now we are where we could have been last night. It was a senseless waste of time, and to top it, we lost Rundstedt also."[110]

First Panzer Army's defensive efforts at Rostov and during the withdrawal to the Mius line were harrowing. In fact, the fighting retreat of the German southern wing might have ended disastrously had it not been for heavy *Luftwaffe* attacks against the advancing Soviets.[111] Kleist's panzer army was composed almost entirely of armored and motorized infantry formations which, as previously explained, were inherently less able to hold ground than were German infantry divisions. This problem was exacerbated by the increasing appearance of new Soviet T-34 tanks, against which the German tank and antitank guns made little impression. In one case, the German 60th Motorized Infantry Division had some of its *Paks* literally "rolled flat" by T-34s during defensive fighting within Rostov itself.[112]

In addition, the German forces held an excessively broad defensive front and did so with units that were badly depleted in strength. The III Panzer Corps, for example, initially held its 100-kilometer-long perimeter around Rostov with only one panzer and two motorized divisions.[113] Russian attacks, characterized by Halder as "well-led" and "numerically far superior," inflicted heavy casualties on these thinly spread German units.[114] On 22 November, for example, the 16th Panzer Division could muster only 350 riflemen in its defensive positions guarding the German flank north of Rostov. Heavy Soviet assaults cost one of the 16th Panzer Division's weakened infantry battalions seventy men in one day, a loss that decimated that unit.[115] The temperature, which dipped to more than -20°C, diminished the obstacle value of streams and rivers by freezing them solid and rendered the ground so hard that defensive positions could only be gouged out with explosives.

Finally, the smooth withdrawal of German forces to the Mius line was interrupted by Hitler's temporary "stand and fight" order. This order reached German forward units after the retreat had already begun, thus resulting in considerable confusion during the following two days as combat forces and rear-echelon service units became entangled in marches and countermarches.[116]

By the end of the first week of December, Army Group South had established a winter defensive line running generally from the Mius River north along the Donets River. Likewise, the Army Group North positions had stabilized in a vast salient extending from Leningrad eastward to Tikhvin and then south to Lake Ilmen and the Valdai Hills. The lines of Leeb's army group fell short of the goal set by Hitler of linking up with the Finns, but no further offensive actions could be expected. Only on the central portion of the front did the Germans cherish hopes of further offensive success.

Bock's Army Group Center had surged forward on 15 November in a last, desperate grab for Moscow. This attack had immediately collided with prepared Soviet defenses manned by newly reinforced Russian armies. Dogged by a deficient logistical system, severe shortages in personnel and equipment, and the onset of harsh winter weather, the German offensive made slow progress. Although Hitler wildly urged Bock to undertake deep envelopments, the fact remained that the armies of Army Group Center had so dwindled in strength and mobility that only frontal attacks could be mounted.[117] By the end of the month, German units had reached the extreme limit of their endurance. Although the maps in Hitler's headquarters still portrayed a great offensive, at the front the scattered and feeble thrusts by German units increasingly resembled the reflexive spasms of a dying animal.[118]

Even before their hopes of capturing Moscow totally died away, German planners hastened to assess the requirements for extended defensive operations through the Russian winter. Whatever the outcome of the Moscow battles, the German armies in Russia would be unable to conduct new offensive operations until the following spring. Consequently, as it became apparent that no final Soviet collapse or capitulation was going to occur, German staff officers bent their efforts to planning for a winter defense on the Russian Front.

As early as 19 November, with Operation Taifun still in full swing, Hitler conferred with his military advisers on the building of an "east wall" defensive line, but the dictator put off any decision until a later date. Four days later, Halder discussed the construction of a rearward defensive line and fortifications with General Hans von Greiffenberg, Army Group Center's chief of staff. On 29 November, after a review of the situation on the Eastern Front with the head of the General Staff's Operations Section, Halder authorized the preparation of orders for a general winter defense.[119] Drafted over the next week, this order became Führer Directive 39, which Hitler signed on 8 December.

Taken at face value, Führer Directive 39 resembled the shrewd 1917 plan to withdraw to the Hindenburg Line that had inaugurated the German Elastic Defense. Although framed in strategic terms, Führer Directive 39 (and the Army High Command's implementing instructions that accompanied it) generally followed the traditional principles of the elastic defense in depth. Brauchitsch, the German Army's commander in chief, was directed to designate a winter defensive line. At his discretion, this line could be located to the rear of current German positions, although rearward fortifications were to be prepared prior to any tactical withdrawals. (Significantly, in light of subsequent events, this showed an initial willingness even on the part of Hitler to relinquish terrain that did not contribute materially to German goals.) The defensive line itself was to be held with minimum forces, allowing combat units—and especially panzer and motorized divisions—to be refitted in reserve positions farther to the rear. These rehabilitation and reserve areas were to be located fairly close to the front lines to facilitate rapid reinforcement of threatened sectors. Defensive positions were to be sited for optimum defensive effectiveness and comfortable troop quartering. Moreover, to provide additional defensive depth, the order emphasized the construction of rearward defensive positions, using whatever manpower could be scraped together.[120]

Führer Directive 39 was historically significant because it implicitly conceded that the German armies had failed to achieve Barbarossa's strategic objectives. The Soviet Union, though suffering enormous losses in the summer and autumn battles, had not been conquered in a "single, lightning campaign." Moscow, belatedly named the climactic operational objective, remained beyond the German reach. Führer Directive 39 blamed these failures on the premature winter weather and resultant supply difficulties. More crucial, however, was the vastly depleted German combat power. The offensive exertions of the previous five months had so sapped German strength that German units had become unfit for combat of any sort, whether offensive or defensive.

In a situation analogous to that encountered by the Allies in 1918 following the Ludendorff offensives, Soviet counterattacks revealed that German units were scarcely able to hold the ground they had recently won. Red Army soldiers, testing German lines outside of Moscow with local counterattacks, discovered to their surprise that German resistance was spotty. Exploiting tactical successes, these Soviet counterblows gradually swelled in scope and intensity. By the beginning of December, the Soviet High Command had recognized the frailty of the German position and threw all available forces into a general counteroffensive. Beginning on 6 December, this counterstroke tore open the German front and created the greatest strategic crisis yet faced by the Germans in the war.

Thus it was that Führer Directive 39, though significant in reflecting German defensive intentions, failed to have any real effect on the conduct of winter operations by the German Army. Whereas the German winter defensive order assumed a smooth, deliberate transition to positional defense, Soviet counterattacks were already forcing battle-weary German units into headlong retreat. Belatedly issued on 8 December, the German defensive order had already been made obsolete by events. As in the defensive battles during Barbarossa's drive eastward, German winter defensive tactics were to be dictated more by local conditions than by doctrinal prescription.

Chapter 3

Winter Battles, 1941—42

The Russo-German War entered its second major phase in December 1941. During the previous five months, the Germans had held the strategic initiative, but on 6 December, the Red Army seized the initiative, counterattacking first against Army Group Center and later against all three German army groups (see map 5). Lasting through the end of February, these attacks upset the calculations of Führer Directive 39, which had assumed that the front would remain quiescent until the following spring.

The Soviet winter counteroffensives prompted significant changes to German strategy and tactical methods. These alterations emerged during the winter fighting and helped shape the German defensive practices that were used throughout the remainder of the war.

At the strategic level, the December crisis on the Eastern Front caused Hitler to override his military advisers' recommendations by enjoining a face-saving no-retreat policy that callously risked the annihilation of entire German armies. His patience with independent-minded officers finally at an end, the German dictator then followed this strategic injunction with a purge of the German Army's senior officer corps that left the Führer in direct, daily control of all German military activities. These events had ominous long-term implications in that Hitler's personal command rigidity, together with his chronic insistence on "no retreat" in defensive situations, eventually corrupted both the style and substance of German military operations.

The winter of 1941—42 left its mark on German defensive tactics as well. During the defensive battles from December to February, German attempts to conduct a doctrinal Elastic Defense were generally unsuccessful. Instead, German units gradually fell to battling Soviet attacks from a chain of static strongpoints. This defensive method was based on tactical expedience and was successful due as much to Soviet disorganization as to German steadfastness.

Standing Fast

The German High Command was slow to appreciate the magnitude of the Soviet winter counteroffensive. For weeks prior to the Russian onslaught, German units had been reporting incessant enemy counterattacks during their own drive toward Moscow. So routine had these counterattacks become that German analysts failed to recognize immediately the Russian shift from local counterattacks to a general counteroffensive. Since the Germans had seemingly ruled out large-scale offensive operations for themselves due to heavy losses, supply difficulties, and severe weather conditions, they supposed the Russians would do the same. In fact, the intelligence annex supporting Führer Directive

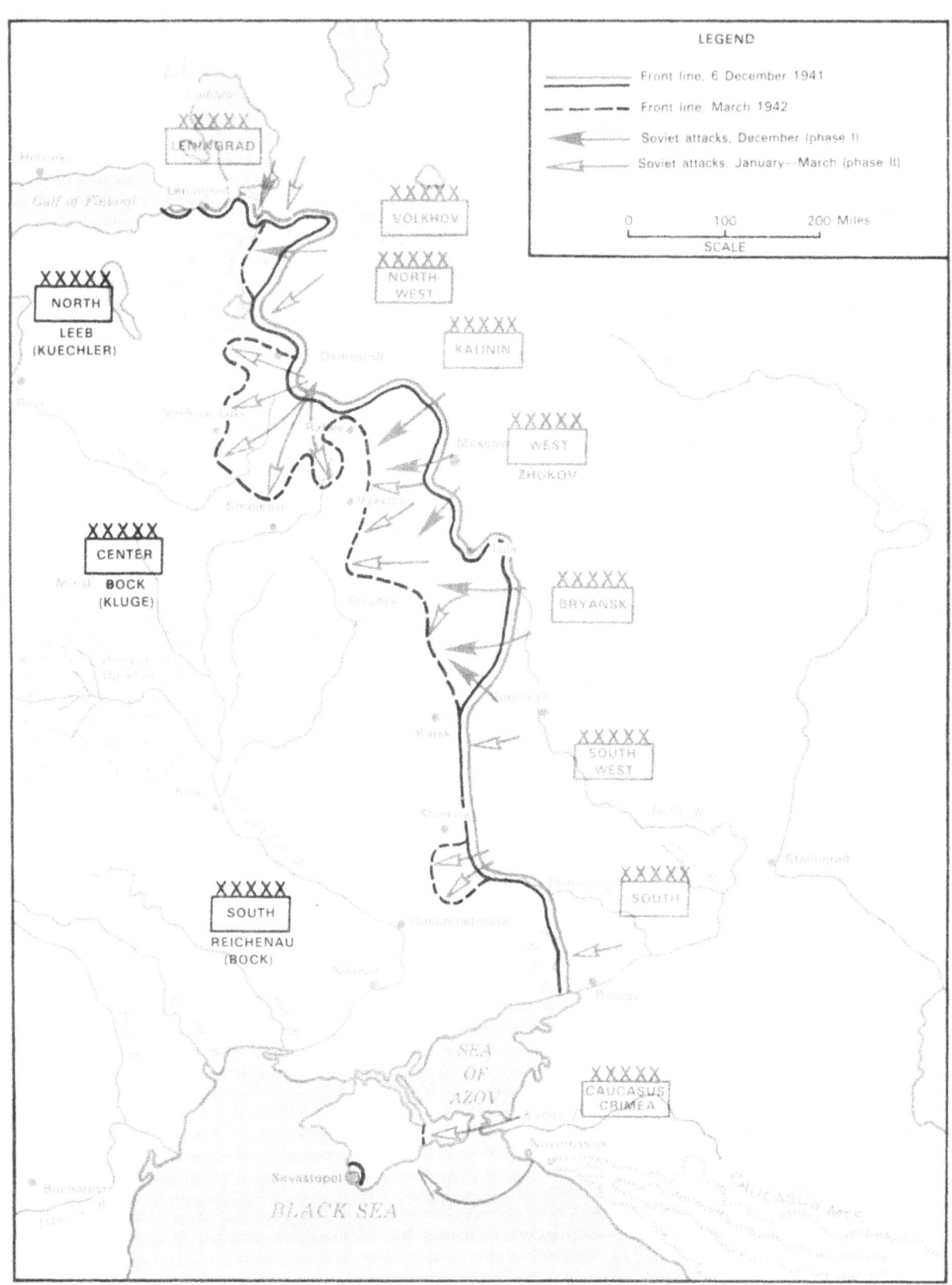

Map 5. Soviet winter counteroffensives, December 1941—March 1942

39 discounted the Red Army's ability to mount more than limited attacks during the coming winter.[1]

High-level German leaders also underestimated the abject weakness of their own units. The Taifun offensive had overextended the German armies in the east, and their spent divisions lay scattered like beached flotsam from Leningrad to Rostov. As a discouraged General Guderian wrote on 8 December: "We are faced with the sad fact that the Supreme Command has overreached itself by refusing to believe our reports of the increasing weakness of the troops. . . . [I have decided] to withdraw to a previously selected and relatively short line which I hope that I shall be able to hold with what is left of my forces. The Russians are pursuing us closely and we must expect misfortunes to occur."[2]

The greatest immediate danger loomed on Army Group Center's front (see map 6). Committed to offensive action until swamped by the Soviet counterblow, the divisions of Field Marshal von Bock's army group had prepared few real defensive works. On 8 December—the same day that Guderian on his own initiative had ordered his Second Panzer Army to begin withdrawing—Bock assessed that his army group was incapable of stopping a strong counteroffensive.[3] The most exposed forces were the 3d and 4th Panzer Groups north of Moscow and Guderian's Second Panzer Army south of the Russian capital. Occupying salients formed during Operation Taifun, these exposed panzer and motorized divisions experienced a cruel reversal. Once again, offensive success had turned into defensive peril for the panzers, as the formations most heavily beset by Soviet attacks were also those least able to sustain a positional defense.

Caught off balance by the Soviet counteroffensive, the Germans lacked any real concept for dealing with the deteriorating situation on the central front. The chief of the German Army General Staff wrote in his diary that "the Supreme Command [Hitler] does not realize the condition our troops are in and indulges in paltry patchwork where only big decisions could help. One of the decisions that should be taken is the withdrawal of Army Group Center. . . ."[4] Still smarting from Army Group South's earlier abandonment of Rostov, however, Hitler was unwilling to countenance any such retreat. Instead, German countermeasures during the first two weeks of the Russian offensive were reminiscent of the frantic half measures taken during the summer defensive crises at Yelnya and Toropets: minor local withdrawals and piecemeal attempts to contain Soviet breakthroughs. For example, the hasty withdrawal of Second Panzer Army's beleaguered divisions from the area east of Tula was done on Guderian's own initiative and not as part of a coordinated general plan.

Although these measures reduced the immediate likelihood that exposed units would be cut off and destroyed, the fundamental German strategic problem was not addressed. The thin lines of exhausted German troops seemed to be on the verge of collapse, few reinforcements were available, and puny local countermeasures merely invited greater danger. For instance, even as Guderian's forces were recoiling from Tula, gaps opened between his units, and sizable Russian forces poured into the German rear.[5] Then, between 9 and 15 December, a massive Soviet attack on Guderian's right flank overran and virtually annihilated the German Second Army's 45th, 95th, and 134th

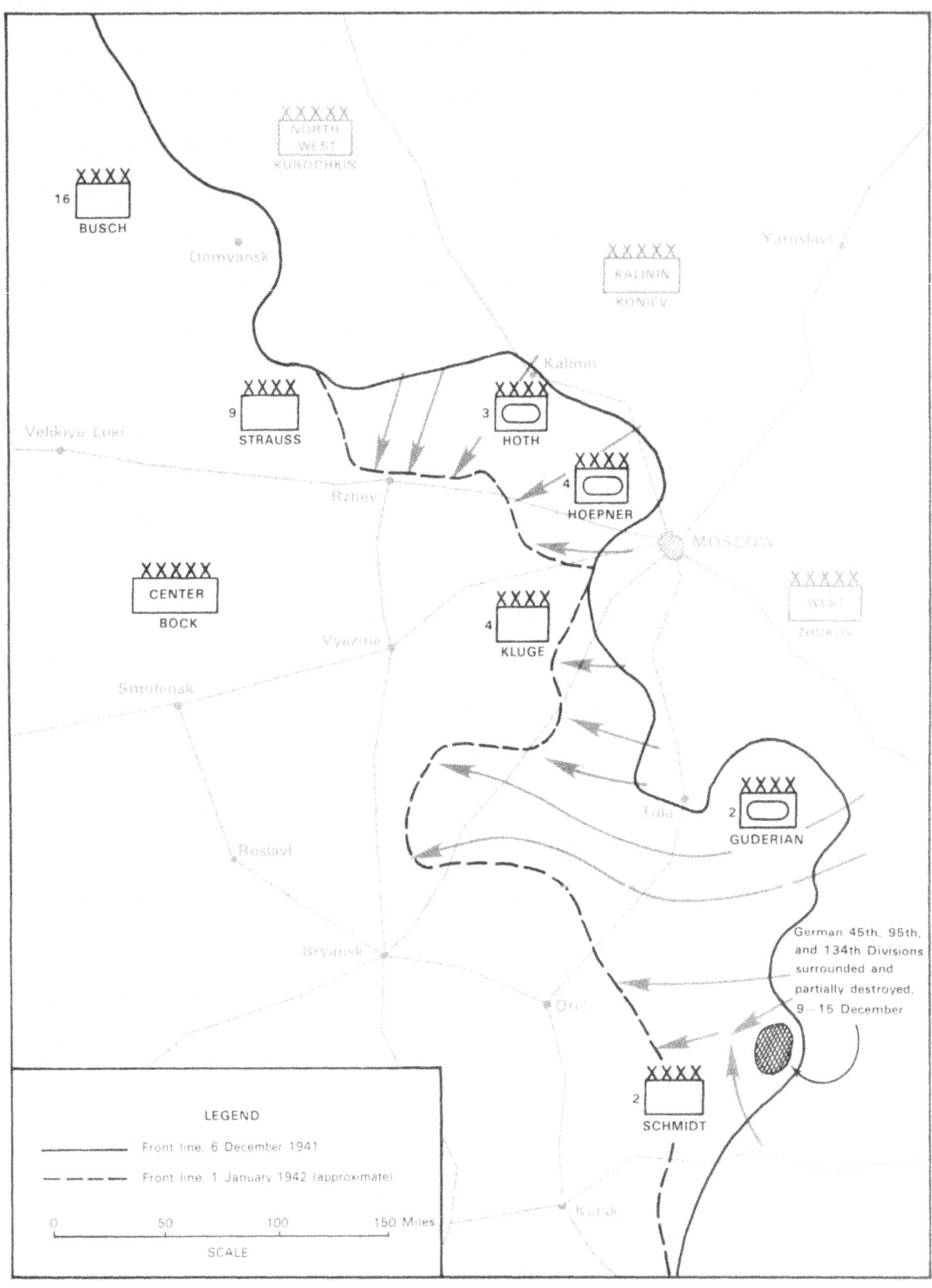

Map 6. Soviet attacks against Army Group Center, December 1941

Infantry Divisions.[6] This complete destruction of German divisions was unprecedented in World War II and an unmistakable omen of impending disaster. By the third week of December, deep Soviet penetrations on both flanks of Bock's army group threatened to ripen into a double envelopment of the entire German central front. After touring the splintered German lines, ailing Field Marshal von Brauchitsch confessed to Halder that he could "not see any way of extricating the Army from its present predicament."[7]

In fact, only two alternatives offered an escape from the deepening crisis. One choice was to conduct an immediate large-scale withdrawal, trusting that German forces could consolidate a rearward defensive line before Soviet pursuit could inflict decisive losses. The other choice was to stand fast and weather the Soviet attacks in present positions. Neither course of action guaranteed success, and each was fraught with considerable risk.

A winter retreat would cost the Germans much of their artillery and heavy equipment, which would have to be abandoned for lack of transport. Because of Hitler's procrastination in November, no rearward "east wall" defensive line had been prepared; therefore, a withdrawal promised little improvement over the tactical situation the Germans already faced.[8] Too, as already shown on Guderian's front south of Moscow, retrograde operations could easily lead to an even greater crisis if enemy units managed to thrust between the retreating German columns. Finally, a retreat through the Russian winter conjured up the shade of Napoleon's 1812 *Grande Armée.* Though morale in the depleted German divisions still remained generally intact despite the harsh conditions, German officers fearfully reminded each other of the sudden moral collapse that had turned the French retreat into a rout nearly a century and a half before.[9]

German equipment abandoned outside of Moscow

The alternative seemed even more desperate. A continued defense from present positions could succeed only if German defensive endurance exceeded Russian offensive endurance—a slim prospect considering the exhausted state of the German forces. The chances for success were best on the extreme northern and southern wings, where the Leningrad siege works and the Mius River line offered some protection. Between these two poles, however, a stand-fast defense would surely cost the Germans heavily. The absence of reserves and the lack of defensive depth ensured that some units would be overrun or isolated during the winter. Moreover, this course of action forfeited the possibility of a new German offensive in the central sector the following spring or early summer, since surviving German divisions of Army Group Center would require substantial rebuilding.

Conditioned by their professional training to weigh risks carefully and to conserve forces for future requirements, German commanders and staff officers preferred the potential dangers of a winter retreat to the certain perils of standing fast. Guderian, for example, regarded "a prompt and extensive withdrawal to a line where the terrain was suitable to the defense ... [to be] the best and most economical way of rectifying the situation," while Brauchitsch and Halder agreed that "Army Group [Center] must be given discretion to fall back ... as the situation requires."[10] In anticipation that this course of action would be followed, Russian civilians and German labor units were hurriedly pressed into work on a rearward defensive line running from Kursk through Orel to Gzhatsk.[11]

Once again, Adolf Hitler confounded the plans of his military advisers. Hitler watched the disintegration of the German front with great dismay and convinced himself that each retreat simply added momentum to the Soviet offensive. On 16 December, the German dictator telephoned Bock to order Army Group Center to cease all withdrawals and to defend its present positions. German soldiers would take "not one single step back." At a late night conference the same evening, Hitler extended the stand-fast order to the entire Eastern Front. A general withdrawal, he declared, was "out of the question."[12]

Hitler marshaled both real and fanciful arguments to justify his decision. Citing information collected by his personal adjutant, Colonel Rudolf Schmundt, Hitler ticked off the disadvantages of retreat: German units were sacrificing artillery and valuable equipment with each withdrawal, no prepared line existed to which German forces could expeditiously retire, and "the idea to prepare rear positions" amounted to "drivelling nonsense."[13] Furthermore, Hitler argued, attempts to create fallback positions weakened the resolve of the fighting forces by suggesting that current positions were expendable. All of these arguments were at least partially correct, even if senior military officers preferred to discount them.

However, Hitler's rationalizations went even further. Contrary to the visible evidence, Hitler insisted that the Russians were on the verge of collapse after suffering between 8 and 10 million military casualties. (This estimate exaggerated Soviet losses by almost 100 percent.) The Red Army artillery, he claimed, was so decimated by losses that it no longer existed as an effective arm—a claim for which there was no evidence whatsoever. Hitler asserted that the enemy's sole asset was the superior numbers of soldiers, an advantage of no real value since they were "not nearly as good as ours." In a strange

Hitler feared the loss of valuable equipment during a general winter retreat

twist of logic, Hitler even argued that the enormously wide frontages held by German divisions proved the enemy's weakness, since otherwise the Soviets would have exploited this vulnerability to a greater extent than they had already done. (Coming at a time when the entire German front was threatening to give way in the face of Soviet offensive pressure, this claim must have seemed totally outrageous.)[14]

One major factor that affected Hitler's decision went largely unspoken by the dictator. Tyrants, it is said, fear nothing so much as ridicule, and Adolf Hitler feared the embarrassment that retreat would cause to the Reich's—and to his own—military prestige. Moreover, on 11 December, Hitler had recklessly declared war on the United States, a move that unnecessarily compounded Germany's military problems. Under the circumstances, the spectacle of German armies in unseemly retreat before Russian *Untermenschen* (subhumans) would have been a serious blow to Hitler's credibility. Therefore, German soldiers were exhorted to "fanatical resistance" in place "without regard to flanks or rear."[15]

Having again rejected the recommendations of his military advisers, Hitler decided to rid himself once and for all of uncooperative senior officers. Not only would this end the tugs-of-war between Hitler and the Army High Command over military strategy, but it would satisfy Hitler's desire to curb the enduring independence of the German Army's officer corps as well.

Adolf Hitler had an irrational mistrust of the aristocratic, apolitical officers who held most of the high positions in the German Army. Their professional aloofness and political indifference had long irritated Hitler, who regarded them as obstacles to his own strategic visions and his personal power. Since becoming chancellor in 1933, he had skillfully worked to curtail the army's independence. When the aged Weimar President von Hindenburg died in 1934, Hitler suborned an oath of personal loyalty from all members of the armed forces, a step that exceeded the doomed Weimar Republic's constitutional practice. In 1938, Hitler engineered the disgrace and removal of Field Marshal Werner von Blomberg and General Werner Freiherr von Fritsch, who were respectively the minister of war and commander in chief of the army. At that time, Hitler absorbed the duties of war minister into his own portfolio as Führer and created a new joint Armed Forces High Command (*OKW*), which diluted the traditional autonomy of the German Army. Hitler then staffed the senior *OKW* posts with sycophants like General (later Field Marshal) Wilhelm Keitel and General Alfred Jodl so that the *OKW* amounted to little more than an executive secretariat for Hitler and an operational impediment to the Army High Command (*OKH*). As his knowledge of military matters grew during the war, Hitler overruled with greater frequency and confidence the campaign advice of his army advisers. During Barbarossa, the army's resistance to Hitler's interference repeatedly antagonized the Führer, and so he resolved to purge troublesome officers.[16]

Field Marshal von Brauchitsch, the German Army's commander in chief, was among the first to follow Rundstedt into retirement. Weakened by a heart attack in November, Brauchitsch had neither the moral courage nor the physical strength to resist the Führer's trespasses. Hitler made no secret of his growing disdain for the ill field marshal, subjecting him to humiliating tongue-lashings and treating him openly as a gold-braided "messenger boy."[17] On 19 December, Hitler finally sacked Brauchitsch and took over the position of army commander in chief.

The timing of Brauchitsch's relief was masterful. Although not stated so officially, Brauchitsch was made the scapegoat for the failure of Barbarossa and for the winter crisis on the Eastern Front. Hitler himself propagated this view to his inner circle, referring to Brauchitsch as "a vain, cowardly wretch who could not even appraise the situation, much less master it. By his constant interference and consistent disobedience he completely spoiled the entire plan for the eastern campaign."[18]

Although Brauchitsch had been a weak and relatively ineffective army commander in chief, the real issue in his relief was not military competence but political loyalty and personal subservience. Lest this lesson be misunderstood, Hitler pointedly informed Halder that "this little affair of operational command is something that anybody can do. The Commander-in-Chief's job is to train the Army in the National Socialist idea, and I know of no general who could do that as I want it done. For that reason I've decided to take over command of the Army myself."[19]

As soon as Brauchitsch was out of the way, Hitler then turned his wrath on balky field commanders. With Hitler directly supervising their operations, frontline officers no longer enjoyed the insulation previously provided by Brauchitsch. Furthermore, with the Führer doubling as the army commander in chief, military subordination effectively became synonymous with political allegiance. Officers who too candidly criticized Hitler's strategic designs or commanders who took independent action at variance with Hitler's instructions were implicitly guilty of affronting the Führer's personal authority. Whereas

Two senior commanders relieved by Hitler: Field Marshal Walther von Brauchitsch (left), commander in chief of the German Army, and General Heinz Guderian (right), commander of the Second Panzer Army

during the war's earlier campaigns such independence might have gone unremarked or unchecked, henceforth such actions might lead to swift relief or even worse.

Hitler, bent on a personal vendetta against the German Army's leaders, was given ample opportunity to make examples of offending officers during the winter defensive crisis. Suffering from failing health, Field Marshal von Bock had already lost the Führer's confidence over Army Group Center's failure to storm Moscow. When Bock persisted in predicting disaster unless allowed to retreat, he was abruptly retired on 20 December. General Guderian evaded orders to stand fast because such actions would endanger his Second Panzer Army and, after a tense face-to-face meeting with Hitler on 20 December, was relieved from active duty on 26 December.[20] General Erich Hoepner, like Guderian an aggressive panzer leader, enraged Hitler in early January by ordering units of his Fourth Panzer Army* to retreat westward to avoid encirclement. Hoepner was summarily relieved of his command, and Hitler ordered that Hoepner be stripped of all rank and privileges, including the right to wear his uniform in retirement.[21] Strauss, the Ninth Army commander who had directed the German defense against Timoshenko's attacks in August and September, was cashiered a week after Hoepner for being overly pessimistic in his reports. Field Marshal von Leeb, the commander of Army Group North, found his prewar defensive theories swept aside by Hitler's insistence on a rigid defense. When Leeb explained that a dangerous and unnecessary

---

*Panzer Groups 3 and 4 were redesignated panzer armies on 1 January 1942.

salient near Demyansk should be abandoned to free badly needed reserves, Hitler countered by arguing that such salients were, in fact, beneficial since they tied down more Russian than German forces. Leeb, "being unable to subscribe to this novel theory," was thus relieved on 17 January.[22] Army and army group commanders were not Hitler's only targets. In fact, during the 1941—42 winter, he relieved more than thirty generals and other high-ranking officers who had been corps commanders, division commanders, and senior staff officers.[23]

Hitler also took other steps to secure control over the German Army. Disregarding seniority and even combat experience, Hitler elevated officers of unquestioning loyalty (such as General Walter Model) or officers of known Nazi sympathies (such as Field Marshal Walter von Reichenau) to senior positions. (Model replaced Strauss as commander of Ninth Army, while Reichenau succeeded Rundstedt at Army Group South. Reichenau's previous position as Sixth Army commander was filled by the loyal but unimaginative General Friedrich Paulus, an energetic staff officer whose unflinching obedience led to tragedy at Stalingrad a year later.) To ensure close future control over promotions and assignments, Hitler promoted Schmundt, his personal adjutant, to general and placed his former aide in charge of the army personnel office. In one further step to cement his authority, Hitler forbade voluntary resignations, thereby denying the German officer corps the traditional soldierly protest against unconscionable commands.[24]

While the removal of unruly senior officers made the German Army more docile, these turnovers adversely affected German military performance in three ways.

First, the cashiering of so many field commanders in the midst of desperate defensive fighting disrupted the continuity of German operations. The newly appointed leaders, who frequently brought with them new chiefs of staff, normally required an adjustment period before they could discharge their new duties with complete confidence. In fact, some of the replacements could not make the adjustment at all. General Ludwig Kübler, who replaced Field Marshal Günther von Kluge as Fourth Army commander when Kluge replaced Bock, found Hitler's stand-fast strategy intolerable and requested his own relief barely a month after assuming command.[25] The net effect of all this turmoil was to minimize bold initiatives at the front and to concede virtually all strategic and operational control to the Führer by default.

Second, by sweeping away those officers who had the temerity to challenge Hitler's strategic views, an important source of advice and assessment was silenced. For the remainder of the war, responsible criticism of the Führer's designs was muted by the threat of punishment. Therefore, for the next three years, German military strategy lurched from disaster to disaster due mainly to Hitler's having banished or intimidated into silence those whose courage, skill, and judgment best qualified them to act as independent advisers.

Finally, by removing so many senior leaders and by inserting himself into the chain of command as army commander in chief, Hitler profoundly altered the command philosophy of the German Army. For generations, commanders in the Prussian and German Armies had been schooled to direct

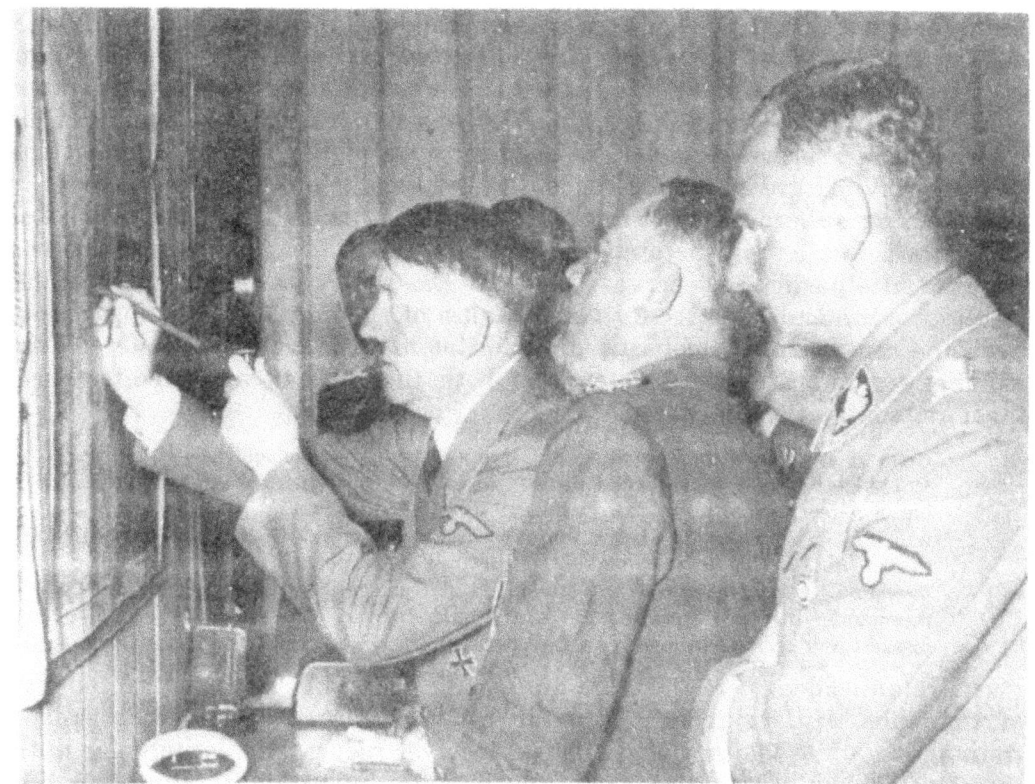
Hitler assumed personal command of the German Army in December 1941 and began interfering in the direction of combat operations

operations according to the principle of *Auftragstaktik*. This principle constrained commanders to giving broad, mission-oriented directives to their juniors, who were then allowed maximum latitude in accomplishing their assigned tasks. Senior leaders trusted implicitly in the professional discretion of their subordinates, and German operations characteristically evinced a degree of imagination, flexibility, and initiative matched by few other armies. So deeply ingrained was this philosophy that actions contrary to orders were seldom regarded as disobedience, but rather as laudable displays of initiative and aggressiveness. According to a German military aphorism, mules could be taught to obey but officers were expected to know when to disobey.[26]

Hitler's rigid and overbearing insistence on the literal execution of all orders corrupted *Auftragstaktik*. That Hitler, the "Bohemian corporal," did not understand this system or, more likely, that he had no patience for it was demonstrated early in the Barbarossa campaign. Halder diagnosed Hitler's leadership style as lacking "that confidence in the executive commands which is one of the most essential features of our command organization, and that is so because it fails to grasp the coordinating force that comes from the common schooling of our Leader Corps."[27]

The harm done to the German command philosophy was not confined to upper echelons only, however. Hitler's stifling, obedience-oriented style was transmitted throughout the German Army so that operations at all levels suffered its stifling effects. Senior field commanders, themselves answerable to the implacable Führer, were thus pressed to control more closely the operations of their own subordinates. This corrosive process was abetted by two features of the World War II battlefield. The first was modern radio communications, which enabled senior commanders to direct even remote combat actions. This not only invited greater interference, but spawned timidity at lower levels by conditioning subordinates to seek ratification of their decisions from their superiors before acting. Second, the chronic lack of German reserve units—a circumstance particularly pervasive on the Eastern Front—reduced the ability of senior commanders to rectify the mistakes of subordinates and thus encouraged the centralization of battle direction at higher levels. As General Frido von Senger und Etterlin, a veteran of both the Russian and Mediterranean theaters, wrote after the war:

> Reserves enable the commander to preserve a measure of independence. He may feel obliged to report his decisions, but as long as his superior authority has his own reserves with which to influence the general situation, that authority will only be too ready to leave the subordinate commander to use his as he thinks best. If the forces shrink so much that these normal reserves are not available ... then the forces so detailed are put at the disposal of the highest commander in the area, while the local commanders ... can no longer expect to exert any decisive influence on the operations.[28]

German leaders were therefore driven to a more and more centralized style of command. Hitler's insistence on literal obedience restricted independence from above, while the lack of battlefield reserves reduced the latitude for initiative from below. The result was a decline in the flexibility that had been traditional in German armies for over a century.

Because real operational flexibility no longer existed in the German Army from the winter of 1941—42 onward, German defensive actions on the Russian battlefield were adversely affected. Hitler's orders to the German Army to stand fast established the framework of German defensive strategy. The cashiering of recalcitrant senior officers gave authority to that strategy and gradually narrowed the discretionary latitude of subordinate leaders to act independently. It remained for the combat units themselves, coping as best as they could with dreadful weather and a tough enemy, to give substance to the German defense.

Strongpoint Defense: Origins

At the tactical level, German defensive practice during the winter of 1941 was dictated by Hitler's stand-fast order, the appalling weakness of German units, and the harshness of the Russian winter weather. These three factors forced the Germans to use a defensive system that consisted mostly of a network of loosely connected strongpoints backed by local reserves. This strongpoint defense had no basis in prewar German doctrine and was, in fact, wholly improvised to fit the particular circumstances existing at the time. As the 197th Infantry Division reported at the end of the winter fighting: "A strongpoint-style deployment can only be an emergency expedient *(Notbehelf)*, especially against the combat methods of the Russians with their skill at penetration and infiltration. On the basis of his previous training, the German soldier is not disposed to a strongpoint-style defense."[29]

Although some Germans later represented the strongpoint defense as being a shrewd method of slowing a superior enemy by controlling road junctions, any such success was largely coincidental. The strongpoint defense was, first and foremost, a tactic of weakness. German commanders did not elect to fight from village-based strongpoints due to any cunning assessment of Soviet vulnerabilities. Rather, the German winter defense coagulated around towns because Hitler forbade voluntary withdrawals, because German divisions were too weak to hold a continuous line, and lastly, because the winter weather lashed at unprotected German units that tried to stand in the open.

When the German armies on the Eastern Front began defensive operations in early December, they did not expect an immediate major Soviet counteroffensive. Therefore, most German divisions deployed into a thin linear defense similar to that used by the Army Group Center units during the August and September defensive battles. Lacking the depth and reserves of a true Elastic Defense, this linear formation merely stretched German forward units into a semblance of a continuous defensive front. Such a tissue-thin deployment could only have served to prevent large-scale infiltration or, at the very best, to fend off local attacks. The 31st Infantry Division, holding a broad divisional sector southwest of Moscow, "had to return more or less to the old [pre-1917] Linear Tactics, and had to foresake a defensive deployment in depth" due to lack of forces. The division's main line of resistance consisted of a "thin string of infantry sentry posts, with large uncovered areas in between" and was held together chiefly by the fire from the 31st Division's few surviving artillery pieces. The artillery gun positions, fitted out as small infantry redoubts, provided the only defensive depth.[30]

The Soviet counteroffensive completely overwhelmed this flimsy German defensive line, and those German units not destroyed outright were swept rearward in a series of running battles against superior Red Army forces. The 31st Division, its own sector quiet until 14 December, had its front lines perforated on that date by several Soviet attacks. When the scratch German reserves failed to restore the division's front, the 31st Division, like most German units on the central portion of the Eastern Front, initiated a fighting withdrawal in the hope of reestablishing a linear defense farther to the rear.[31]

Pitifully weak in men and firepower and generally inferior to the Russians in winter cross-country mobility, the Germans found it difficult to break contact with the enemy and to slip across the frozen landscape unmolested. German infantry companies and battalions were so understrength that they could not be subdivided any further in order to create rearguards. Consequently, an entire battalion (scarcely amounting to a single undermanned rifle company in most cases) commonly had to remain in place to cover the remainder of a regiment as it withdrew. The outlook for these rearguards was grim: "[The rearguard carried] the large burden of the fighting. Frequently they had to stop and delay the pursuing enemy, while other Russian elements were already attacking their flanks or rear. Then they had to fight their way out, or pass through the enemy lines at night to join their own forces."[32] Needless to say, many rearguard detachments were swallowed whole by the advancing Soviets.

Even with the occasional sacrifice of the rearguards, units clambering rearward over the snowy wastes remained extremely vulnerable to attack or ambush by fast-moving Soviet pursuit columns. During a withdrawal, one battalion of the 289th Infantry Regiment (98th Division) was attacked by Soviet forces and nearly annihilated, losing all of its antitank weapons and machine guns.[33] To protect itself from such peril, the 35th Infantry Division put its engineers to work blasting hasty defensive positions into the frozen ground along proposed withdrawal routes in order to provide emergency cover during retreats. However, on occasion, this action backfired, as when Soviet cavalry and ski troops slipped into the German rear, occupied the intermediate positions, and raked the approaching Germans with deadly small-arms fire.[34] Seemingly beset by relentless Red Army forces from all sides, many German units began to exhibit an acute fear of being encircled or outflanked.[35]

Soviet tanks posed the greatest threat to the retreating Germans. The Russian T-34s had excellent cross-country mobility and had little to fear from German light antitank weapons. The few heavy guns that the Germans still possessed tended to wallow helplessly in the deep snow, unable to deploy or to engage the Russian armor.[36] German officers noted that epidemics of tank fear were again afflicting entire units, and local withdrawals sometimes turned into headlong, panic-stricken flight at the first appearance of Soviet tanks.[37] Though kept well in hand by their own leaders, retreating soldiers of the 31st Division passed telltale evidence of disintegration in other units: quantities of artillery, engineering equipment, supplies, and motor vehicles all abandoned in place by fleeing German forces.[38]

Standing fast: German infantry occupying a thin defensive line in snow trenches during the 1941—42 winter. The weapon in the revetment is a 20-mm flak gun.

Such local incidents aroused concern not only for German morale, but also about German small-unit leadership. The wastage in combat officers and noncommissioned officers since the beginning of Barbarossa had been tremendous. By mid-December, lieutenants were commanding many German infantry battalions, while sergeants or corporals led nearly all platoons and many companies. The continued effectiveness of even these remaining leaders was suspect due to the cumulative strain of fatigue and uninterrupted combat.[39]

The Germans first began to use strongpoint defensive positions during these hazardous early withdrawals. Frequently out of contact with neighboring forces and lacking sufficient time to prepare real defensive works, retreating units formed self-defense hedgehog perimeters like the rapidly advancing panzers had done during the previous summer. The 31st Infantry Division, for instance, abandoned all pretense at linear defense as soon as its own withdrawals began.[40] Likewise, the 137th Infantry Division pinpointed its own adoption of strongpoint tactics to the beginning of difficult retrograde engagements southeast of Yukhnov. According to the division's former operations officer, from that point on "for all practical purposes the campaign consisted of a battle for villages. Positions in open terrain were seldom possible due to the weather conditions, and only then when we remained several days in one position and the engineers could aid in blasting through the meter-deep frost."[41]

Hitler's 16 December no-retreat order curtailed the flurry of piecemeal withdrawals. By forbidding even local retreats without permission from the highest authority, this directive forced German units into a positional defense. The strongpoint style of defense, having come into wide use as a protective measure during the pell-mell retrograde operations, was extended into a general defensive system across most of the German front. Bearing little visible resemblance to the Elastic Defense postulated in prewar manuals, the strongpoint defense therefore evolved solely in response to the peculiar conditions of the winter battles.

The second factor necessitating a strongpoint scheme was the weakness of German units. In fact, German units stood at such low levels that no continuous front could realistically be sustained. This was true not only at the operational level where gaps between German divisions, corps, and armies had been routine since July, but even at the tactical level as well. At the start of the Soviet drive, the "continuous" line held by Army Group Center was, in fact, already a discontinuous series of unit fronts. Divisions of the German Fourth Army were allotted sectors thirty to sixty kilometers wide, although most infantry companies contained only twenty-five to forty men.[42] Such strengths were clearly insufficient to man a solid defensive front.

Losses during the first days of the Soviet counterthrust extinguished any lingering possibility of a continuous linear defense. In the Ninth Army's 35th Infantry Division, cold and Soviet attacks whittled the average rifle company strength from ten noncommissioned officers (NCOs) and sixty men on 7 December to five NCOs and twenty men just five days later.[43] Panzer Group 3, bearing the brunt of the Soviet counteroffensive northwest of Moscow, reported on 19 December that its XLI Corps and LVI Panzer Corps fielded only 1,821 and 900 total combatants respectively.[44] In a desperate attempt to create greater infantry strength, officers and men from nonessential rear services

German troops dig defensive trenches in the snow

were hurried forward, as were troops from artillery and antitank batteries whose weapons had been destroyed or abandoned. Though providing some relief, the relatively small number of additional riflemen thus created had no substantial impact.[45]

Losses in weapons and equipment paralleled those in personnel. By mid-December, field artillery pieces, antitank guns, motor vehicles, and tanks were all in particularly short supply. Panzer Group 4 estimated on 18 December that only 25 to 30 percent of its heavy weapons remained in action, while Panzer Group 3 counted only twenty-one artillery pieces of 100-mm or larger still operational among its six divisions. Similarly, the LVI Panzer Corps had lost so much of its equipment that it remained a corps-size unit in name only: its four panzer divisions together mustered only thirty-four tanks, and its 6th Panzer Division had no running tanks whatsoever.[46] This lack of heavy weapons further diminished the Germans' ability to hold continuous positions, while the shortage of effective motorized forces foreclosed the possibility of any type of mobile defense.

This overall weakness of German units made a renewed linear defense impossible. Not only could assigned frontages not be covered, but any such extended deployment would further disperse what few troops and weapons remained. Consequently, to prevent German combat power from evaporating altogether, German company and battalion commanders instinctively drew their beleaguered units into small strongpoint garrisons when Hitler ordered them to "fanatical resistance" in place.

The severe winter weather was the third major reason that caused German defenders to adopt village-based strongpoints. Even by Russian standards, the 1941—42 winter was particularly harsh. From December until early March, military operations were hampered by heavy snowfall and by the few hours of winter daylight. Yet the extreme cold was by far the most significant aspect of the winter weather. During the winter battles, German and Russian forces clashed in temperatures routinely ranging from -10°C to -30°C, with brief cold spells exceeding -40°C.[47] Contrary to German belief, the cold was an impartial adversary that dogged the operations of both sides with equal intensity. However, the Germans were generally more vulnerable to the debilitating effects of the subzero temperatures due to a near-total lack of winter clothing and equipment.

Hitler blamed the Army High Command for the failure to provide winter necessities, ignoring any intimation that he might bear some blame for the German military predicament. In a clever propaganda stroke, Nazi Party functionaries launched a massive emergency drive in late December to collect winter clothing from the German public. Direct action by the party and the people, it was implied, would rapidly correct the scandalous frontline conditions wrought by General Staff bungling.[48] Coming at a time when Hitler was relieving "incompetent" and "disloyal" officers left and right, this program confirmed the popular impression that Adolf Hitler's personal intervention into the German Army's affairs was not only warranted but even overdue. So persuasive was this logic—and so thorough the propaganda effort to sell it—that even some high-ranking German military officers remained convinced after the war that slipshod General Staff planning had produced the shortage of winter equipment.[49]

German armored vehicles in snow revetments, December 1941

However, the truth was far different. German soldiers fought without winter clothing or special equipment simply because the German supply system could not transport the items forward from rear depots. Normal winter-issue items (woolen vests, caps, earmuffs, scarves, and sweaters) were stocked in Germany and Poland, and General Halder had repeatedly discussed the need to provide these and other essentials to the fighting forces before the onset of winter. On 10 November, however, Halder learned that transportation difficulties would delay deliveries of winter clothing to the front until late January 1942 or even later.[50]

The German logistical system, already tottering from the strain of providing fuel, food, and ammunition to three army groups over the primitive Russian transportation net, was brought to the brink of total collapse by the arrival of winter. Sporadic partisan activity and an epidemic of locomotive breakdowns greatly curtailed German rail-haul capacity. (For instance, the number of German supply trains to the Eastern Front totaled only 1,420 in January 1942, compared to 2,093 in September 1941.)[51] Losses of motor vehicles and draft horses further snarled supply distribution, and frantic attempts to press Russian pony-drawn *panje* wagons into service provided little immediate relief. Moreover, the severe cold increased the consumption rate of certain commodities. For example, German soldiers used large quantities of grenades and explosives to fracture the frozen earth in order to create makeshift foxholes. Likewise, fuel consumption did not decline in proportion to vehicle losses since drivers idled their motors round-the-clock to prevent engine freeze-up.[52]

Because the supply lines could not handle all the supplies that the Germans needed, the limited transportation space was devoted to such vital cargoes as ammunition and medical supplies. Since winter clothing is inherently bulky and therefore relatively inefficient to transport, it remained, for the most part, crated in warehouses in Poland and Germany, awaiting a lull in the logistical crisis when it could be shuttled forward without displacing other commodities.[53] In the meantime, German soldiers had to fend for themselves as best they could.[54]

Without winter clothing to protect them against the subzero temperatures, German units gravitated to Russian towns and villages to find shelter. This shelter was, quite literally, essential to German survival as troops without winter clothing quickly contracted frostbite unless treated to periodic warm-ups. Also, units deployed in the open overnight courted wholesale death by freezing. Even with the Soviet winter counteroffensive in full swing, cold-weather casualties exceeded combat losses in most German units. One German infantry regiment, heavily engaged at the beginning of the Soviet attack, estimated that its losses in two days of fighting amounted to only 100 battle casualties compared to 800 cases of frostbite.[55] As the LVII Panzer Corps' war diary succinctly stated on 26 December, "The weather increasingly stands as the troops' greatest enemy."[56]

Russian villages not only offered immediate protection from the cold, but they also provided relief from many of the collateral problems of winter warfare as well. Food could be warmed and drinking water thawed, thereby reducing the cases of stomach dysentery that lengthened German sick lists. Wounded soldiers could receive medical care without immediate fear of death

Horse-drawn sleds carry German supplies forward near Roslavl, December 1941

due to gangrene or exposure. Villages normally had supplies of straw, with which German soldiers could pad their boots and uniforms against the cold. Indoors, soldiers could more easily attend to personal hygiene—a matter of some consequence considering that German units reported more than 10,000 cases of typhus before spring.[57] Finally, small arms and other items of equipment could be cleaned and warmed inside heated huts. This last task had a significance beyond normal preventive maintenance, for the extreme cold made gunmetal brittle and weapons kept outside tended to jam or malfunction due to broken bolts and firing pins.[58]

By mid to late December, much of the German defensive front in Russia consisted of a series of local strongpoints, where battered German units defended themselves as best they could against waves of Russian attacks.* Since the combat strength of units had wasted away to where a continuous defensive line could not be held or even manned, and because Hitler had forbidden any large-scale withdrawal, this strongpoint defensive system emerged as the only plausible solution to the difficult winter situation. This system offered German forces a chance to defend themselves in place by concentrating what few resources remained without abandoning large chunks of territory entirely to Russian control. In addition, the village-based strongpoints provided essential shelter, since the harsh winter weather posed as dangerous a threat as the enemy.[59]

When combat reports characterized a strongpoint defense as the price of standing fast under the existing battlefield conditions, Hitler quickly issued a new directive giving his own approval to this expedient technique. Dated 26 December, this secret order began by reiterating Hitler's command that no ground be relinquished voluntarily. Glossing over the problems that had forced

---

*Hitler, with an orator's ear for colorful metaphor, preferred the term "hedgehog" (*Igelstellung*) to the more bland term "strongpoint" (*Stützpunkt*). By the end of the war, many officers were emulating the Führer's verbal usage, though *Stützpunkt* remained the technically correct term appearing in German doctrinal publications.

the strongpoint system onto the German armies, the Führer then emphasized the ways in which this technique could be turned against the Russians:

> The defensive system must be strengthened to the utmost, especially by converting all towns and farms into strongpoints and by *maximum echelonment in depth*. It is the duty of every soldier, including support troops, to use every means to hold these shelters to the last. The enemy will therefore be denied use of these localities. He will thus be exposed to the freezing cold, and will be denied use of the roads for supply purposes, thereby hastening his collapse. . . . These principles must be fully communicated to the troops [italics in original].[60]

German soldiers at the front scarcely needed the Führer's advice on how to fight their Russian foes. The prevailing circumstances left no feasible alternative to the holding of village strongpoints. What remained to be seen was how effective this system would be in halting the Soviet counteroffensive and in saving German units from piecemeal annihilation.

Strongpoint Defense: Conduct

Driven to the shelter of Russian towns and villages as an emergency measure, German troops did their best to fortify these positions against the inevitable Soviet assaults. Defensive techniques varied from division to division according to local conditions and experiences. A major difficulty, now becoming apparent to German commanders for the first time, was that previous defensive training had been deficient. As one senior officer later wrote, German troops "so far had been inexperienced in this sort of thing. . . . It is surprising indeed how often and to what extent veteran officers, who had already participated in World War I, had forgotten their experiences of those days. The fact that [German] peacetime training shunned everything connected with 'defensive operations under difficult *winter conditions*' proved now detrimental for the first time [italics in original]."[61]

To compensate for their inexperience, German units shared combat knowhow by exchanging hastily prepared battle reports. An early memorandum of this type, prepared by Fourth Army on 23 January 1942, recounted techniques used effectively by the 10th Motorized Division. Reduced to the strength of a mere infantry regiment, the 10th Motorized Division had for three weeks used a strongpoint defense to defend a fifty-kilometer sector against an estimated seven Red Army divisions.

The 10th Motorized Division's report explained how, in preparing to defend a village strongpoint, officers began by surveying the available buildings to identify those best suited for defensive use. Houses that did not aid in the defense were razed, both to deny the Red Army future use of them as shelter and also to improve German observation and fields of fire. Houses selected as fighting positions were then transformed into miniature fortresses capable of all-around defense: snow was banked against the outer walls and sheathed with ice, overhead cover was reinforced, and firing embrasures were cut and camouflaged with bedsheets. When available, multibarreled 20-mm flak guns were integrated into the defense in special positions, which consisted of houses with their roofs purposely torn off, the floors reinforced (to hold the additional weight of guns and ammunition), and the exterior walls covered with a snow-

A German combat group prepares to leave a Russian village with sleds carrying supplies and heavy weapons, February 1942

and-ice glacis to gun-barrel height. These "flak nests" helped keep both Soviet aircraft and infantry at bay.[62]

Russian farming communities were usually located on hills and ridges, and defensive strongpoints established within them normally had commanding observation and fire over the surrounding cleared fields.[63] Defensive combat from such positions was, again according to a 10th Motorized Division report, primarily "a question of organization," requiring careful use of all available heavy weapons and artillery. When enemy attacks seemed imminent, German artillery fire and air attacks (when available) were directed against known and suspected enemy assembly areas. As Soviet forces approached the strongpoint, the fire of heavy mortars, antitank guns, and heavy machine guns joined in. Such fire was carefully controlled, since experience showed that "it is inappropriate to battle *all* targets with single artillery pieces and batteries. It is much more important to strike the most important targets using timely, concentrated fire to destroy them." If enemy forces were able to get close enough to launch a close assault against the fortified buildings, the careful preparations of the defenders kept the odds strongly in their favor. Any enemy infantrymen who worked their way into a village were either cut down by interlocking fires from neighboring buildings or wiped out by the counterattacks of specially designated reserves. Armed with submachine guns and grenades, these reserve squads were launched against any penetrating enemy troops before they had a chance to consolidate.[64]

During this winter fighting, German units soon realized that strongpoints confined to small villages had serious drawbacks as well as advantages. For

A German machine-gun team defends a village strongpoint, February 1942. A destroyed Soviet tank is in the background.

one thing, Soviet armor posed a deadly threat to house-based defenses. Since camouflage could not hide buildings, Russian tanks had little difficulty in identifying and engaging the German positions concealed therein. Moreover, if successful in driving the Germans from their building shelters and into the open, the enemy tanks could slaughter the fleeing Germans almost at leisure.[65]

Second, strongpoints sited entirely inside villages virtually conceded control of the surrounding area to the Red Army. This reduced German reconnaissance and left the strongpoints susceptible to encirclement or night attack by stealth. (Even in its early report, the 10th Motorized Division conceded that night attacks were a major problem for village strongpoints. Noting that the Russians frequently used night attacks to disrupt the carefully orchestrated German fire plans, 10th Motorized Division officers felt compelled to keep a minimum of 50 percent of their strongpoint garrisons on full alert at night "with weapons in hand" to guard against surprise Soviet assaults.[66])

Finally, most rural Russian villages occupied only a relatively small area, with huts and houses clustered close together. According to an 87th Infantry Division after-action report, strongpoints restricted to such congested areas formed "man traps" since they made ideal targets for Soviet artillery.[67] The 35th Division's report concurred with this assessment, declaring emphatically that "the defense of such a [village] strongpoint must be made in the surrounding terrain."[68] Likewise, the 7th Infantry Division learned to avoid unduly concentrating troops in villages even when no other positions had been prepared.[69]

Based on these considerations, German units gradually refined their strongpoint defenses by pushing defensive perimeters beyond village limits. This helped to conceal the German positions, increased security against surprise attack, and gave sufficient dispersion to avoid easy annihilation by Soviet artillery. These extended perimeters also reduced the distance between neighboring units and made it more difficult for Russian patrols to locate the gaps between strongpoints. Though tactically sound, the extended perimeter was accepted only reluctantly by cold and tired soldiers, and "rigorous" measures were sometimes needed "to convince the troops of the necessity of occupying as uninterrupted a front line as possible in spite of the cold weather."[70]

Within these extended strongpoints, command and support personnel, artillery, and reserve detachments were normally located in and around the built-up area itself. An outer defensive perimeter, consisting of interconnected infantry fighting positions, encircled this central core (see figure 6). Although each unit developed its own priority of work, the construction of the outer defensive works usually began with the building of hasty fighting positions. Then followed, in varying order, the construction of small, warmed living bunkers; the improvement of fighting positions; the clearing of communications paths through the snow; the clearing of fields of fire; and the emplacement of mines and obstacles.[71]

As a rule, German soldiers kept "living bunkers" that were separate from their fighting positions (see figure 7). The quarters bunkers, replete with overhead cover, cots, stoves, and charcoal heaters, were built in sheltered pieces

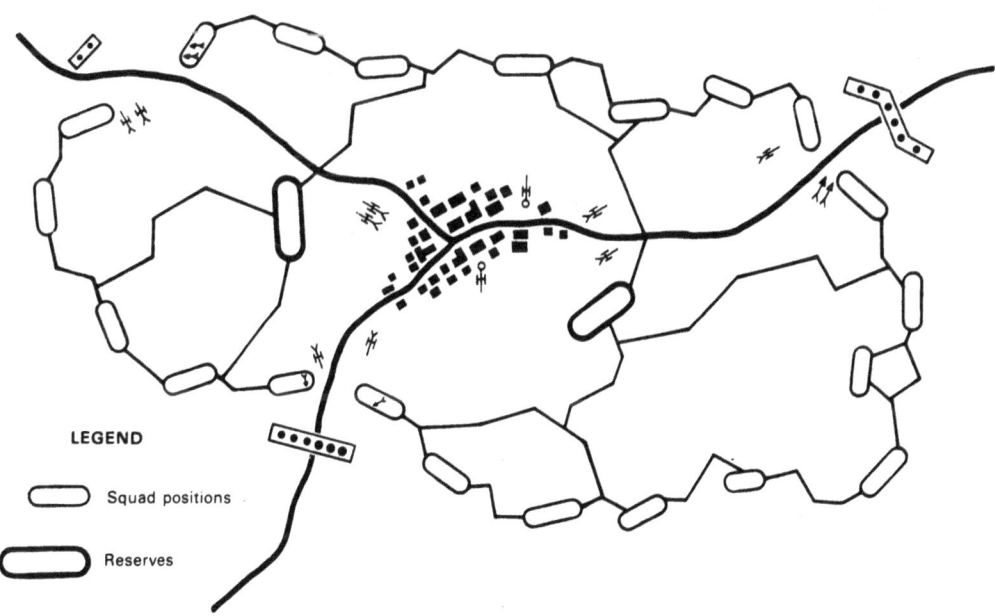

Figure 6. Extended strongpoint

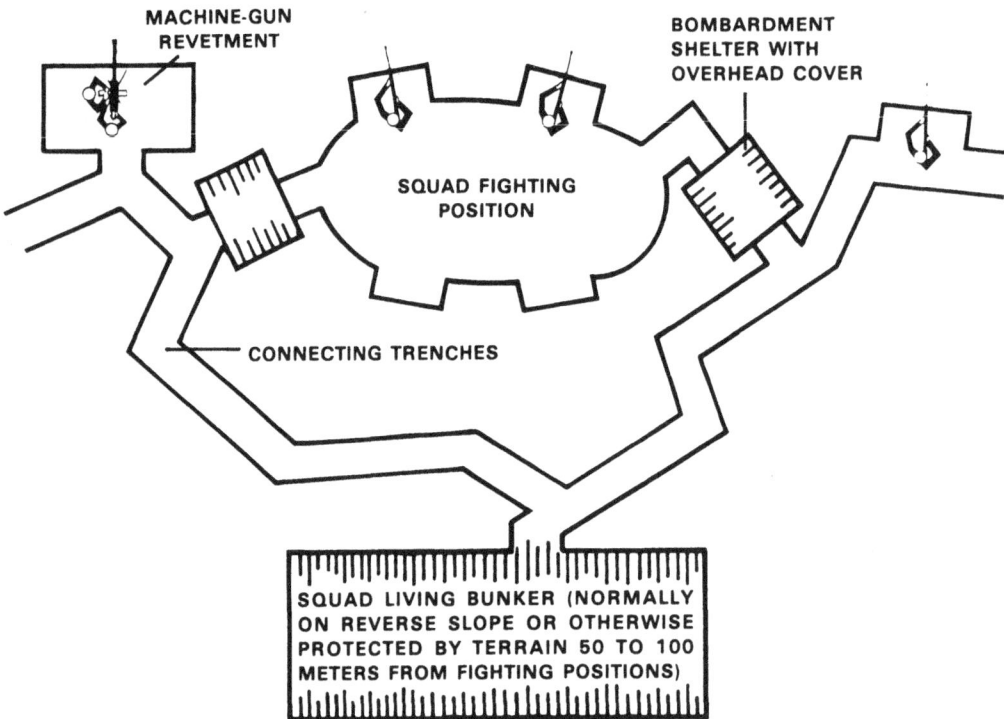

Living bunkers were sturdily built and had strong overhead covers. They normally contained cots, charcoal stoves, and wooden flooring, and served as a field barracks for German troops.

Figure 7. German squad fighting positions and living bunker

of ground and were connected to the fighting positions by short trenches. If outpost sentries sounded an alarm, soldiers would scramble from their warm quarters to their battle stations. The living bunkers for forward troops were just large enough to accommodate "the smallest combat unit (squad, machine-gun crew, or antitank team). Thus, these bunkers generally [held] about six men; otherwise they [became] *Menschenfallen* [man traps] under heavy bombardment." Reserve forces deeper inside the strongpoint perimeter were commonly sheltered in larger, platoon-size bunkers.[72]

Not only did German infantry squads live together in warmed bunkers, but they also fought together from squad battle positions. These squad positions were normally protected by individual rifle pits to the flanks and acted as alternate locations for nearby machine-gun teams.[73] The use of thick ice walls, armored by pouring water over poncho-covered bundles of sticks and logs, was a favored method for protecting the fighting positions and the connecting trenches.[74] The 35th Division found that the squad battle positions should be uncovered so embattled troops could observe, fire, and throw

German troops man trenches in extended village strongpoints. Defensive advantages were gained by siting positions away from buildings.

A sketch of inside a German living bunker

grenades in all directions. Walk-in bombardment shelters with overhead cover, constructed at intervals throughout the defensive trench system, protected troops from enemy artillery. By day, crew-served weapons were kept inside the living bunkers to protect them from the cold; at night, they were prepositioned outside ready for immediate use.[75]

The Russian winter caused special problems for laying minefields and constructing obstacles. Pressure-activated antipersonnel mines proved to be singularly unreliable. Enemy ski troops could glide over fields of pressure mines without hazard, and the heavy accumulations of snow cushioned the mines so that detonation even by footslogging infantry was uncertain. The snow also smothered the blast of those mines that did explode. Therefore, tripwire-detonated mines were more reliable and more effective than pressure mines, posing a threat even to Soviet ski troops. (The 87th Infantry Division suggested that tripwires be strung with excessive slack so they would not contract in the extremely cold temperatures and cause the mines to self-detonate.)[76] Placement of antitank mines was generally restricted to roads and other obvious avenues of approach for armor, as neither mines nor engineers were available in sufficient numbers to lay belts of antiarmor mines elsewhere. Since the Germans used pressure-detonated antitank mines, they ensured that the mines were laid on hard surfaces and that snow did not muffle the explosive effects. In fact, after the blast of buried mines failed to damage the tracks of enemy T-34s, the 35th Division painted its antitank mines white so they could be left nearly exposed on hard-packed road surfaces.[77]

The construction of effective obstacles required some ingenuity. Deep snow, of course, was a natural obstacle to cross-country movement for troops lacking skis and snowshoes. (One German attributed the survival of encircled German forces at Demyansk to the fact that "even the Russian infantry was unable to launch an attack through those snows."[78]) However, as snowbanks did not always locate themselves to maximum defensive advantage, the Germans devised effective supplemental barriers. Simple barbed-wire obstacles were helpful, with a double-apron-style fence being most effective, especially when coupled with antipersonnel mines and warning devices. Unfortunately, barbed wire remained generally in short supply due to the ruinous German logistical system, and wire fences could be covered by drifting snow. Thus, the 7th Infantry Division believed that its few flimsy wire obstacles were valuable only for the sake of morale and early warning.[79] To compensate for the barbed-wire shortage, German troops contrived a variety of expedient entanglements. Some units gathered large quantities of harvesting tools from Russian villages and fashioned "knife rest" obstacles consisting of sharpened scythe blades supported by wooden frames. Even when covered by snow drifts, these nasty blade fences impeded or injured Soviet infantrymen wading through deep snow toward German positions.[80] In and near wooded areas, the Germans felled trees to make abatis-type barriers. Snow walls, measuring two to three

German soldiers exit a living bunker, winter 1941

A German reconnaissance patrol, supported by a sled-borne machine gun, prepares to depart a village strongpoint, January 1942

meters high and thick, were built—mostly with civilian labor—to impede Russian tanks.[81] Some German units tried to keep Soviet forces at arm's length by burning down all Russian villages forward of their own positions. Denied the warmth and shelter of these buildings, Red Army troops would have to spend their nights sheltered some distance away from the German lines and could attack only after a lengthy approach march.[82]

However fortified and protected by barricades, the village strongpoints still occupied only a small fraction of the German front line. Thus, although German officers continued to use the doctrinal term "*HKL*" (*Hauptkampflinie* or main line of resistance) to describe the German forward trace, a line existed only in a general sense. Recalling the large gaps between strongpoints, the former commander of the 6th Infantry Division later complained that even the use of "the term *HKL* was misleading. The *HKL* was a line drawn on a map, while on the ground there stood only a weak strongpoint-type security zone."[83] The Sixth Army's war diary also noted this discrepancy, describing the German winter positions as a mere "security line" of strongpoints that did not amount to an "*HKL* in the sense envisioned by *Truppenführung*."[84]

The intervals between strongpoints were the Achilles' heel of the German defensive system. Russian forces seemed to have an uncanny ability to locate unoccupied portions of the German front. If left unmolested, Red Army troops would maneuver through these gaps to encircle individual strongpoints. If cut off from outside aid and resupply, the besieged German defenders could then be forced either to capitulate or to conduct a desperate breakout. Alternatively, Soviet units could force their way between strongpoints and move directly against valuable objectives deeper in the German rear. While posing a less immediate tactical threat to German regiments and divisions, this option imperiled the fragile German logistical network and, indirectly, the long-term survival of entire German armies. The Red Army even found ways to exploit gaps in sectors where current Soviet plans did not call for major operations. Russian press gangs brazenly shuttled through a large wooded gap between Demidov and Velikiye Luki, for example, to raise Red Army conscripts in the German rear. In other areas, the Soviets used openings in the German front to convey cadre, weapons, and equipment to fledgling partisan bands behind the German lines.[85]

As combat experience revealed the gravity of these problems, the Germans became more determined in their efforts to exert some control over the space between strongpoints. The 5th Panzer Division, discussing the problems of strongpoint defense in its after-action report, concluded that "constant control of the territory between builtup areas (strongpoints) is of decisive importance. Only thus can envelopment attempts by the enemy be promptly frustrated."[86]

Complete control of the entire front was, of course, inherently beyond the capacity of the strongpoint garrisons. Where adjacent strongpoints could adequately observe the surrounding open spaces, German units used artillery and mortar fire to disrupt large-scale Soviet infiltration. However, darkness, poor weather, wooded terrain, and distance all reduced the German ability to detect and to interdict clandestine Soviet movement by fire. For these reasons, as the 87th Infantry Division reported, "the closing of gaps by fire alone [was] not always sufficient."[87] German patrols also stalked the gaps between strongpoints, trying at least to detect, if not to prevent, Russian encroachment. Even this limited patrolling strained German resources, particularly at night: few strongpoint contingents could confidently spare many infantrymen for nocturnal patrols for fear of Soviet night attacks on the strongpoints themselves.[88] German commanders, therefore, came to realize that neither artillery fire nor ground patrols could thwart determined Russian efforts to pass between widely separated strongpoints.

Where strongpoints were sited closer together, the Germans relied on traditional doctrinal methods to expel Russian penetrations. With the bulk of their modest infantry strength confined to strongpoints, German forces could not exercise small-unit maneuver as described in *Truppenführung*; however, the Elastic Defense principles of depth, firepower, and counterattack effectively neutralized all but the most overwhelming Soviet attacks (see figure 8).

Since infantry strength was so limited, defensive depth had to be improvised. One technique was to arrange the forward strongpoints checkerboard style so that backup strongpoints guarded the gaps between advanced positions. The 331st Infantry Division, in fact, reported that one of the essential conditions for a successful strongpoint defense was that the redoubts be staggered one behind another to create defensive depth of sorts.[89] In a memorandum reflecting its own winter experiences, the 98th Division described how this arrangement entangled enemy breakthroughs "in a net of strongpoints."[90] Where sufficient forces allowed the luxury of this technique, the strongpoint system most nearly resembled the defense in depth set forth in *Truppenführung*.

Insufficient numbers of troops or broad unit frontages often prevented the overlapping of combat strongpoints in depth, however. Another expedient

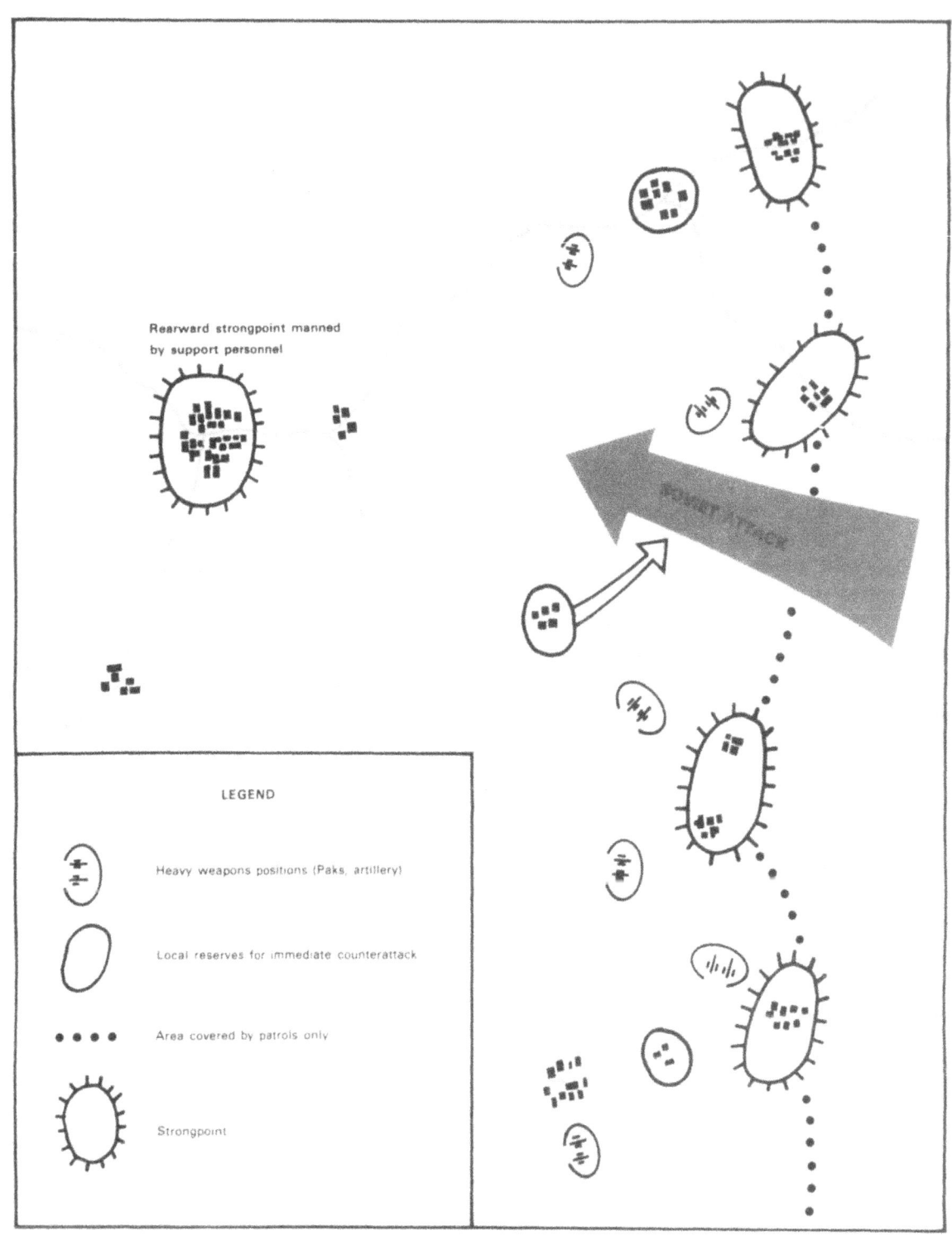

Figure 8. German strongpoint defense tactics, winter 1941—42

method of generating defensive depth—and the one specifically ordered by Hitler's 26 December directive—was to convert all rearward logistical installations into additional strongpoints. Though manned only by supply and service personnel (occasionally augmented by *Landeschutz* security units composed of overage reservists), these strongpoints prevented the Soviets from freely exploiting tactical breakthroughs. Such support strongpoints also protected the valuable logistical sites from surprise attack and served as rallying points for German personnel separated from their units in the confusion of battle.[91]

One other technique for giving depth to the German defense was to array heavy weapons (light "infantry" howitzers, antitank guns, flak guns, artillery pieces) and artillery observers in depth behind the forward strongpoints. Enemy forces penetrating beyond the strongpoint line could thus be continuously engaged by direct and indirect fire to a considerable depth. (The 197th Infantry Division actually recommended graduating artillery assets for a distance of five kilometers behind the main line of resistance.) Though weakening the direct-fire capabilities of the forward strongpoints somewhat, this technique did not require the displacement of the snowbound German guns in order to fire on penetrating Soviets. Furthermore, the fortified gun positions also served as additional pockets of resistance against further Russian advance.[92] The 87th Division saw in this a confirmation of prewar doctrinal methods, noting that "the arrangement of heavy weapons and their deployment in depth according to the tactical manuals proved successful."[93] Even though this technique complied with doctrine, under the circumstances it was a desperate expedient because it risked sacrificing the precious German artillery simply to contain ground assaults.

The German heavy weapons were far more valuable for their ability to smash advancing Soviet formations by fire. By careful fire control, German commanders used their concentrated firepower to slow, disrupt, and occasionally even destroy Soviet penetrations outright. As explained in one after-action report, "Rapid concentration of the entire artillery on the enemy's main effort is decisive."[94] To that end, German divisions meticulously integrated the fires of all major direct- and indirect-fire weapons (including infantry mortars and heavy machine guns), as well as the fires of neighboring units, into a single division fire plan. This prearranged fire plan was then executed on order of designated frontline commanders so that attacking Russian troops were suddenly ripped by simultaneous blasts of concentrated artillery and small-arms fire. The 35th Division explained that intense flurries of shells falling on Soviet assault units "just at the moment of attack [could] stampede even the best troops."[95]

However clever the Germans were in fabricating defensive depth and however skillfully they brandished their limited firepower, determined Soviet attacks could not be vanquished by these means alone. More often, depth and firepower were mere adjuncts to the counterattack, the third traditional ingredient of German defensive operations. German unit combat reports unanimously cited immediate, aggressive counterattacks (*Gegenstösse*)—even when conducted using limited means—as the best way to defeat Russian penetrations. Deliberate counterattacks (*Gegenangriffe*)—which doctrinally were those more carefully coordinated counterblows using fresh units—were regarded as less effective due to the shortage of suitable uncommitted forces and the

German infantry counterattacking, January 1942. Note the lack of winter camouflage overgarments.

German lack of winter mobility. The operations officer of the 78th Division stated that "a *Gegenstoss* thrown immediately against an enemy break-in, even if only in squad strength, achieves more than a deliberate counterattack in company or battalion strength on the next day."[96] However, a fine line existed between aggressiveness and recklessness, and few German units could afford to suffer even moderate personnel losses from an ill-conceived counterattack. Consequently, the 35th Division counseled that, where the Russians had been allowed any time at all to consolidate or where the depth of the enemy penetration made immediate success unlikely, German reserves were to be used only to contain the enemy rather than to be squandered in weak or uncoordinated piecemeal counterattacks.[97]

The immediate counterattacks were normally performed by small reserve contingents positioned in villages behind the forward strongpoints. According to one division commander, these forces were assembled despite the consequent weakening of the forward positions. The strength of these counterattack detachments varied in that some units held as much as one-third of their total strength in reserve, while others made do with smaller forces. Invariably, however, the counterattack forces were given as much mobility as possible. Where available, skis and snowshoes were issued to the reserve units; where these were unavailable, Russian civilians were put to work trampling paths through the snow along likely counterattack axes. To ensure the proper aggressive spirit, some units disregarded unit integrity and assembled their reserves from "especially selected, capable, and daring men."[98] These desperadoes were armed "for close combat" with machine pistols and hand grenades. For maximum shock effect, these counterattack forces were launched against the open flanks of enemy penetrations, preferably in concert with heavy supporting fires from all available weapons.[99]

Thus, though the strongpoint defensive system did not conform exactly to the doctrine in *Truppenführung*, the German expedient methods bore the unmistakable imprint of traditional principles in their use of depth, firepower, and especially counterattack. General Maximilian Fretter-Pico, who served through the 1941—42 winter battles with the 97th Light Infantry Division, described the German improvisations in words that captured the essential spirit of the Elastic Defense: "These defensive battles show that an active defense, well-organized *in the depth of the defensive zone* and using every conceivable means to improvise combat power, can prevent a complete enemy breakthrough. A defense must be conducted offensively even in the depth of the defensive zone in order to weaken [enemy] forces to the maximum extent possible [italics in original]."[100]

In many cases, the strongpoint style of defense did achieve remarkable successes against great odds. Fretter-Pico's division, for example, held its own against some 300 separate Soviet attacks between January and March 1942, with its subordinate units executing in that time more than 100 counterattacks.[101] Other units were less successful, however, with some divisions being almost completely torn to pieces by the Russian counteroffensives. Therefore, the varied effectiveness of the German defensive expedients is best understood in the context of the overall strategic situation.

The Winter Campaign: Overview and Analysis

The Soviet winter counteroffensive unfolded in two distinct stages. The first stage, beginning on 6 December and lasting approximately one month, consisted of furious Russian attacks against Army Group Center. These blows were to drive the Germans back from the gates of Moscow and, in so doing, destroy the advanced German panzer groups if possible. These attacks breached the thin German lines at several points and sent Hitler's armies reeling westward until the stand-fast order braked their retreat. By the end of December, the front had temporarily stabilized, with most German units on the central sector driven to a form of strongpoint defense.

Encouraged by the success of these first attacks, Joseph Stalin ordered an even grander counteroffensive effort on 5 January 1942. This second stage mounted major Soviet efforts against all three German army groups and aimed at nothing less than the total annihilation of the *Wehrmacht* armies in Russia. Tearing open large gaps in the German front, Soviet armies advanced deep into the German rear and, in mid-January, created the most serious crisis yet. Grim reality finally succeeded where professional military advice had earlier failed, and Hitler at last authorized a large-scale withdrawal of the central German front on 15 January. Even with this concession, the German position in Russia remained in peril until Soviet attacks died out in late February.

To appreciate the tactical effectiveness of the German winter defensive methods, it is important to understand the nature of the Soviet counteroffensives. German defensive actions did not take place in a tactical vacuum; rather, their value must be measured in relation to the peculiarities of Russian offensive methods during the 1941—42 winter.

Throughout the winter, the hardscrabble German defensive efforts benefited from the general awkwardness of Soviet offensive operations. The strongpoint defensive tactics adopted by German units exploited certain flaws in Russian organization, leadership, and combat methods. However, this exploitation was not purposeful, for as already discussed, other factors compelled the Germans to use strongpoints. Also, many of the particular Soviet internal handicaps were unknown to the Germans. Nevertheless, the effectiveness of the German strongpoint measures was enhanced by peculiar Red Army weaknesses.

Though achieving great success in their winter counteroffensives, the Soviet armies possessed overwhelming strength only in relation to their enfeebled German opponents. The Barbarossa campaign had inflicted frightful losses on the Red Army, and the Russian forces that assembled for the December attacks were a mixture of fresh Siberian divisions, burned-out veteran units, and hastily raised militia. At almost every level, these Russian forces were troubled by inadequate means and inferior leadership.

The first Soviet attacks against Army Group Center were executed by the Western *Front*, now under the command of the ubiquitous General Zhukov. Planning for the assault had begun only at the end of November, and preparations were far from complete when the counteroffensive began. Though nine new Russian armies were concentrated around Moscow, the assaulting forces also included many divisions ordered straight into the attack after weeks of fierce defensive fighting. Except for some Siberian units, the newly deployed formations were generally understrength, poorly trained, and lacking in equipment. The rebuilt Soviet Tenth Army, for example, had no tanks or heavy artillery and was short infantry weapons, communications gear, engineering equipment, and transport. Although the Tenth Army nominally fielded ten rifle divisions, its overall strength, including headquarters and support troops, scarcely amounted to 80,000 men. Ammunition shortages also afflicted Zhukov's command, with many units having only enough stocks to supply their leading assault elements. Large mobile formations were virtually nonexistent; for example, Western *Front* forces included only three tank divisions, two of which had almost no tanks. Most of the available tanks were instead scattered among fifteen small tank brigades, each having a full establishment strength of only forty-six machines.[102]

These problems were compounded by amateurish leadership and faulty doctrine. Instead of concentrating forces on narrow breakthrough sectors, inexperienced Soviet commanders and staffs assigned wide attack frontages (nine to fourteen kilometers) to each rifle division by the simple method of "distributing forces and equipment evenly across the entire front."[103] Marshal S. I. Bogdanov, recalling his experiences in the Moscow counteroffensive, noted a similar deficiency in using the few Soviet tank forces, namely, "the tendency to distribute tanks equally between rifle units ... which eliminated the possibility of their massing on main routes of advance." Furthermore, the Soviet tanks were cast solely in an infantry support role. "All tanks," continued Bogdanov, "which were at the disposal of the command, were assigned to

Dead Russian troops and destroyed Soviet tanks litter the snowy field in front of German defensive positions, winter 1941—42

rifle forces and operated directly with them ... or in tactical close coordination with them...."[104] These errors further diluted the Soviet combat power and weakened the Russian capacity to strike swiftly into the enemy rear with sizable mobile forces.

Nevertheless, Zhukov's Western *Front* armies possessed more than enough brute strength to overwhelm the weak German lines opposite Moscow. They did so with a notable lack of finesse, however, often butting straight ahead against the flimsy German positions when ample opportunity existed to infiltrate and outflank the invaders. As one Soviet analyst criticized, "Although the [German] enemy was constructing his defense on centers of resistance and to slight depth (3—5 km), and there were good opportunities for moving around his strongpoints, our units most frequently conducted frontal assaults against the enemy."[105] When breakthroughs were achieved, follow-up thrusts minced timidly forward as Soviet commanders looked fearfully to their flanks for nonexistent German ripostes.[106] Oafish Red Army attempts to encircle German formations closed more often than not on thin air. Impatient at these mistakes, General Zhukov issued a curt directive to Western *Front* commanders on 9 December, decrying the profligate frontal attacks as "negative operational measures which play into the enemy's hands." Zhukov ordered his subordinates to avoid further "frontal attacks against reinforced centers of resistance" and urged instead that German strongpoints be bypassed completely. The bypassed German strongpoints would hopefully be isolated by the Soviet advance and then later reduced by following echelons. To lend speed and depth to his spearheads, Zhukov also ordered the formation of special pursuit detachments composed of tanks, cavalry, and ski troops.[107]

Although these measures increased the pace of the Russian drive, they failed to increase appreciably the bag of trapped German units and even may have helped to save some retreating German forces from destruction. As previously discussed, German units turned to strongpoint defensive methods during this chaotic retreat period. These strongpoints massed the slender German resources in a way that the diffuse Soviet deployment did not, thereby reducing the relative German tactical vulnerability. Zhukov's *Front* Directive of 9 December prohibited Russian divisions from breaking down these centers of resistance by direct assault, even though the Red Army forces could certainly have achieved this in many instances. In accordance with Zhukov's instructions, the Russian forces tried instead to snare the retreating Germans by deep maneuver. At this stage of the war, however, the Red Army possessed neither the skill, experience, nor (except for the few pursuit groups) mobility to accomplish these operations crisply and effectively. Time and again, German divisions dodged would-be envelopments or, when apparently trapped, carved their way out of clumsy encirclements.[108] Even Zhukov's sleek pursuit groups failed to cut off German forces. These mobile detachments—often acting with Soviet airborne forces—caused alarm in the German rear areas, but the Russian cavalry and ski troops were generally too lightly armed to do more than ambush or harass German combat formations.

The first stage of the Soviet winter counteroffensive drove the Germans back from Moscow but failed to destroy the advanced German panzer forces. The divisions of Army Group Center, slipping into a strongpoint style of defense as they retreated, by luck adopted a tactical form that the advancing Russians were not immediately geared to smother. Even though many German divisions were mauled at the outset of the Red Army counteroffensive, other German units probably owed their subsequent survival to the purposeful Soviet avoidance of bludgeoning frontal attacks and to the maladroitness of Soviet maneuver.

When Hitler ordered the German armies to stand fast on 16 December, the opening Soviet drives had already spent much of their offensive energy. The initial Russian attacks had been planned, as Zhukov later explained, merely as local measures to gain maneuver space in front of Moscow.[109] The near-total dissolution of Army Group Center's front exceeded the most optimistic projections of the Soviet High Command. Having planned for a more shallow, set-piece type of battle, the Russians were unable to sustain their far-ranging attacks with supplies, replacements, and fresh units. On the contrary, Russian offensive strength waned drastically as Red Army divisions moved away from their supply bases around Moscow. Consequently, Hitler's dogmatic no-retreat directives, issued at a time when some Soviet units were already operating 50 to 100 miles from their starting lines, stood a much greater chance of at least temporary success than would have otherwise been the case.

During the latter part of December, both sides struggled to reinforce their battered forces. Hitler ordered the immediate dispatch of thirteen fresh divisions to the Eastern Front from other parts of German-occupied Europe.[110]

The arrival of these units proceeded slowly, retarded by the same transportation difficulties that dogged the German supply network in Russia. To speed the transfer of badly needed infantrymen, *Luftwaffe* transports airlifted several infantry battalions straight from East Prussia to the battle zone—in retrospect, a measure of questionable merit since the reinforcements arrived without winter clothing or heavy weapons.[111] The frantic German haste to introduce these new units into the fighting led to bizarre incidents. In one case, the detraining advance party of a fresh division was thrown straight into battle even though many of the troops involved were only musicians from the division band.[112] In still another case, elements of two separate divisions were combined into an ad hoc battle group as they stood on railroad sidings and then hurried into the fray without further regard to unit integrity or command structure.[113]

In a curious parallel to Hitler's command actions, Soviet leader Joseph Stalin assumed personal control over the strategic direction of Russian operations in late December. In Moscow, Stalin saw in the Red Army's surprising early success the makings of an even grander counteroffensive to crush the invaders and win the war at one stroke. Pushing Russian reinforcements forward as fast as they could be assembled, Stalin sketched out his new vision for this second stage of the Soviet counteroffensive. The Leningrad, Volkhov, and Northwestern *Fronts* would bash in the front of Army Group North and lift the siege of Leningrad. The Kalinin, Western, and Bryansk *Fronts* would annihilate Army Group Center by a colossal double envelopment. In the south, the Soviet Southwestern and Southern *Fronts* would crush Army Group South while the Caucasus *Front* undertook amphibious landings to regain the Crimea (see map 7).

This Red Army avalanche fell on the Germans during the first two weeks of January, thus beginning the second stage of the winter campaign. As during the first stage, German defensive actions benefited from Soviet offensive problems.

A fundamental flaw in the new Soviet operation was the strategic concept itself. Whereas the first-stage counterattacks had been too cautious, the second-stage objectives were far too ambitious and greatly exceeded what could be done with Red Army resources. The attacking Soviet armies managed to penetrate the German strongpoint belt in several areas, but once into the German rear, the Soviets did not retain sufficient strength or impetus to achieve a decisive victory. Stalin had willfully ignored the suggestions of Zhukov and other Soviet generals that decisive operational success required less grand objectives and greater concentration of striking power.[114] Instead, Stalin insisted that the opportunity had come to begin "the total destruction of the Hitlerite forces in the year 1942."[115]

The advantage to German defensive operations from this conceptual fault was profound. Lacking the necessary reserves to assure the defeat of major breakthroughs, German armies were spared decisive encirclement and possible annihilation by the dissipation of Soviet combat power. After breaking through the German strongpoint crust, Russian attacks eventually stalled on their own for lack of sustenance. On several occasions, major Soviet formations became immobilized in the German rear, slowly withering until mopped up by German reinforcements. For example, the Soviet Second Shock Army, commanded by

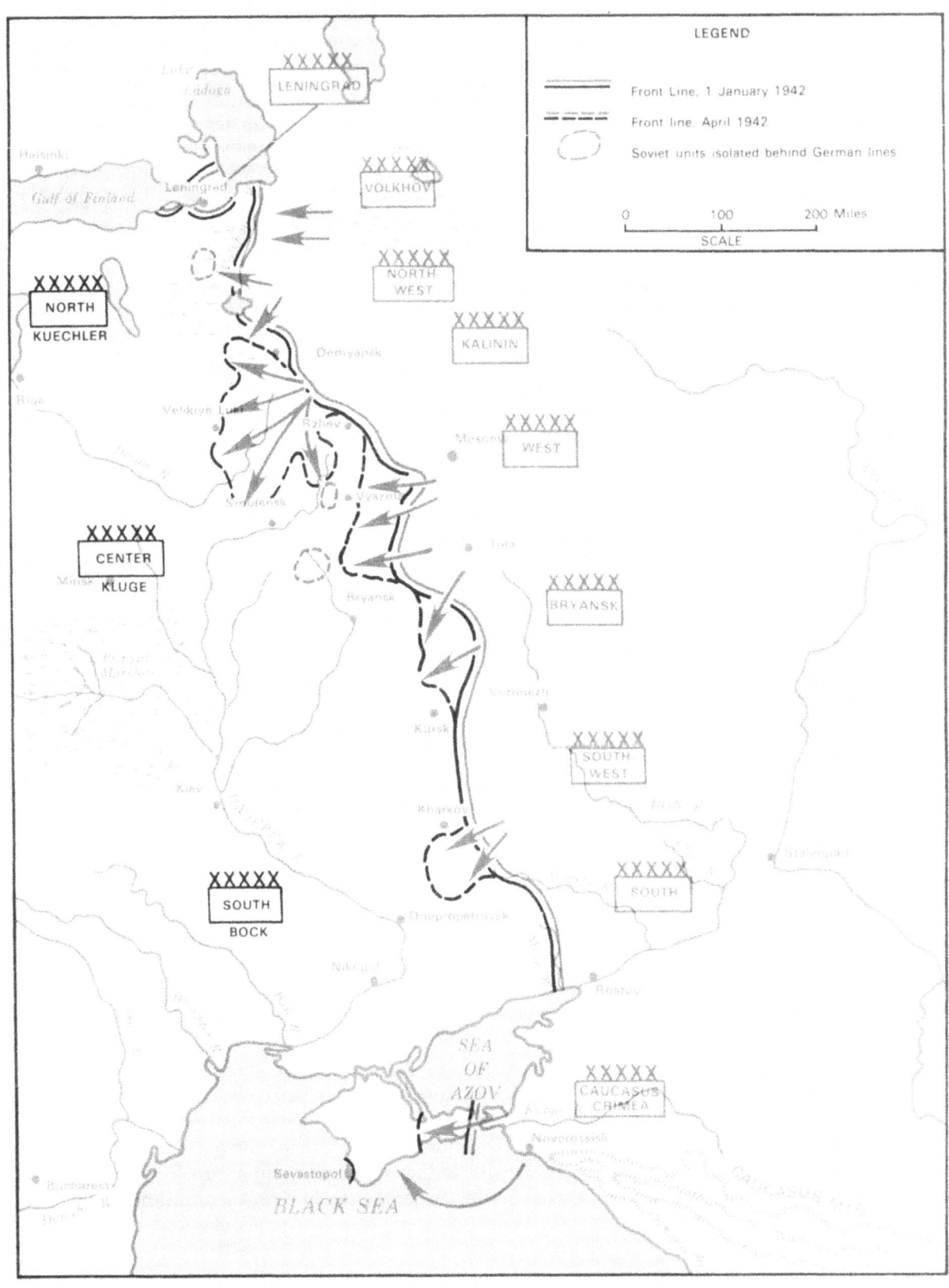

Map 7. Second phase of the Soviet winter counteroffensive, January—March 1942

General A. A. Vlasov, slashed across the rear of the German Eighteenth Army in January only to become bogged down there in forest and marsh. Unsupplied and unreinforced, Vlasov's nine divisions and several separate brigades remained immobile in the German rear until finally capitulating in June 1942.[116] Likewise, the Soviet Thirty-Third Army and a special mobile operational group composed of General P. A. Belov's reinforced I Guards Cavalry Corps struck deep into the vitals of Army Group Center near Vyazma only to be stranded there when German troops blocked the arrival of Russian support forces. A similar fate befell the Russian Twenty-Ninth Army near Rzhev.[117] In these and other cases, the dispersion of Soviet combat power in pursuit of Stalin's grandiose objectives prevented the reinforcement or rescue of the marooned forces.

Although failing to provoke a general German collapse, these deep drives unnerved the German leadership. As Soviet forces groped toward Army Group Center's supply bases and rail lines of communication in mid-January, the German stand-fast strategy grew less and less tenable. Near despair, General Halder wrote on 14 January that the Führer's intransigent leadership "[could] only lead to the annihilation of the Army."[118] The next day, though, Hitler relented by authorizing a belated general withdrawal of Army Group Center to a "winter line" running from Yukhnov to Rzhev. However, Hitler imposed stiff conditions on the German withdrawal: all villages were to be burned before evacuation, no weapons or equipment were to be abandoned, and—most distressing of all to German commanders with vivid memories of the piecemeal withdrawals in early December—the retreat was to be carried out "in small steps."[119]

Indicative of Hitler's penchant for meddling in tactical detail, this last constraint proved particularly painful. Senior German commanders, conforming to Hitler's preference for a more centralized control of operations, dictated the intermediate withdrawal lines to their subordinate divisions. Often, the temporary defensive lines were simply crayon marks on someone's command map, and several units suffered unnecessary casualties in defense of hopelessly awkward positions laid out "on a green felt table" at some higher headquarters.[120] Even with this retreat to the winter line, then, it was fortunate for the German cause that the Soviet High Command had obligingly dissipated its forces.

Logistics also hampered Soviet operations to the Germans' benefit. In his eagerness to exploit the December successes, Stalin ordered the January wave of offensives to begin before adequate logistical preparations had been made.[121] Zhukov later complained bluntly that, as a result, "[logistical] requirements of the armed forces could not be met as the situation and current tasks demanded." To emphasize this point, the Western *Front* commander recited his own ammunition supply problems:

> The ammunition supply situation was especially bad. Thus, out of the planned ammunition supplies for the first ten days of January, the *Front* actually received: 82mm mortar shells—1 per cent; artillery projectiles—20-30 per cent. For all of January: 50mm mortar rounds—2.7 per cent; 120mm shells—36 per cent; 82mm shells—55 per cent; artillery shells—44 per cent. The February plan was no improvement. Out of 316 wagons of ammunition scheduled for the first ten days, not one was received.[122]

The general shortage of artillery ammunition directly affected the Red Army's failure to crush the German strongpoint system. Because German defenders regarded Soviet artillery to be an extremely dangerous threat to their strongpoints, the Germans took such measures as were possible to disperse their defensive positions and reduce the effectiveness of the Russian fire. Even so, that more German strongpoints did not become fatal "man traps" stemmed from the fact that, in general, "the [Soviet] artillery preparation was brief... due to a shortage of ammunition, and was of little effectiveness."[123] Zhukov's units, for example, were limited to firing only one to two rounds per tube per day during their renewed offensive advances. In a report to Stalin on 14 February, Zhukov complained that "as shown by combat experience, the shortage of ammunition prevents us from launching artillery attacks. As a result, enemy fire systems are not suppressed and our units, attacking insufficiently neutralized enemy positions, suffer very great losses without achieving appropriate success."[124]

Misguided tactics also undermined the Soviet artillery's effectiveness. In accordance with faulty prewar tactical manuals, Red Army gunners distributed their pieces as evenly as possible along the front, a practice that prevented the massing of fires against separated strongpoints. Moreover, Russian artillery units frequently located themselves too far to the rear to be able to provide continuous fire support to attacking units battling through a series of German strongpoints. Instead, according to Artillery General F. Samsonov, "the artillery often limited its operations only to artillery preparation for an attack. All this slowed down the attack, often led to the abatement of the attack, and limited the depth of the operation."[125]

A German patrol brings in prisoners and a captured machine gun, March 1942

These artillery problems were symptomatic of the general lack of Soviet combined arms coordination during this period. Attacking Russian tanks often outdistanced their accompanying infantry, leaving the infantry attack to stall in the face of German obstacles and small-arms fire while the tanks barged past the German strongpoints. Accordingly, the Soviet armor, shorn of its infantry protection, was more vulnerable to German antitank measures. Occasionally, Soviet tanks would halt in full view of German gunners and wait until the assigned Russian infantrymen could catch up, or the tanks would turn around and retrace their path past German positions in search of their supporting foot soldiers.[126] Both of these measures played into the hands of German antitank teams. As a result of the general confusion and lack of tactical cooperation between artillery, infantry, and armored forces, Soviet commanders conceded the vulnerability of their own assaults to German counterattack.[127] Indeed, the German use of strongpoint tactics preyed mercilessly on these Soviet blunders: German fire concentrations separated tanks and infantry, antitank guns located in depth throughout the strongpoint network picked off the naked Russian armor, and the carefully husbanded German reserves—maneuvering without fear of Soviet artillery interference—delivered the *coup de grace* by counterattacking the groggy remnants of any Red Army attack.

In an attempt to rectify these shortcomings, Stalin issued a directive to his senior commanders on 10 January that commanded better artillery support, closer tank-infantry cooperation, and—like Zhukov's directive a month earlier to the Western *Front*—greater use of infiltration and deep maneuver. As a diagnosis, this document showed great insight into the Red Army's tactical faults. As a corrective measure, this directive (and supplementary orders that succeeded it) came too late, for most Soviet forces were already heavily engaged in the second-stage offensives by the time it was issued. Also, there was little opportunity to reorganize and retrain Soviet units before spring.[128]

By the end of February, Stalin's great offensive had run its course. German armies, reinforced at last by the few fresh divisions that Hitler had summoned to the Eastern Front, reestablished a continuous defensive front, relieved some German pockets isolated behind Russian lines, and stamped out those Red Army forces still holding out in the German rear. The front line itself stood as stark evidence of the confused winter fighting: instead of spanning the front in a smooth arc marred by a few minor indentations, it snaked tortuously back and forth, its great swoops and bends marking the limits of Russian offensive and German defensive endurance.

On the German side, the best that could be said of the winter campaign was that the German *Wehrmacht* had survived. Strapped by Hitler's strategic rigidity, their strength exhausted, and lacking proper winter equipment, the German eastern armies had successfully withstood the two-stage Soviet onslaught using an improvised strongpoint defensive system. Though fighting as well as could be expected under the circumstances and even incorporating those aspects of their doctrinal Elastic Defense that could be made to fit the situation, German Army officers recognized that they had come within a hairbreadth of disaster. Shaking their heads at their own good fortune, they dimly realized that the survival of the German armies owed as much to Russian tactical clumsiness and strategic miscalculation as to German steadfastness. This realization clouded German attempts to draw doctrinal conclusions from the winter fighting.

German Doctrinal Assessments

Adolf Hitler regarded the winter defensive battles to be his own personal triumph, won against heavy military odds and in spite of the advice of the German Army's senior officers. In rhetorical terms that made it seem as if he had personally braved Russian bullets (Hitler in fact had not visited front commanders since late November), the Führer gave his own assessment of the campaign to Dr. Joseph Goebbels on 20 March 1942. As the propaganda minister wrote in his diary:

> Sometimes, the Führer said, he feared it simply would not be possible to survive. Invariably, however, he fought off the assaults of the enemy with his last ounce of will and thus always succeeded in coming out on top. Thank God the German people learned about only a fraction of this.... The Führer described to me how close we were during the past months to a Napoleonic winter. Had he weakened for only one moment, the front would have caved in and a catastrophe ensued that would have put the Napoleonic disaster far into the shade.[129]

Hyperbole aside, the winter fighting had borne Hitler's peculiar stamp, first in the refusal to allow withdrawals and then, after 15 January, in his insistence that Army Group Center's retreat be conducted in small costly steps. Moreover, the Führer's leadership style was already corroding the bonds of trust and confidence between various field commanders. As a precaution against the dictator's wrath, some officers kept written copies of their orders to subordinates as proof that Hitler's instructions had been passed on unaltered. (Field Marshal von Kluge, since December the commander of Army Group Center, was a master practitioner of this artifice.) Recriminations were another symptom of this disease. On 30 April 1942, for example, Kluge demanded an official inquiry to ascertain why the 98th Division (whose

Soviet troops attack a German strongpoint, March 1942

A lone German sentry stands guard over snowed-in vehicles, February 1942

combat strength was less than 900 men) had failed to carry out impossible orders to crush a fortified Soviet bridgehead at Pavlovo held by superior enemy forces. That 12 officers and 450 men had fallen in the German counterattack mattered little to Kluge, who needed scapegoats.[130]

The Russian winter battles left their imprint on the Führer as well. The success (if the avoidance of total disaster could be described as such) of the stand-fast strategy reinforced Hitler's conviction that his own military instincts were superior to the collective wisdom of the front commanders and the General Staff. It also convinced him that will and determination could triumph over a materially stronger enemy. Armed with these delusive notions, Hitler ordered German troops to stand fast on many future battlefields, though more often with disastrous than with victorious results. The seeds of future stand-fast defeats at Stalingrad and El Alamein, as well as in Tunisia, the Ukraine, and Normandy, were planted in Hitler's mind during the 1941—42 winter struggle.

On a less grand level, the German Army set about drawing its own conclusions about the winter fighting. Responsibility for these assessments was divided. The Operations Branch of the Army General Staff was responsible for seeing that major lessons learned were immediately reported and disseminated to interested field commands. The General Staff's Training Branch had responsibility for the more deliberate adjustment of doctrine through the publication of new field manuals and training directives. Finally, field commanders from army group level downward all had some latitude and authority in modifying the tactical practices of their own forces.

A camouflaged German antitank gun defends a village strongpoint, winter 1941

After-action reports from frontline units constituted the primary information base on which these agencies depended. When necessary to amplify this information, General Staff officers visited forward units or interviewed officers returning to Berlin from frontline duty. (Even General Halder, the chief of the Army General Staff, frequently conducted such firsthand consultations.[101])

Fourth Panzer Army ordered the most thorough early assessment of the winter fighting. On 17 April 1942, it sent a memorandum to its subordinate units ordering them to prepare comments on general winter warfare experiences. As guidance, this memorandum posed more than forty specific questions about tactics, weapons, equipment, and support activities. Thirteen of these questions dealt directly with defensive doctrine and included such matters as the choice of a linear defense versus a strongpoint system, the siting of strongpoints, the construction of obstacles, patrolling, and the composition and role of reserves.[132] While the resulting reports provided valuable technical information in all areas, comments on antitank defense and on strongpoint warfare in general caused the greatest doctrinal stir.

The German Elastic Defense had been designed primarily for positional defense against infantry, and opposing tanks had previously been regarded simply as supporting weapons for the enemy's foot troops. The Barbarossa campaign and winter fighting had exposed the woeful inadequacy of German antitank guns against Russian armor; therefore, Soviet tank attacks—with or without infantry support—had emerged as a major threat in their own right.

In its response to the Fourth Panzer Army memorandum, the German XX Corps noted that, due to the weakness of German antitank firepower, otherwise weak enemy attacks posed a severe danger to German defenses if the attacking force was supported by even one heavy tank.[133] Overall, the reports that were returned to Fourth Panzer Army emphasized this fact and gave careful considerations to the defensive measures necessary to defeat Soviet tanks.

German prewar antitank doctrine had focused on separating enemy tanks and infantry. Since June, battles against Russian armor had confirmed the theoretical effectiveness of this technique. Under attack by Red Army tank-infantry forces, German units frequently succeeded in driving off or pinning down the Soviet infantry with artillery, small-arms, and automatic weapons fire. This tactic was abetted by the generally poor Soviet combined arms cooperation, as Stalin admitted in his 10 January directive. In fact, several German commanders noted how easily Russian tanks and infantry could be separated and the surprising tendency of the enemy occasionally to discontinue otherwise successful tank attacks when the accompanying infantry was stripped away.[134] Confirming the general thrust of German antitank doctrine, the 35th Division's report declared that "the most important measure [was] to separate the tanks from the infantry."[135]

What troubled German commanders was not the splitting of enemy armor and infantry but the practical difficulties in destroying Soviet tanks. German prewar thinking, reflecting the wisdom passed down from the Great War, had regarded tanks without infantry support to be pitiable mechanical beasts whose destruction was a relatively simple drill. Given the ineffectiveness of German antitank guns, such was clearly not the case on the Russian Front.

Most German antitank guns needed to engage the well-armored Russian tanks at extremely close range in order to have any chance at all of destroying or disabling them. To accomplish this, the antitank guns were placed in a defilade or reverse-slope position behind the forward infantry. Hidden from direct view, the *Paks* then had a good chance for flank shots at enemy tanks rolling through the German defenses. The disadvantage of this system, of course, was that the *Paks* could not engage Soviet armor until it had actually entered the German defensive area.[136]

The only German weapon able to kill Soviet tanks at extended ranges was the 88-mm flak gun. However, this weapon was so valuable and, due to its high silhouette, so vulnerable that it, too, was commonly posted well behind forward German positions. Thus hidden, the heavy flak guns were safe from suppression by Russian artillery and from early destruction by direct fire; they could not, however, use their extended range to blast enemy tanks far forward of the German lines.[137] Thus, neither the lighter *Paks* nor the heavy 88-mm flak guns provided an effective standoff antitank capability.

The lack of powerful antitank gunfire placed enormous pressure on German infantrymen in two ways. First, it was not uncommon for German infantry positions to be overrun by Soviet tanks. Assaulting in force, Russian armored units were virtually assured of being able to rush many of their tanks through the German short-range antitank fire, over the top of German fighting positions, and into the depths of the German defenses. This shock effect wracked the nerves of German soldiers, who found little comfort in an antitank concept that, in practice, regularly exposed them to the terror and danger of being driven from their positions by Soviet T-34s. Echoing sentiments first voiced by German commanders twenty-five years earlier, one officer warned, "The fear of tanks (*Panzerangst*) must disappear. It is a question of nerves to remain [in fighting positions being overrun]."[138]

Second, German infantrymen were routinely given the dangerous task of destroying Russian tanks by close combat measures (mines, grenades, fire bombs). Though such methods had been discussed in prewar manuals and journals, the powerlessness of the German antitank guns forfeited to the beleaguered infantry a far greater burden than anyone had foreseen. For an infantryman, attacking a Soviet tank was not easy. He had to crouch undetected until the tank passed close to his hiding place and then spring forward to attach a magnetic mine to the tank's hull or to disable the tank's tracks or engine with a grenade. In doing so, the soldier exposed himself to machine-gun fire from other tanks (which, naturally, were particularly alert for such attacks) and also risked being crushed by a suddenly swerving tank or even wounded by the explosion of his own antitank device. To facilitate the close assault of enemy tanks and to cloak the movements of the German infantry, some German units released smoke on their own positions as the enemy tanks closed. However, this tactic was dangerous, as such smoke interfered with aimed German fire against any Russian infantry and also tended to enhance the shock value of the menacing armor.[139] Protesting the

A drawing of German infantrymen attacking Soviet T-34 tanks with grenade clusters

Captured German War Art Collection

unbearable strain that infantry-versus-tank combat placed on German soldiers, the 7th Infantry Division stated bluntly in its report: "It is wrong to pin the success of antitank defense on the morale of the infantry." The 7th Division's report strongly advocated a thickening of forward antitank weapons, including the forward placement of 88-mm flak guns "to smash [Soviet] tank assaults *forward* of the German defensive line [italics in original]."[140]

German strongpoint tactics during the winter fighting increased the problems of antitank defense. Strongpoints were subject to attack from all directions, thereby complicating the siting of the relatively immobile German antitank guns. When attacking enemy armor, German infantrymen preferred the protection of continuous trenches, since these gave them a covered way to scuttle close to the tanks without undue risk of detection.[141] However, strongpoints—particularly those confined to villages—were difficult to camouflage. Therefore, Russian tanks could circle outside the defensive perimeter, blasting away at the German positions and probing for a weak spot, without fear of a surprise attack by hidden German infantry. In the same way, Soviet armored thrusts through the gaps between strongpoints also avoided the lurking German infantrymen. For this reason, many German commanders prepared connecting trenches between strongpoints solely to move infantry antitank teams into the path of bypassing Russian tanks.

After nearly one year of brutal combat in Russia, antitank defense thus loomed as a major vulnerability in German defensive operations. German antitank guns lacked penetrating power and were relatively immobile. Soviet tank assaults exposed German infantrymen to terrific strain, both from the general likelihood of being overrun and from the necessity to combat Russian tanks with primitive hand-held weapons. If anything, the experiences of winter combat had shown that these difficulties were even greater then than during earlier battles. Fortunately for the Germans, the Soviets' tactical ineptitude and early tendency to disperse armor into small units spared the Germans even harsher trials.

Early combat reports, such as those ordered by Fourth Panzer Army, spurred adjustments to German antitank measures. Efforts to improve German antitank weaponry were greatly emphasized, resulting in the eventual introduction of heavier guns. The production of German self-propelled assault guns was also accelerated, partly in answer to the need for a more mobile antitank weapon. Moreover, new German tanks received heavier, high-velocity main guns capable of duelling the Soviet T-34s, and older-model German tanks were refitted with heavier cannon as well.[142]

Efforts to improve the German antitank capability went beyond technological remedies. Since it remained necessary in the short term to rely heavily on infantrymen (and, in some units, combat engineers) to destroy tanks in close combat, the German Army did its best to prepare German soldiers for that task. Various instructional pamphlets were printed giving detailed information on the vulnerabilities of Russian tanks and the most effective methods for disabling them. For example, in February 1942, the Second Army rushed a "Pamphlet for Tank Destruction Troops" to its own units even before the winter battles had subsided.[143] General Halder reviewed the reports of frontline units and conferred with the German Army's Training Branch on the preparation of a new manual on antitank defense.[144] Also, the

German leaders did not neglect the psychological dimension of antitank combat: beginning on 9 March 1942, soldiers who had single-handedly destroyed enemy tanks were authorized to wear a new Tank Destruction Badge, which helped improve morale.[145]

German combat reports also generated a great deal of interest in the strongpoint defensive system. The assessments culled by Fourth Panzer Army contained sharp differences of opinion on this point. The 252d Infantry Division dismissed the strongpoint methods, arguing that "village strongpoints [had] not proven themselves effective in the defense. After short concentrated

A soldier of the *Grossdeutschland* Division receives the Tank Destruction Badge. In the background is a Soviet T-34 tank.

bombardment they [exacted] heavy losses. A continuous defensive line [was] in every case superior to the strongpoint-style deployment." The 252d Division rejected the supposed strongpoint advantages, pointing out that "experiences with the strongpoint defense were muddy. . . . It did not prevent infiltration by enemy forces, especially at night. It [strongpoint defense] cost considerable blood and strength to destroy penetrating enemies by counterattack."[146] Other assessments were less harsh, conceding the value of strongpoints as an expedient measure. Though expressing a strong preference for a doctrinal linear defense in depth, the XX Corps grudgingly acknowledged the importance of strongpoints under certain conditions: "A continuous defense line is successful and strived for. A strongpoint-style defense may be necessary when insufficient forces are available for a continuous front. It is only tolerable for a limited time as an emergency expedient."[147]

Although no unit suggested a general adoption of strongpoint defensive measures over the Elastic Defense system, the widespread use of strongpoints seemingly warranted closer study. General Halder therefore decided on a formal investigation into the strongpoint issue. On 6 August 1942, the chief of the General Staff ordered a survey of frontline units on the terse question, "Strongpoints, or continuous linear defense?"[148] The purpose of this study was not to reach a consensus; rather, it was to seek information of doctrinal value from as many different sources as reasonably possible. Fourth Army, for example, submitted responses that were prepared by every subordinate corps and division commander and by most regimental and many battalion commanders as well.

The monographs returned as a result of General Halder's inquiry provided a thorough critical assessment of German defensive tactics during the previous winter. In practice, all German units had compromised doctrinal Elastic Defense methods to some extent, and most divisions had at least experimented with strongpoint measures. In their reports, the surveyed commanders argued the relative merits of the strongpoint system and tried to define precisely its advantages, disadvantages, and suitability for general defensive use.

Predictably, the most commonly cited advantages were the obvious ones of shelter and concentration of limited resources. However, several veteran officers also pointed out other less-obvious benefits of strongpoint warfare. Units disposed in strongpoints were more easily controlled than those arrayed in a linear defense, thus simplifying the leadership problems of the few remaining officers and NCOs.[149] Within strongpoints, wrote the commander of the 289th Infantry Regiment, even poorly trained soldiers could be kept under tight rein by their junior leaders.[150] Similarly, the chief of staff of the Second Army considered strongpoints beneficial to discipline and training, a vital matter since "the training status of the troops and the quality of the infantry junior leaders had noticeably declined."[151] Strongpoints also bolstered the sagging morale and pugnacity of individual soldiers: troops spread out in a linear defense tended to perceive themselves as solitary fighters and often were less steadfast under fire than those fighting in the close company of strongpoint garrisons. In this regard, the 331st Division expressed concern about its growing numbers of young and inexperienced replacements.[152]

Against these advantages, German officers listed the serious problems that, in their experience, had attended the use of strongpoints. Individual strongpoints invited isolation and destruction in detail by superior Soviet forces. Since separated strongpoints had been unable to secure the German front against enemy penetrations, strong Russian forces had frequently managed to shoulder their way between strongpoints and deep into the German rear. Also, smaller Soviet infiltration parties had wrought havoc throughout the German defensive area. Because of the lack of doctrinal guidance, the use of nonstandard strongpoint tactics by some divisions had unintentionally exposed the flanks of neighboring formations deployed in a linear defense.[153]

Although German officers also found fault with their own occasional use of linear defenses, the faults were generally attributed to insufficient resources (excessively wide sectors, lack of depth, unavailability of mobile reserves). However, the systematic criticisms of the strongpoint style of defense pointed out inherent, fundamental flaws in the strongpoint concept. Strongpoints, in the view of German commanders, would *always* be subject to isolation, and Soviet forces would *always* be able to force passage between strongpoints, even if the Germans disposed of larger forces. These flaws cast into doubt Hitler's prediction that the mere control of villages and road junctions would arrest Soviet offensive momentum. As one divisional report delicately put it, this contention remained "unproven in practice."[154]

Consequently, German officer sentiment ran strongly against a general reliance on strongpoint defenses. To most German field commanders, a strongpoint system remained an emergency expedient prompted by the exceptional conditions of the 1941—42 winter campaign. In their answers to Halder's query, many leaders quickly pointed out that, as combat conditions had allowed, their units had abandoned their exclusive reliance on strongpoints in favor of more traditional methods. As one battalion commander explained: "Except as under the special conditions reigning during the 1941/42 winter campaign, one should reject the strongpoint system and strive for a continuous HKL [main line of resistance]. The strongpoint system can only be an emergency measure for a short time, and must form the framework for a continuous line as was the case during the winter."[155]

Some unit commanders, though firm in their endorsement of an orthodox defense in depth, expressed their intent to incorporate some strongpoints into any future defensive system. With the passing of winter, German divisions on the Eastern Front began organizing their positions, aided by the arrival of fresh divisions and a trickle of replacements. As this occurred, German lines increasingly resembled the Elastic Defense prescribed in *Truppenführung*. Within this burgeoning defense in depth, strongpoints were occasionally retained as combat outposts or, more commonly, as redoubts within the depth of the main battle zone. In contrast to the winter strongpoints, however, these positions generally were smaller and were knitted into the defensive system with connecting trenches. The XLIII Corps, summarizing the views of its subordinate divisions, saw nothing new in this: "The best style of defense is that laid down in *Truppenführung*—many small, irregularly-located nests, deployed in depth, composing a defensive *zone* whose forward edge constitutes the HKL [italics in original]."[156] In the overall context of German defensive doctrine, this addition of greater numbers of small strongpoints was relatively minor. (Small squad-size redoubts had been part of the original German Elastic

Defense as early as 1917, and a few officers even cited passages from *Truppenführung* allowing for such measures.[157]

The stream of winter after-action reports prepared by German units did not result in any major new doctrinal publications. Therefore, *Truppenführung* remained the German Army's basic doctrinal reference for defensive operations. In fact, after extensive study, the winter defensive crises were dismissed as products of extraordinary circumstances. The exceptional conditions of the previous winter—which, the Germans hoped, would not be repeated in the future—invalidated any general doctrinal judgments that might otherwise have been made. Furthermore, any hasty revision of German defensive doctrine would have seemed, in the summer of 1942, to be a superfluous and even a defeatist gesture. While General Halder and other members of the General Staff sifted through the grim after-action reports about the winter fighting, German armies were again on the march in Russia. On 5 April 1942, Hitler ordered preparations for a new German summer offensive to win the war in the east in one more blitzkrieg campaign.

Chapter 4

New Victories, New Defeats

Operation Blau, the German 1942 summer offensive in Russia, was vital to Germany's hopes for victory in World War II. Both a revived Britain and a newly belligerent United States could soon be expected to open new fronts in Africa, the Mediterranean, or France. Consequently, in terms of the Third Reich's grand strategy, a failure to knock Russia out of the war in 1942 would leave Germany embroiled in a hopeless multifront war against stronger adversaries.

Operation Blau entailed substantial military risk for the Germans. The recent winter battles had left the German eastern armies so drained of strength that they could not all be fully rebuilt to pre-Barbarossa levels with the limited resources available. By concentrating the flow of replacements and new equipment to selected units, a powerful offensive phalanx could be created on only a narrow portion of the front. This could only be done at the expense of the remainder of the German forces in the east, in which combat strength would remain at relatively low levels. If the few assault armies failed to land a knockout blow, the burden of sustained combat would then fall on the other, less-capable German divisions. Thus, Hitler's 1942 summer offensive implicitly gambled German long-term combat endurance against the chance for a rapid blitzkrieg-style victory over the Russians.

The main objective of Blau was the seizure of the Caucasian oil-producing regions. While Army Groups North and Center stood on the defensive, a reinforced Army Group South would be split into two separate maneuver elements. Army Group B, the more northerly fragment, would drive forward south of Voronezh, extending the German defensive front along the Don River. Its eastern terminus anchored at the Volga River industrial city of Stalingrad, Army Group B's lines would face generally northeastward, protecting the flank and rear of Army Group A's operations. Army Group A, in turn, would attack due east as far as Rostov and then wheel southward toward the prized oil fields (see map 8).[1]

For such a crucial undertaking, Operation Blau suffered from surprisingly muddled strategic thinking. Even if successful, the Caucasian offensive would leave most of the Soviet armed forces intact. Following its recent winter counteroffensives, the bulk of the Red Army remained massed along a 300-mile front west of Moscow, with other significant concentrations opposite Leningrad and Kharkov. Though strong Soviet forces would probably be drawn into the southern fighting, it was unlikely that they could be subjected to encirclement and *Kessel*-style destruction as during the previous summer. (The German strategic deception plan for Blau intentionally aimed at keeping

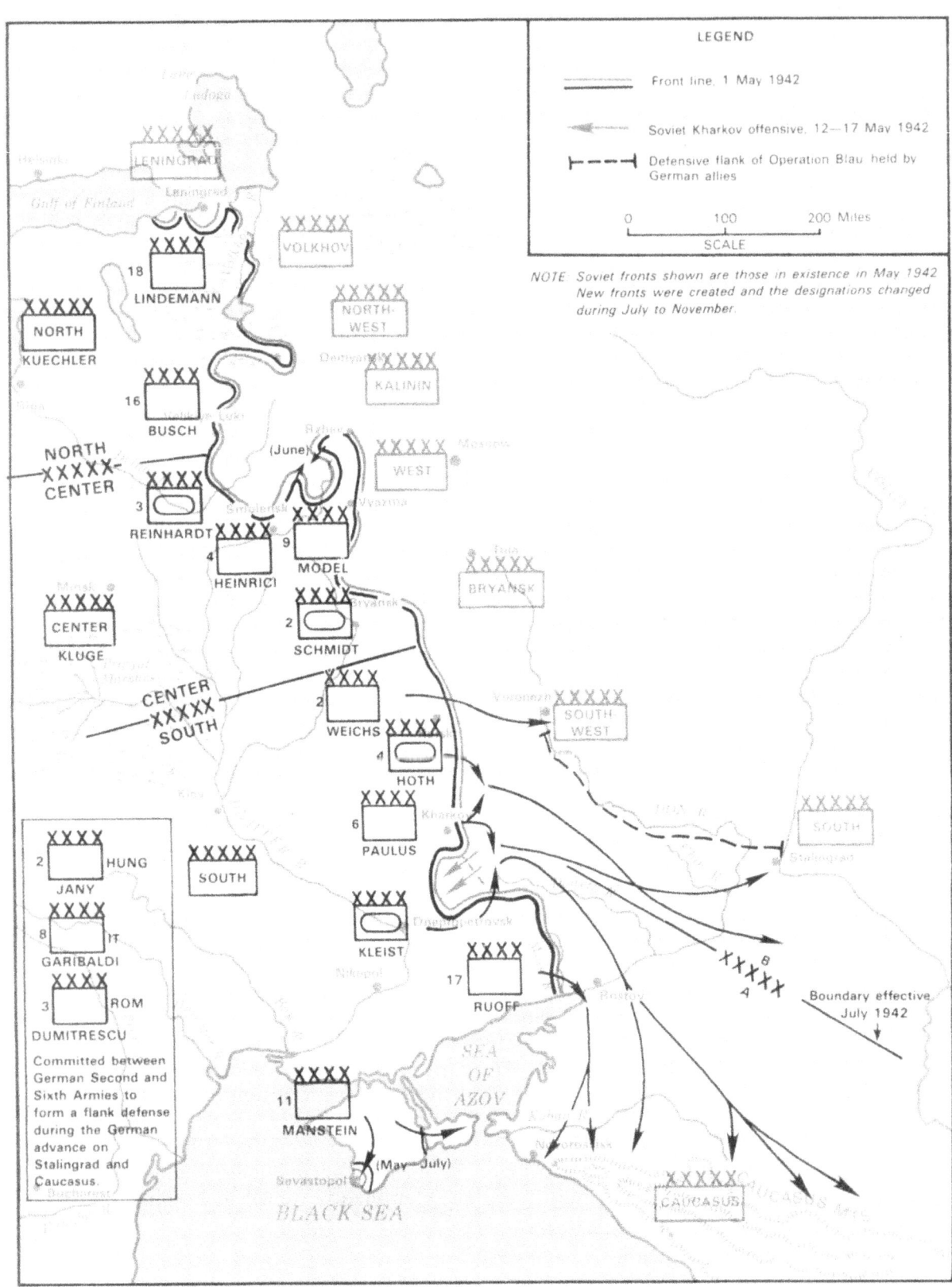

Map 8. Plan Blau and German offensive operations, May—November 1942

Soviet forces in place before Moscow.²) Consequently, for a plan whose overriding strategic purpose was the timely and conclusive completion of operations in the Russian theater, Blau made no provision for dealing with the greater portion of Soviet military might.

Instead of striking at the Soviet armed forces, the Germans aimed at winning the war by economic means. And yet, even though the Caucasian oil regions were a valuable economic target, the precise strategic purpose to be served by their seizure remained vague. German analyses emphasized how Germany would benefit from the capture of the oil fields rather than how the Soviets would suffer from their seizure. Caucasian petroleum would certainly help Germany's own war economy; however, that its loss would fatally undermine the war-making potential of the Soviet Union—which had access to other, albeit lesser, sources of oil—was less certain.[3] Moreover, any harm to the Soviet war economy resulting from the German southern drive would, at best, develop only gradually and would not serve the German goal of swiftly terminating the war in the east. German planners, including not only Hitler but the Army General Staff as well, therefore had not considered completely the relationship between Germany's strategic ends and Operation Blau's military means.

These faults, however, were not immediately apparent amid the renewed optimism of June 1942. What was obvious was the clear division of tasks between the "defensive front," composed of Army Group North and Army Group Center, and the "offensive front" poised farther to the south. (German officers actually used the terms "offensive front" and "defensive front" as a sort of verbal shorthand to describe the missions of the various army groups.[4]) The development of German defensive doctrine through 1942 is most easily pursued in a separate evaluation of these two fronts.

Problems on the Defensive Front

The German defensive front twisted for nearly 1,000 miles, stretching from the area north of Voronezh to the Gulf of Finland. The German armies holding this area were, broadly speaking, those that had suffered the most during the Soviet winter counteroffensives. Concurrent with their development of the Blau attack plans, German planners bolstered the defensive strength of the lines held by Army Group Center and Army Group North.

During February and March of 1942, Hitler and other senior leaders again toyed briefly with the idea of fortifying an "east wall" defensive barrier along a portion of the front. The main inspiration for this scheme came from General Friedrich Olbricht of the German Army Supply Office. On his own authority, Olbricht had undertaken some preliminary studies for such a bulwark, and as German plans for the coming summer began to take shape, he shared his ideas with other influential officers. Since the weakened frontline divisions could not be expected to provide work parties for such a project, Olbricht proposed shifting army training facilities temporarily into the combat zone and using trainees as the principal east wall labor force. General Friedrich Fromm, the commander of the Replacement Army, was being pressured to muster replacements for the shattered combat divisions as quickly as possible and therefore was reluctant to agree to any program that might interfere with that process. However, Fromm conceded that such a construction project, using replacement personnel supervised by limited-duty officers with recent combat experience, might be possible provided that no more than six hours a day was devoted to construction work.[5]

With Fromm's concurrence in hand, Olbricht ordered his staff to prepare a detailed "Proposal for the Construction of a Strategic Defense Line in the East" at the end of January. Elaborating his basic concept, Olbricht requested that a fortified defense in depth be built along a line to be designated by the army chief of staff. Provided that adequate materials and support personnel were made available, Olbricht estimated a total actual construction time of just over three months. Olbricht circulated this written proposal to interested agencies within the German Army and High Command staffs, making occasional amendments to accommodate minor criticisms. Since the general response to the east wall concept was almost unanimously favorable, Olbricht submitted a formal written recommendation through General Halder to the Führer at the beginning of February.[6]

Hitler, with the winter defensive trials behind him and the prospect of a new win-the-war offensive in front of him, bluntly rejected the east wall construction scheme as an unnecessary diversion of precious resources. In a written memorandum to Olbricht, Hitler forbade further consideration of such an elaborate fortified line with the words, "Our eyes are always fixed forward." By way of further explanation, Hitler said that such a grandiose defensive project would convey an unfavorable impression to Germany's allies.[7] At the time, Hungary, Romania, and Italy were all being pressed to invest more troops in the forthcoming summer campaign, and Hitler wished to forestall any doubts that these satellites might have had about Blau's prospects.

Instead of an east wall, the German defensive front in Russia was to be built up from the existing strongpoint lines. As a preparatory step, forward units had been ordered on 12 February 1942 to reestablish a continuous defensive line as soon as possible after the spring muddy period.[8] On 26 April, after Hitler had issued his final directive for the conduct of Blau, General Halder ordered the strengthening of the German defensive front: engineer troops were to assist in preparing field fortifications, key rearward towns and installations were to be converted into major strongpoints, and "fortified areas" were to be designated behind the German front to act as supplemental defensive lines if needed.[9]

Despite the Army High Command's efforts to strengthen the defensive front of Army Groups Center and North, it remained shaky due to insufficient forces. In preparation for Operation Blau, Army Group South* was given strict priority of replacements in order to bring its divisions up to full complement by June. Because of this preferential rehabilitation, two distinct classes of German units existed on the Eastern Front. The assault forces mustering in the south were generally well equipped and ready offensively, while the ninety-odd divisions assigned to the two northern army groups were second-class

---

*The division of Army Group South into Army Group A and Army Group B did not become effective until the beginning of July.

organizations in which major deficiencies in personnel, weapons, and equipment had to be tolerated indefinitely.

The personnel shortages in the divisions manning the defensive front were particularly acute. Replacements reaching Army Groups Center and North in May and June scarcely covered the combat losses of those months alone, to say nothing of filling the ranks ravaged by the winter fighting.[10] The quality of the replacements trickling into the northern army groups was also cause for concern: in order to flesh out the spindly divisions assigned defensive missions, General Halder had authorized these groups to receive men who had completed only two months' training.[11] Even so, the manpower shortfall remained so intractable that sixty-nine of the seventy-five infantry divisions assigned to the defensive front had their infantry component reduced from nine to six battalions.[12] This one-third curtailment of authorized infantry strength—accompanied by a proportional reduction in divisional heavy weapons in some cases—left these German infantry divisions permanently less combat worthy than the "standard" divisions still deployed in Army Group South. All problems considered, the average infantry division in Army Groups North and Center probably deployed about one-half the combat power of a full-strength division.[13] In defensive terms, these reduced-strength divisions were less able to hold terrain in a positional defense and were less suited for prolonged attritional combat than the nine-battalion divisions fielded at the outset of Barbarossa.

Because of the need to endow Army Group South's forces with as much mobility and striking power as possible, the defensive front's infantry divisions were also starved of vehicles and weapons. Infantry divisions along the static front received no replacement motor vehicles and few replacement horses. In some cases, motor vehicles were actually taken away from northern units and reallocated to divisions assigned to the southern attack. These measures reduced the mobility of the defensive units, leaving them almost totally unsuited for fluid operations.[14]

The few mobile reserves held by Army Groups North and Center were also deprived of equipment. Noting that the southern buildup would completely

Soldiers of a bicycle-mounted reconnaissance battalion. For lack of motor vehicles, bicycles were often used for mobility of local reserves on the German defensive front in 1942.

exhaust the German stock of tanks, vehicles, and weapons, General Halder concluded that the mobile reserves for the defensive front could expect to "get nothing and must try to get along on what they still [had], acting as 'fire brigades' on the defensive front." Furthermore, unlike the panzer and motorized divisions assembling in the south, the northern front divisions were not allowed to stand down for rehabilitation. On the contrary, these divisions were actually stripped of some of their organic support vehicles and even had their offensive edge blunted by other makeshift compromises. The panzer divisions, for example, were allotted few replacement tanks and therefore fielded only a single understrength armored battalion each. Also, divisional reconnaissance units for the panzer and motorized formations were frequently remounted on bicycles, and logistical support for the mobile units (which previously had been fully motorized) was partially transferred to horse-drawn wagons, a stopgap that severely reduced the mobile forces' sustained effectiveness in fluid combat.[15]

Neglected by the Army High Command's allocations of fresh resources, the defensive army groups thus held their designated fronts with stunted infantry divisions. The reserve underpinnings of the defensive front were also weak: the panzer and motorized forces, which according to German doctrine were to be used in defense as a mobile counterattack force, had had much of their mobility and shock power siphoned away. In many ways, Operation Blau thus wrought the same transformation of the German Army as had the 1918 Ludendorff offensives. A few selected units would carry the burden of attack, while lower-quality "trench divisions" were trusted only to hold ground in relatively quiet sectors. That the old Imperial German Army had disintegrated when the trench divisions proved unequal to the demands of the Elastic Defense seems to have gone unremarked in 1942.

Thawing snow and spring rains impeded the construction of German defensive works, since neither trenches nor bunkers could be properly excavated in the muddy gumbo. Luckily, the liquefied landscape also brought a halt to Russian attacks, as dismayed German soldiers watched their winter snow trenches and ice parapets dissolve into the slush.[16] Not until late May or early June had the ground dried enough to allow the laying out of serious defensive positions.

Insofar as their blighted units and broad sectors allowed, the German armies along the defensive front tried to organize their defenses according to established doctrine. The actions of the German I Corps, settling into a portion of the Eighteenth Army's front south of Leningrad, were typical in this respect.

The four divisions of I Corps got a late start on their defensive preparations, having first to eradicate the so-called Volkhov *Kessel* in the German rear containing Soviet General Vlasov's ill-fated Second Shock Army.[17] With that bit of operational housekeeping done, the I Corps began digging in along its assigned portion of the German front in early July. An 8 July corps order guided the organization of the defense and spelled out an abbreviated Elastic Defense (no advanced position was possible due to the proximity of the enemy). The corps commander directed that "the course of the HKL [main line of resistance] and of the Combat Outposts are to be set strictly in accordance with the principles of *Truppenführung*."[18] Particularly urgent was the need for subordinate commanders to ensure that a continuous trenchline be linked to all positions along the main line of resistance. Throughout the entire depth of the main battle zone, all weapons pits, command bunkers, and reserve dugouts were to be transformed into small strongpoints capable of sustained all-around defense. The order further specified the depth of the main battle zone in each subordinate unit's area and directed that "in each division sector a minimum of one infantry battalion [would] be held back as division reserve. Moreover, each sub-sector [would] designate its own local reserve, its strength depending on the situation."[19]

Due attention was also paid to fire support and antitank measures. The I Corps defensive order thoroughly discussed the coordination of artillery fire necessary to block enemy attacks against the German defensive front. Displaying an uncommon sensitivity to the shock effect of overrunning armor, the corps commander stated that "the prevention of enemy tank break-ins [was] decisive to the coming defensive battles." Conceding that German antitank fire alone was unlikely to hold enemy armor at bay, dense thickets of mines and antitank obstacles were prescribed to keep Russian tanks out of the German defensive positions.[20]

The German Army's doctrinal defensive methods required a high degree of skill and aggressiveness from individuals and small units—qualities easily dulled by prolonged periods in the trenches. Recognizing this, the I Corps commander warned that "alertness, combat proficiency, and morale should not be allowed to suffer due to increased construction work [on fortifications]" and directed that a refresher combat training program be conducted continuously within the defensive positions. Furthermore, he noted that small-unit leaders played a key role in maintaining the daily combat readiness of their men and therefore needed to be spared burdensome administrative duties:

> Positional warfare brings the danger of the over-exuberant growth of memo-writing, and with it a bureaucratization of the war. This development is to be resisted from the beginning. The preparation of defensive positions can be promoted without voluminous documentation. Small unit leaders belong with their men and at their workplaces, not at the writing table. The number of written reports required of forward units is therefore to be kept to an absolute minimum.[21]

Following the winter battles, in which tactical methods had been largely improvised to fit special conditions, such orders were helpful in restoring direction to German defensive efforts. Though striving to follow these doctrinal methods, German units still found that their defensive operations remained plagued by practical difficulties, with the result that actual defenses seldom approached the ordered standards.

The abiding shortage of infantry posed the greatest stumbling block. A General Staff officer, reporting his findings after a trip to Second Army's static front in early August, noted that rifle companies numbering only forty to fifty men were defending sectors in excess of three kilometers in width.[22] Such low troop densities caused some abridging of German doctrine; therefore, few units actually conducted a full-blown Elastic Defense. The traditional defensive principles of maneuver and depth were especially compromised, placing even greater importance on firepower and counterattack.

Small-unit maneuver had been an important ingredient of the German Elastic Defense since its inception during World War I. German soldiers were taught to avoid local Allied pressure by moving to advantageous positions within the defensive zones until the enemy attack faltered under German artillery and small-arms fire. This idea of small-unit maneuver had been revived in *Truppenführung* in 1933 and remained part of the German doctrinal concept through the early years of World War II. Small-unit maneuver had proved awkward during the winter strongpoint battles and, in practice, remained difficult on the Russian Front during the summer of 1942.

For want of riflemen, German company and battalion commanders were allowed far less freedom to maneuver their units than doctrinal texts recommended. Due to German numerical weakness, any penetration of the forward defensive lines was extremely dangerous and needed to be promptly contained or swiftly eliminated by counterattack. The key lay in keeping enemy incursions as small as possible, and German commanders struggled, virtually at all costs, to resist any widening of Soviet break-ins. German soldiers were therefore taught to "pinch" relentlessly inward against the shoulders of local penetrations, a movement that did constitute maneuver of sorts.[23] However, such rigidity was contrary to the doctrinal ideal, which promoted a less-structured shifting of units. Moreover, the peculiar problems of antitank defense precluded excessive movement within threatened sectors. On the contrary, German soldiers were told to remain in place so they could attack any Russian tanks with mines and grenades. Finally, Hitler's rabid "no-retreat" dictum continued to enervate German defensive operations, and even tactical withdrawals in the heat of combat were discouraged. The I Corps commander, for example, warned his subordinates that "my explicit approval is required for every rearward displacement of the HKL [main line of resistance]."[24]

After-action reports also confirmed the extent to which lack of manpower robbed German defenses of their desired depth. As the 1st Infantry Division admitted in its report on 1942 summer defensive operations, "the demanded depth was seldom achieved due to the wide sectors and low combat strength."[25] Orders like those issued by I Corps directing the preparation of deep defensive zones frequently went unfulfilled for lack of personnel. Elsewhere, when rearward positions were actually constructed, they often remained almost totally vacant. In many units, the only manned positions in the depth of the German main battle zone were *Pak* nests, artillery firing positions, and battalion and regimental command posts. Some units hurried signalers and supply personnel into rearward trenches when Soviet attacks seemed imminent, while others emptied forward dispensaries of walking wounded and posted them in the support positions. The shortage of riflemen prevented some units from distributing their heavy weapons in depth as they desired, as all available machine guns were needed along the main line of resistance to help cover the impossibly wide frontages. This weakened German resistance in depth and also caused the unnecessary loss of valuable weapons to Soviet artillery preparations and long-range direct fire.[26]

The 121st Division found the manpower squeeze to be so excruciating that its frontline companies were unable to man even combat outposts forward of the main line of resistance. The division's total defensive deployment actually amounted to a dangerous charade: a single continuous trench with little forward security or rearward depth. As the division's after-action report explained, even a strongpoint style of defense was impossible since enemy infiltrators would then have quickly ascertained how weak the German positions truly were.[27]

In the face of such desperate weakness, the traditional principles of firepower and counterattack became the real pillars of the German defense. The most desirable qualities of German fire support were the ability to mass fire on Russian main efforts, a process that required careful planning and coordination, and the ability to shift fire quickly from target to target as frontline crises demanded. In some cases, however, the extreme width of division sectors spread German artillery assets to such an extent that any echeloning of guns in depth would have seriously diluted available firepower. Where this was the case, reports recommended abandoning artillery deployment in depth in favor of concentrating maximum fire along the thinly manned forward edge of the German defense.[28] Even though rearward battery locations would still be improved to act as emergency strongpoints, this recommendation reflected the criticality of smashing Soviet assaults by fire as far forward as possible since little resistance could be mustered in the empty depths of the German defenses. German antitank guns were deployed in some depth, but they were almost the only weapons that were not drawn forward by the severe manpower shortage.[29]

The role of reserves was equally critical. Where Soviet units ruptured the thin forward trenchlines, immediate counterattack offered the best, and often the only, chance of averting a major breakthrough. German commanders still considered speed to be more important than mass: small reserve forces stationed close behind the front were preferred to larger, though more distant, counterattack forces.[30] In a reluctant concession to improved Soviet tactics, German commanders occasionally parceled out tanks, self-propelled assault guns, and additional antitank weapons to their reserves in order to generate

German tanks and infantry counterattack a Soviet penetration near Orel, August 1942

maximum striking power against enemy combined arms forces. (As the war progressed, the dispersing of tanks and assault guns to forward units for local counterattack became an increasingly contentious doctrinal issue.)

The German strengths and weaknesses could not be concealed from the Soviets. A shrewd summary of German problems was discovered in captured Russian documents and distributed in an Army High Command Training Branch report entitled "Experiences With Russian Attack Methods in Summer 1942." Published in September, this report listed the Soviet assessment of German defensive problems:

> Weakness of units. Strongpoint system. Defense therefore contains gaps and lacks depth. Clinging to towns and wooded areas, where they are easily trapped. Only tiny local reserves, and counterattacks with distant reserves are therefore mostly too late.... Numerical weakness in tanks facilitates [Russian] antitank measures against counterattacks. Poor construction of positions and obstacles makes it possible to break through their fire and overwhelm infantry.

The report also warned that, although Soviet training and tactical skill currently lagged behind that of the Germans, "the Russian is building his attack techniques on these supposed weaknesses and strengths of the German defense."[31]

This Soviet knowledge was built up during dozens of probing attacks against the German lines throughout the summer. Though diminished in strength by diversion of forces to the southern battles, these Russian assaults placed considerable pressure on the German defensive front.

In July and August, Soviet thrusts punctured Army Group Center's front on several occasions, causing local crises that were controlled only by repeated counterattacks of Field Marshal von Kluge's meager armored reserves. According to General Halder, a "very heavy penetration" of the Ninth Army's front during the first week of August placed "severe strain" on the German forces despite the intervention of three understrength panzer divisions.[32] In Army Group North's area, a powerful Russian attack south of Lake Ladoga in late August penetrated eight miles into Eighteenth Army's sector. This breakthrough could not be contained with available reserves, and a major portion of Field Marshal von Manstein's Eleventh Army (reassembling for an attack on Leningrad after mopping up the Crimean Peninsula) had to be thrown into a major counterattack.[33] Even though mastered after fierce fighting, these repeated crises clearly demonstrated the frailty of the German defensive front.

While not achieving major victories, the Russian attacks on the German defensive front succeeded in wearing down those forces beyond tolerable levels. By September, the German High Command admitted that defensive capabilities would have to be improved drastically before winter.

The German leadership addressed the worsening defensive problem from two different directions. First, Hitler investigated the status of German defenses and issued a new Führer Defense Order decreeing improved defensive standards and procedures. Second, several programs were begun to increase the infantry strength of German forces on the Eastern Front.

The Führer Defense Order of 8 September 1942

Adolf Hitler blamed the German Army leadership for the growing defensive difficulties in Russia. From the experiences of the past winter, Hitler had concluded that the Army's senior officers were timid and lacked the stomach to face crises. Further evidence of this, in the dictator's view, had come throughout the summer of 1942. It appeared to the Führer that, whenever Russian attacks breached the German lines, frontline commanders did little but whine about insufficient forces and submit panicky requests to conduct local retreats. Despite standing orders against withdrawals, many recalcitrant commanders continued to allow their subordinate units freedom of maneuver within the depths of their defensive zones, a policy that, in Hitler's mind, was merely an excuse for retreat. Furthermore, based on his own Western Front combat experience as an infantry soldier during World War I, Hitler considered himself to be an expert on defensive tactics and his military advisers to be fuzzy-headed theorists without personal knowledge of defensive combat. Stirred by these perceptions, Hitler decided to personally oversee the conduct of German operations.

On 8 September 1942, Hitler issued his most detailed defensive instructions of the entire war. Besides addressing current projects for upgrading German defenses, this Führer Defense Order soared into a rambling discussion that mixed general operational principles and detailed tactical instructions into a confusing melange. Woven into this exposition were occasional personal reminiscences and dubious historical examples. Written in Hitler's ranting style, the entire document was over eleven pages long. General Halder, who had vainly protested the unprofessional tone and content of earlier Führer missives, found the whole document to be so objectionable that he refused to allow his own name to appear on the published version, even though it bore the Army General Staff letterhead.[34]

In the Führer Defense Order, Hitler developed several confused themes that showed an ominous misunderstanding of German doctrinal theories and Russian Front combat realities. Hitler emphasized the desirability of crushing Soviet attacks forward of German trenches, thereby avoiding altogether the problem of enemy penetrations into the German defensive positions. Seizing on the experiences of many weakened units, Hitler declared that it was always essential for overmatched troops to stand and fight rather than to disengage by maneuver. Although this idea had some validity in certain cases (as reported by those frontline commanders who felt that maneuver by weak forces fatally widened penetrations), it was flatly contrary to the entire concept of the elastic defense in depth.[35]

Hitler then vented his displeasure with the Army's combat leaders. In the Führer's jaundiced view, many (perhaps even most) Russian penetrations occurred due to a lack of determination and will on the part of German commanders. "There is no doubt," he declared, "that some positions have been abandoned without absolute necessity." The arguments in favor of local retreats, he continued—namely, that the loss of terrain was of little consequence in the vast Russian reaches or that more advantageous conditions could be created by withdrawal—"are basically false." Gathering steam, Hitler cited examples in which immobile German artillery had been abandoned in place when Russian forces had overrun certain sectors. Where artillery pieces lacked sufficient mobility to redeploy, Hitler fumed, then the artillerymen, too, should be prepared as a matter of honor to stand and defend their positions with hand weapons until, the last round fired and no help arriving, they blow up their own cannons.[36]

What Hitler really wanted, and what the disjointed Führer Defense Order gradually made clear, was a return to the rigid, terrain-holding linear defense that the Germans had practiced before the adoption of the Elastic Defense during the winter of 1916—17. "I deliberately turn back with this concept [of a continuous linear defense] to the style of defense such as was employed with success in the harsh defensive battles *up to the end of the year 1916* [italics added]." In these battles, Hitler recalled, the enemy had possessed overwhelming superiority in men and materiel, even "incomparably higher than [was] the case at some places on the Eastern Front," and had managed to inflict heavy casualties on the defenders. "In spite of this, the enemy achieved only insignificant advances after weeks of fighting at heavy loss to himself."[37]

As historically minded German officers recognized, Hitler's use of the 1916 combat example was counterfeit. In holding up the Imperial German Army's sacrifices in the Battle of the Somme as a model of tactical virtuosity, Hitler ignored the resulting denouement: the German Army had purposely altered its defensive doctrine after the costly 1916 battles precisely because its own losses were unacceptable using the rigid linear tactics and because the Elastic Defense made more efficient use of Germany's limited manpower. Although more efficient, the Elastic Defense required a temporary relinquishing of terrain when tactical necessity dictated—a notion that went against the grain of Hitler's megalomania and which he therefore desired to banish from the minds of his battle leaders.

Even though his general observations were implicitly critical of the Army's doctrinal practices, Hitler stopped short of an outright rejection of the Elastic Defense. Indeed, one of the most confusing aspects of the Führer Defense Order was the way in which Hitler glibly combined established doctrinal concepts (depth, firepower, counterattack) with his own fevered visions of defensive warfare. However, careful readers noted that buried within Hitler's prose were three specific concepts that were patently incompatible with standard German practices.

First, Hitler proposed shifting units in order to mass forces in the path of Russian attacks: "When the attacker himself uncovers a particular section of the front in order to concentrate strong forces in another attack sector, so must the defense respond by the same method and to an equal extent. . . . It is necessary immediately to pull divisions out of thickly defended areas so that they can be shifted to the threatened sectors."[38] Under normal circumstances, reinforcing threatened sectors would amount to little more than ordinary military prudence. However, combined with Hitler's obsessive insistence on holding terrain, such lateral shifting of forces promised only to place greater concentrations of German troops on the Red Army's anvil, causing them to be hammered to pieces by the weight of Russian blows. The Elastic Defense sought to wear out enemy attacks by depth, maneuver, and firepower and then to defeat enemy assault forces by timely counterattacks against enemy weakness. Hitler's scheme planned to mass German strength against greater Soviet strength, thickening German defenses at points threatened by Russian attack. Such a procedure might be successful in blunting Soviet offensives without significant loss of territory; however, it would invariably do so—as on the Somme in 1916—at enormous cost in German lives.

Second, Hitler announced his personal intention to intervene even more frequently in the conduct of defensive operations in the east. In yet another historical allusion of doubtful veracity, Hitler compared this to actions during the Great War in which Hindenburg and Ludendorff had taken direct control of operations on the Western Front. Therefore, so he would have all relevant information available to exercise close personal control over future battles, the Führer ordered front commanders to provide him with detailed maps (down to a scale of 1:25,000) of their positions, assessments of unit capabilities, and their current supply status.[39] Enlarging on Hitler's previously displayed proclivity to interfere in battlefield operations, this announcement—which portended Hitler's direction of even division-level engagements—struck yet another blow at *Auftragstaktik* and the independence of subordinate leaders.

Finally, Hitler reiterated his insistence on standing fast in the face of defensive crisis. In an underlined passage, the Führer Defense Order stipulated that "no army group commander or army commander has the right to allow on his own authority the execution of a tactical withdrawal without my specific approval." Rather than worrying about withdrawal or evasive maneuver, frontline commanders were ordered to undertake a prodigious new entrenchment program under the slogan: "Trenches and always more trenches."[40]

With these instructions, Hitler signaled to his combat commanders his desire for an unrelenting positional defense, one that would hold terrain without regard to casualties or doctrinal niceties. He also made it clear that he was prepared to exert his own authority to the utmost to ensure compliance. This Führer Defense Order must have made German officers uneasy, promising as it did to paralyze their conduct of defensive operations with still more of Hitler's doctrinal quackery.

For the short term, the damage to German defensive doctrine remained potential rather than actual as autumn rains interrupted operations for a time. Furthermore, in implementing the Führer Defense Order instructions, frontline commanders tried to minimize its disruptive impact by heeding only those portions that supported existing methods and by selectively ignoring Hitler's more obnoxious suggestions. Army Group Center contented itself with issuing a brief order directing improved trenchworks and a second directive prescribing the further fortification of logistics centers and the construction of large-scale antitank obstacles (mostly ditches) in its rear using civilian labor.[41]

General Gotthard Heinrici, the commander of Fourth Army, discussed the Führer Defense Order and its implications with his subordinates at a formal command and staff meeting on 25 September, but he limited his written implementing instructions to a defensive memorandum dealing exclusively with technical matters.[42] The commander of the LVI Panzer Corps, noting that the Führer's order required "the construction of a defensive position of a sort equivalent to those of the 1914–1918 World War," ingeniously forwarded a requisition for construction materials that included 75,000 rolls of barbed wire, 68,000 antitank mines, and 50,000 antipersonnel mines.[43] (This request was hopelessly optimistic, as these quantities were more than triple the amounts previously delivered during the entire summer. However, such requests were part of "playing the game" and allowed one to blame future failure on the nondelivery of required supplies.)

German infantrymen occupy forward trenches. Note the shellproof bombardment shelters at intervals along the trenchline.

The most visible immediate effect of the Führer Defense Order was some improvement and standardization of German defenses. The Fourth Army, for example, condensed Hitler's instructions into a directive specifying a standard defensive layout. Hitler's confused guidance notwithstanding, the Fourth Army's prescribed deployment replicated the Elastic Defense to a degree that should have satisfied the most pedantic doctrinal purist. Aside from some differences in nomenclature (for example, the successive positions within the defensive area were no longer referred to as independent "zones" but, rather, were regarded more as parts of a common whole), the Fourth Army's scheme almost completely agreed with combat practices of 1917–18 and later doctrinal publications.[44]

Of course, commanders could not evade all of Hitler's guidance, and some important shifts in emphasis made their way into frontline instructions. The use of local reserves, for example, shifted subtly: instead of awaiting the enemy's disruption and exhaustion within the depths of the defense, reserves were now expected to confront enemy penetrations as soon as they occurred in order to win back the original front. This change was motivated by Hitler's impatience at even the temporary loss of ground and implied that the commitment of German reserves would henceforth be triggered more by the loss of terrain than by the enemy's vulnerability to counterattack. Likewise, new instructions included some of the ambiguity of Hitler's own thinking. For all the emphasis on holding forward along the main line of resistance, there frequently appeared a concurrent, and apparently contradictory, emphasis on improving defensive positions in depth and often on creating a duplicate second position far behind the original front.[45]

Although German commanders were duty-bound to implement Hitler's general designs, they were not blind to either the contradictions or the impracticalities of the Führer Defense Order. Even as he was dutifully ordering his Fourth Army to implement the Führer's directive, General Heinrici dispatched a secret letter to Army Group Center, decrying the impossibility of achieving those standards. Because of the scarcity of combat troops, Heinrici had already spread his divisions to the uttermost limits, leaving no manpower whatsoever to undertake new construction or to man more extensive positions. For example, along the Fourth Army's front, it was not uncommon for trenches to be posted at night with only one two-man team for every 60 to 100 meters of trench. Furthermore, competing daily requirements for local security, patrols, trench repair, training, equipment maintenance, and rest made it impossible to fulfill current tasks adequately, much less to bring Hitler's plans for a massive fortification project to life. The simple fact was, Heinrici declared, that present positions could not even be fully secured with existing forces, as evidenced by the steady loss of prisoners and casualties to Soviet raiding parties.[46]

Heinrici's complaints emphasized Germany's main defensive problem: lack of men. Even though Hitler planned to banish the German Army's defensive problems by issuing a frothy directive, the Führer Defense Order could not be fully implemented for the same reason that I Corps' instructions had gone unfulfilled earlier in the summer. Whatever Hitler's headquarters might decree, the German divisions manning the defensive front lacked sufficient numbers of soldiers to conduct more than an expedient defense. For any real improvement in German defensive dispositions, the troop strength would have to be raised substantially. Finally, in midsummer 1942, the German High Command attempted to rectify its continuing defensive problems by generating additional manpower strength.

Bolstering Combat Manpower

In gross terms, the *Wehrmacht*'s manpower problems were insoluble. Germany simply had too few men of military age to meet its expanding requirements. Also, Germany's consistent mismanagement and misuse of the manpower it did possess made this reality even harsher.

Adolf Hitler's Third Reich allocated its manpower resources similar to an oriental bazaar, forcing the German Army to jostle its way through various military, paramilitary, economic, governmental, and Nazi Party organizations like a none-too-wealthy rug merchant in search of a bargain. Each of these competing agencies jealously defended its claims to draft-age men by patronage and political intrigue, thereby robbing the army of choice manpower badly needed at the front. The two greatest offenders (and the ones with the most influence with Hitler) were the *SS* and the *Luftwaffe*.

A German machine gunner on the Eastern Front

Germany's conscription apparatus was managed by the Armed Forces High Command, which denied the SS a share of the draftees. The SS, which preferred to fill its ranks with pure volunteers anyway, circumvented this exclusion by energetically recruiting younger men who were not yet eligible for the draft. (At the beginning of the war, German conscription called only men twenty years old or older; many SS recruits were as young as sixteen.) Benefiting from Nazi Party propaganda and Hitler youth indoctrination, the SS was thus able to siphon off large numbers of highly motivated volunteers for service in its own *Waffen SS* field units.[47] Although *Waffen SS* units served at the front under army control, the duplicate training machinery and administrative bureaucracy maintained by the *Waffen SS* wasted thousands of men who could otherwise have been used as combat troops. Moreover, many of the high-quality enlistees drawn to the *Waffen SS* as private soldiers were needed in the army as potential noncommissioned officers (NCOs) and technical specialists.

At the beginning of Barbarossa in 1941, *Waffen SS* field units numbered six full divisions and a handful of separate battalions and regiments. Battle losses and a gradual enlargement of *Waffen SS* forces continued to draw men away from the army at a steady rate until August 1942, when Hitler sanctioned a massive enlargement of SS units that would double *Waffen SS* forces within a year.[48] Therefore, precisely at the time that the German Army was frantically searching for ways to raise its own frontline strength in late summer 1942, the *Waffen SS* was becoming an even more voracious consumer of German manpower.

Even more frustrating to the German Army was the conduct of Reichsmarschall Herman Göring's *Luftwaffe*. Like the *SS*, the *Luftwaffe* benefited from an elitist image among German youth and consistently attracted large numbers of zealots who were prime soldier material. With the curtailment of its offensive air activities since the 1940 Battle of Britain, the *Luftwaffe* found itself with an excess of ground support personnel. An attempt by the army to claim these men for retraining as infantry replacements during the summer of 1942 was parried by Göring, who argued to Hitler that transferring these "genuinely National Socialist" young men to the army would contaminate them by exposure "to an army which still had chaplains and was led by officers steeped with the traditions of the Kaiser."[49]

Instead, in mid-1942, Göring ordered that 170,000 surplus air personnel be organized into twenty-two *Luftwaffe* field divisions for employment as ground units at the front. In the army's view, this remedy promised no relief since these *Luftwaffe* units would almost certainly be of low quality due to inexperience and lack of trained leadership. As Field Marshal von Manstein explained in his memoirs: "To form these excellent troops into divisions within the framework of the Luftwaffe was sheer lunacy. Where were they to get the necessary close-combat training and practice in working with other formations? Where were they to get the battle experience so vital in the east? And where was the Luftwaffe to find divisional, regimental, and battalion commanders?"[50] These questions were tragically answered in late 1942, when several *Luftwaffe* field divisions fell apart at their first taste of combat on the Russian Front. These 170,000 men, who as infantry replacements could have nearly replenished the bedraggled divisions of Army Groups Center and North, thus added very little combat strength to the German forces in the east.

The German Army shared some blame for the shortage of infantrymen. The infantry, respected in the Prussian and German Armies since the days of Frederick the Great as the "Queen of the Battlefield," had been eclipsed in popular affections by the glamour and publicity given to the mobile troops during World War II's early campaigns. Although conscripts could still be made to fill the ranks of infantry divisions, flocks of enterprising young soldiers avoided infantry service by volunteering for the new darlings of the German Army, the panzer and motorized forces. By late summer 1942, some senior officers even detected a growing "unpatriotic" tendency on the part of recruits to abhor infantry duty and to seek assignment to other, less-demanding jobs.

In an attempt to counteract these perceptions, General Halder authorized an information campaign on 27 July 1942, intended to "glamoriz[e] the infantry."[51] A 1 August memorandum to field commanders from the German Army's chief of infantry invited suggestions from field commanders for regenerating the German infantry forces. In reply, General Heinrici suggested a number of wide-ranging reforms, including preferential career development for infantry NCOs, improved pay and benefits, and a better effort to counter the recruiting guiles of the *Waffen SS*, *Luftwaffe*, navy, and Reich Labor Service. Heinrici also cited a pervasive "east complex" as a major deterrent to infantry enlistments, explaining that the reports of the desolate Russian landscape and harsh battle conditions in the east were causing widespread melancholia among frontline soldiers and discouraging recruits from volunteering for infantry service.[52]

Another measure taken to ease the infantry crisis included using volunteer laborers—most of whom were paroled Russian prisoners of war—on work projects behind the German front. While not directly increasing the number of infantrymen, the use of these laborers at least reduced the demand for German auxiliary personnel somewhat.[53] In addition, officers of frontline infantry units were allowed to make recruiting sweeps through service and support units, attempting to persuade rear-echelon soldiers to volunteer for infantry duty. To prevent rear-echelon units from protecting their favorite personnel, an Army High Command order warned that even "indispensable clerks" were to be released if willing, since "only the Front Fighter is indispensable. For all others will a replacement be found."[54] To enforce this edict, Hitler deputized General Walter von Unruh to comb rear area units to identify excess personnel. Unruh's writ as "hero snatcher" included absolute authority to order individuals transferred to the front in the Führer's name.[55] Such policies offered minor relief but could not greatly affect the overall combat worthiness of German units.

More substantial measures soon followed. In yet another Führer order, Hitler announced his displeasure at the intolerably low combat strengths of fighting units in relation to their support units and ordered all army commanders immediately to account for their subordinate divisions' total ration strength versus infantry combat strength.[56] In a companion directive, General Kurt Zeitzler (who succeeded the disenchanted General Halder as chief of staff in September) ordered an immediate 10 percent reduction in all Army High Command, army group, army, corps, and division headquarters personnel. All freed manpower was to be sent to the front as combat replacements. Zeitzler also directed that the personnel in rearward support units regularly be reduced in proportion to forward combat losses, with the dislocated officers, NCOs, and soldiers sent forward. In this way, Zeitzler reasoned, the support units would share the inconvenience of reduced establishments and even actual casualties along with the fighting forces, thereby eliminating the traditional estrangement between "combat troops" and "rear echelons."[57]

General Zeitzler also ordered all rearward forces on the Eastern Front, including high-level staffs, supply troops, and signal personnel, to organize combat-ready "alarm units." In addition to performing their normal duties, these units were to receive refresher infantry training and, ideally, were to be rotated periodically into the front lines for a few days' exposure to real combat. In crisis situations, these alarm units were assembled and placed at the disposal of forward commanders for use as supplementary reserves.[58]

His energy and enthusiasm for his new job as yet undimmed by Hitler's stultifying command style, Zeitzler dashed off other memorandums addressing morale, leadership, and unit organization. In a 29 October 1942 order entitled "Front Fighters," Zeitzler charged all officers with ensuring that the fighting troops receive the best possible treatment and creature comforts, even if this meant that service troops went without.[59] Worried that the constant attrition of junior leaders might jeopardize the esprit of small units, Zeitzler directed that all junior officer and NCO requests for transfer to combat duties be given immediate, unconditional approval. The new chief of staff also specified that all leaders returning to duty from convalescent leave were to be returned, if possible, to their old units, as were officers and NCOs serving on detached duty at training depots or elsewhere.[60] Noting that combat losses and lack of adequate replacements had caused many divisions to disband one-third of their infantry battalions, Zeitzler urged on 20 November that all veteran companies be kept intact regardless of losses, even if reassigned to new parent units: "Every soldier is attached to his own particular company. Cohesiveness takes a long time to develop in new units—often it never develops at all. Thus it is better to keep together original companies...."[61]

Collectively, these measures showed the growing German awareness of the severe pressures placed on their divisions by the lack of adequate manpower. For want of men, German commanders were being forced to compromise doctrinal Elastic Defense methods, sacrificing especially the traditional use of depth and small-unit maneuver to absorb enemy attacks without inordinate loss. The manpower shortage caused internal strain as well, wearing away at the morale, training, and general combat worthiness of German units. The desperate expedients taken to redistribute personnel within the German Army eased the stresses somewhat, but the ultimate solution to Germany's manpower problems lay far beyond the army's control. Moreover, catastrophic losses during the coming winter at Stalingrad and elsewhere would strain Germany's already overtaxed eastern armies even more severely.

Volunteers from logistics units are formed into a combat ski unit near Kharkov, 1942

Winter Battles on the Defensive Front

In the unfolding autumn of 1942, German soldiers and civilians were haunted by the specter of a second winter campaign in Russia. Seeking to allay those fears, the *Luftwaffe*'s Reichsmarschall Göring told a cheering crowd in the Berlin *Sportpalast* in early October that "this time we are immune. We already know what a Russian winter is like."[62]

With respect to the weather, Göring's prediction proved accurate. Drawing on their own experiences plus the knowledge exchanged in after-action reports, German divisions braced themselves for the expected cold temperatures and harsh conditions. In supplies, training, and shelter, German units were far better prepared for winter warfare than they had been the previous year. However, protection against the weather did not make German forces immune from Russian bullets. Even though Soviet strength had shifted to the south, the Red Army forces facing Army Groups Center and North remained sufficiently powerful to batter the German defensive front, causing several defensive crises during the course of the winter fighting.

The autumnal stiffening of German defenses prompted by the Führer Defense Order had also served as early preparation for winter. On 17 September, for example, the 58th Infantry Division directed that the mandated improvements in its own defenses be made so "the troops [could] spend the winter in the position."[63] One criterion emphasized at all levels was the construction of a continuous defensive line so as to avoid the costly and hazardous strongpoint tactics of the previous winter. (One specific passage of the Führer Defense Order had even addressed this issue. Noting that a strongpoint style of defense had been compelled in "certain sectors" as an "emergency measure" during the 1941—42 winter, Hitler had made it clear that he considered such expedient measures to be peculiar to the previous winter and in no way a doctrinal model for winter defensive tactics. Instead, Hitler demanded a continuous defensive line even during winter months, a requirement that, for once, corresponded exactly with the opinions of frontline commanders as expressed in their own earlier after-action reports.[64])

Hitler added specific operational guidance on 14 October 1942 by issuing Operations Order 1. This order gave instructions for winter activities and implicitly conceded that Germany's strategic ambitions for 1942 had not been realized. Instead, Hitler promised that success in the coming winter battles would protect recent German gains, creating favorable conditions for the "final destruction of our most dangerous enemy" sometime in 1943. While directing the continuation of German attacks at Stalingrad and in the Caucasus, Hitler ordered the armies along the defensive front to prepare for a winter campaign. Reiterating the constraints of the September Führer Defense Order, he directed that winter positions be defended to the last under all circumstances. Hitler added that German units were not to avail themselves of evasive maneuvers or withdrawals, that enemy penetrations were to be contained as far forward as possible, and that any units isolated by Russian breakthroughs were to hold in place until relieved. Moreover, "the significance of a *continuous HKL* [main line of resistance] must once more be especially emphasized." And in what was becoming virtually a personal trademark, Hitler warned darkly that every leader was unequivocally responsible for the "unconditional execution" of his instructions.[65]

Three weeks later, with intelligence reports predicting the imminent onset of powerful Russian attacks, Hitler directed the chief of the Army General Staff to remind army commanders of their defensive responsibilities. At a situation conference on 2 November, Hitler told General Zeitzler to issue a new memorandum "based on the Führer's Winter Directive [Operations Order 1] setting forth again the principles according to which operations [were] to be conducted." Apparently forgetting for the moment his own proscriptions against strongpoint defenses (the Führer did not hold himself to the same standards of obedience that he demanded from field commanders), Hitler added that "particular emphasis is to be given to the demand that every *Stützpunkt* [strongpoint] is to be defended to the last."[66] While the reference to strongpoints may have caused some officers to blink in momentary confusion (for a continuous defensive line was still the prescribed standard, and strongpoint defenses remained officially anathema), Hitler's basic message was clear. In the coming winter battles, German defenders would fight bitterly to retain their initial positions, and no tactical flexibility would be granted for the execution of "elastic" defensive methods that required the relinquishing of any terrain.[67]

While Hitler rattled orders to his generals, German soldiers continued to gird for winter warfare. Where time and manpower allowed, defensive positions were improved to meet Hitler's qualifications. Foraging parties hunted through Russian villages for sleds and snowshoes, while German panzer units received extra-wide snow tracks for their tanks and assault guns to give greater cross-country mobility over snow and slushy ground. (Unfortunately, since the wider tracks did not fit German railroad flatcars or standard military bridging, they had to be removed each time the vehicles used a flatcar or a bridge.[68]) Most divisions assembled special ski units, earmarking them for use as local counterattack forces. In the 132d Infantry Division, for example, troops of the division's "bicycle battalion" traded their bicycles for skis and continued as the division's only mobile reserve.[69]

As is often the case, actual conditions at the front did not always match the hearty standards decreed by higher headquarters. Frontline visits by General Georg Lindemann, the commander of the Eighteenth Army, revealed enduring deficiencies among his units. Touring the front of the L Corps outside Leningrad in early November, Lindemann found that, in spite of repeated orders to the contrary, gaps still existed in the forward trenchlines. Explaining the lack of improvements, the corps commander pointed out to Lindemann that "due to the tremendous shortage of personnel only maintenance of the [existing] position is possible."[70]

Though somewhat stronger than during the last winter, German divisions still manned extended fronts with understrength units. The 121st Infantry Division, holding part of Army Group North's line, had an average battalion strength of only 200 men and could muster only one composite bicycle-ski company and one alarm company (composed of service troops) as division reserves.[71] In the 254th Division, each regiment held only one infantry and one pioneer platoon in reserve behind frontline troops that, according to the division commander, were "extremely tired."[72]

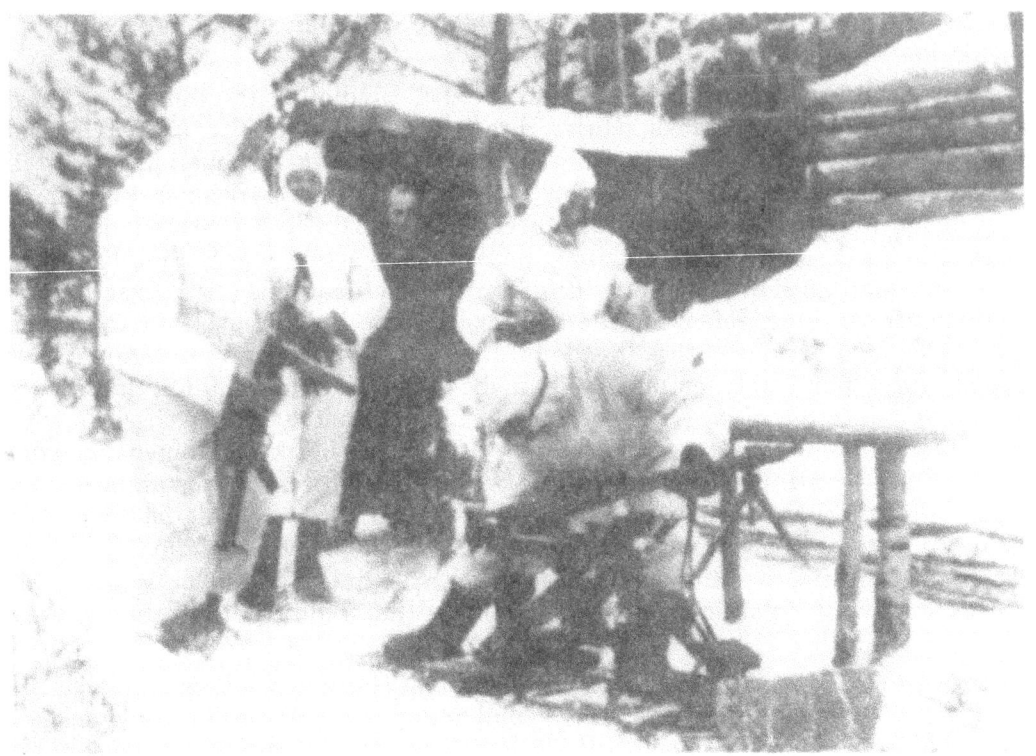
Troops of Army Group North ready a machine-gun sled for a reconnaissance patrol, December 1942

Manned by worn-out and understrength divisions in haphazard positions, the German defensive front invited Russian penetrations. The defensive lines of Army Groups Center and North zigzagged back and forth, their twists and turns adding hundreds of unnecessary miles to the trenches held by German troops. The two army group commanders each requested Hitler's permission to conduct limited withdrawals in order to straighten their lines. These retreats, they argued, would free troops to thicken German defenses and form reserves. Hitler rebuffed both, scorning the notion that the surrender of terrain could in any way work to German advantage.

The most vulnerable portions of the German lines were the so-called Rzhev salient in Army Group Center, the Demyansk salient south of Lake Ilmen, and the narrow neck of land held by the Eighteenth Army east of Leningrad around Schlüsselburg. In each of these areas, German forces were geographically exposed. The Rzhev and Demyansk positions had been occupied since the 1941—42 winter fighting and represented stand-fast lines held by German divisions despite deep Soviet envelopments on each flank. At Schlüsselburg, the strip of land held by the Germans along the southern shore of Lake Ladoga was all that kept outside Soviet forces from lifting the land siege of Leningrad. A Russian breakthrough at any one of these points could have easily resulted in the encirclement and destruction of sizable German forces, especially considering Hitler's repeated injunctions against local retreats.

Soviet attacks during the winter of 1942—43 tested the German front in each of these sectors but failed to achieve the catastrophic breakthrough desired. At Schlüsselburg, the Russians managed to seize a thin sliver of land linking Leningrad with their main forces, but they did so without inflicting any decisive German losses. The Russian onslaughts pinned down nearly all the reserves belonging to Army Group Center and Army Group North, however, leaving virtually no forces available for transfer to the southern front once the Stalingrad debacle had begun.[73]

Soviet sappers approach German lines near Leningrad, February 1943

The one Soviet offensive that managed to destroy even a division-size German force on the defensive front occurred at Velikiye Luki. There, though less exposed than the forces in the Demyansk or Rzhev salients, the Germans tolerated gaps in the rough terrain areas to the north and south of the town. Even the German main positions were not completely tied together, for only lightly manned trenches linked platoon and company strongpoints. A Soviet advance through these gaps on 25 November surrounded 70,000 German troops from two different divisions in and around Velikiye Luki. For the next two months, German forces were embroiled in a savage battle to spring open the Velikiye Luki trap, an effort that eventually consumed elements of three additional divisions in desperate rescue attempts.[74]

The battles around Velikiye Luki, as with the fighting at Schlüsselburg, Demyansk, and Rzhev, produced few surprises in defensive doctrine. As had already been demonstrated dozens of times in other places, inadequately manned German positions could be swamped by superior Soviet forces in winter combat. Unlike during the 1941—42 winter, the divisions on the northern front made little attempt to use strongpoint tactics, instead clinging grimly to their continuous defensive lines per Hitler's orders. The lack of manpower doomed this effort to failure. As one former corps commander wrote:

> To be sure, there were no gaps—the reader will recall their serious consequences in the winter campaign of 1941/42—in the ... front. The positions formed a continuous line during the early fighting, but it was impossible to man them adequately (a division had to hold a sector of from forty to fifty kilometers). Neither were there any major reserve forces. Only small, local reserves were available. Whatever could be spared had been transferred to the armies on the southern front.[75]

German troops, stolidly holding on to the intact bits of front in accordance with the Führer's instructions, managed to sustain pathetic little islands of resistance against the Russian flood (see map 9). Ultimately, however, the retention of such points proved completely meaningless in the absence of strong mobile reserves. The German forces pocketed around Velikiye Luki, for example, eventually became a substantial operational liability, tying down precious reserves to no purpose other than to rescue them from a trap wrought largely by Hitler's rigid constraints. The commitment of German forces to such relief expeditions weakened German defenses at still other points and prevented the shifting of additional divisions to the concurrent decisive battles between Stalingrad and Rostov.

The same was generally true at Demyansk and Rzhev. There, German reserves were drawn into attritional battles that, although preventing Soviet breakthroughs and the consequent encirclement of the exposed German forces, accomplished little apart from satisfying Hitler's bent for holding ground. In early 1943, with the forces of Army Group Center and Army Group North near utter exhaustion and with no further reserves available to prevent future Russian penetrations of the defensive front, Hitler finally authorized the abandonment of both the Demyansk and Rzhev salients. These withdrawals substantially shortened the front—in Rzhev, for example, Operation Büffel reduced the German frontage from 340 to 110 miles—but they came too late to allow either the building of a new fully manned defensive line or the transfer of additional units to other sectors.[76]

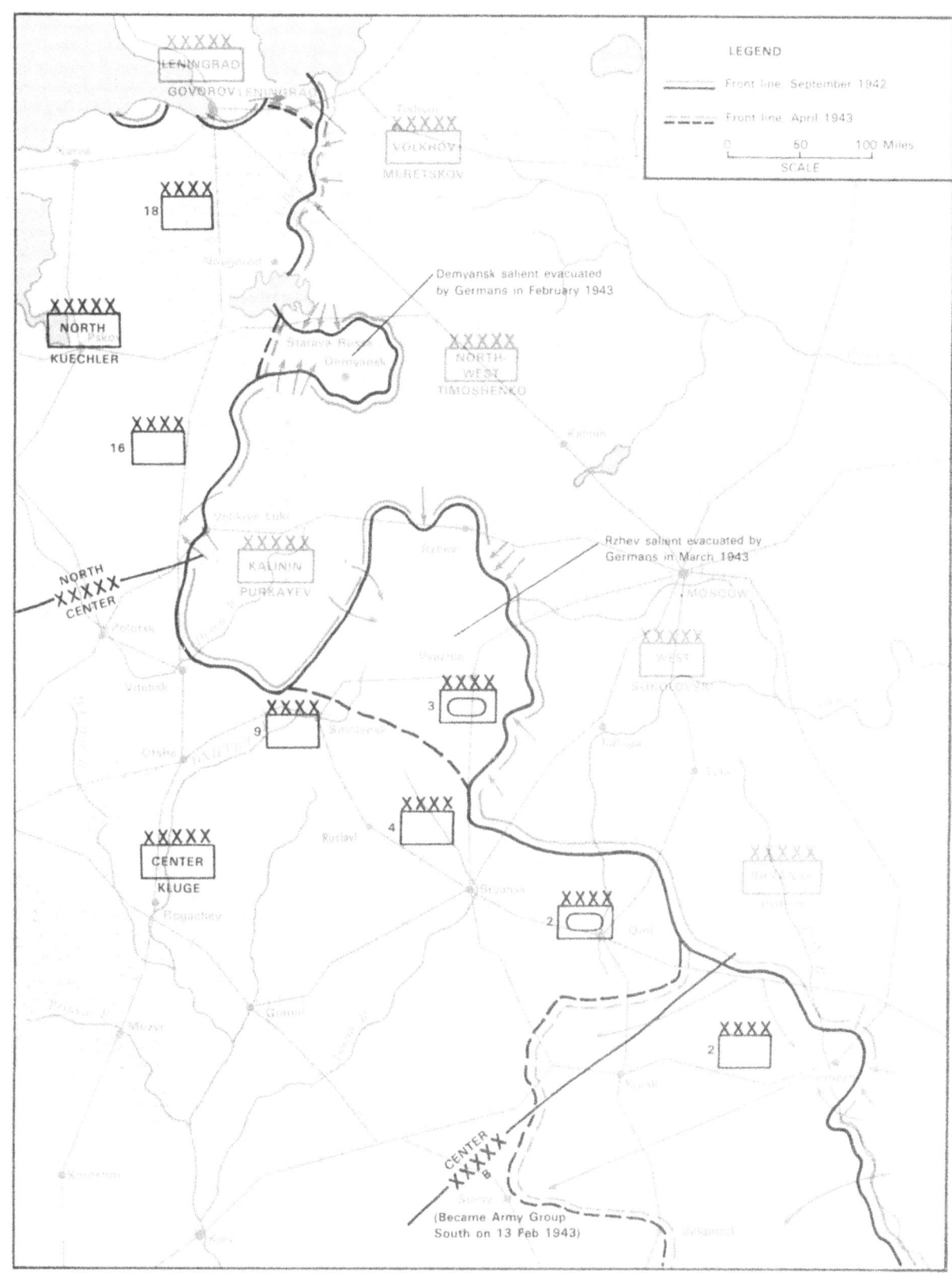

Map 9. Soviet attacks on Army Groups Center and North, winter 1942—43

Destroyed Soviet tank provides additional cover for German trench dugout, February 1943

German infantrymen retake a village south of Orel, March 1943

Hitler refused to acknowledge that his rigid defensive instructions hampered field commanders by precluding the potential advantages of the elastic defense in depth. Hitler, it seemed, could be convinced to authorize retreats or line-shortening withdrawals only after entire German armies had been shredded in positional warfare under disadvantageous conditions. Even when the Führer finally authorized rearward movement, such withdrawals offered little tactical relief since German losses in the interim had usually been so great that even the new, shorter lines could not be properly secured.

The Offensive Front

Compared to the stripped-down divisions left holding the defensive front, the German southern attack forces that assembled for Operation Blau seemed sleek and powerful. However, this appearance was deceiving. The divisions assigned to Army Group South (later divided into Army Groups A and B) suffered from many deficiencies that compromised their offensive and defensive capabilities.

In May 1942, most of the infantry divisions in Army Group South stood at about 50 percent strength. Although brought nearly up to strength over the next six weeks, the southern divisions had little time or opportunity to assimilate their new troops. Only one-third of the infantry divisions committed to the upcoming attack could be taken out of the line in early spring for rehabilitation; the remaining divisions stayed in their old winter defensive positions and tried to train and integrate their replacements even as they fought desultory defensive battles against minor Russian attacks.[77] As a result, the general training standards in the southern assault forces were far below those of the 1939—41 German armies. Losses in officers, NCOs, and technical personnel during the 1941 winter battles had further sapped the combat abilities of the German forces. In fact, many German units now regretted the use of artillerymen, signalers, and other specialists as infantry during the winter months since they were so hard to replace. Moreover, even after stripping vehicles and equipment from the northern forces, Army Group South's divisions lacked their full complement of motor transport. According to a General Staff study in late May, the spearhead forces (those divisions that would actually lead the attacks toward Stalingrad and the Caucasus) would embark with only 80 percent of their vehicles, and the follow-on infantry divisions and supply columns would be slowed by shortages of both horses and vehicles.[78] For all of the ruthless economies inflicted on their poorer relatives to the north, Army Groups A and B would therefore be more clumsy, be less mobile, and have less logistical staying power than the German armies that had launched Barbarossa a year before.

Army Group B had two distinct missions in Operation Blau: first, to carve its way eastward along the southern bank of the Don River some 300 miles to Stalingrad, and second, to post a defensive screen along its northern flank as it went, protecting its own rear and the further unfolding of Army Group A's attack to the south. Though not the decisive thrust (Army Group A would actually push into the Caucasus toward the strategic oil fields), Army Group B's mission was crucial to German success.

German infantrymen prepare to attack during Operation Blau, July 1942

German motorized infantry forces cross the Don River, July 1942

Army Group B's far-flung tasks could not be accomplished with the German divisions at hand. Consequently, the most critical jobs were given to the more powerful German armies, and the less-demanding tasks were allotted to a polyglot of allied contingents. The Sixth Army and the Fourth Panzer Army were to attack toward Stalingrad, while the veteran Second Army was to seize Voronezh and then form the link between Army Group Center's defensive front and Army Group B's flank pickets. The job of covering the long flank in between was handed to allied armies of lesser fighting value.

In the spring of 1942, Hitler prevailed on the Reich's military partners to provide additional combat forces to augment the German armies. Romania, Hungary, and Italy all reluctantly consented to deploy additional forces on the Eastern Front, though they each insisted that their contingents fight under their own army headquarters rather than as separate divisions in German corps and armies.[79] By early August, thirty-six allied divisions were committed in the southern portion of the front, roughly 40 percent of the total number of Axis divisions in that region. Even though German liaison staffs were assigned to these forces, the combat effectiveness of the allied armies was generally poor.[80] By relegating the allied forces to purely defensive missions along the German flanks, the German High Command figured to minimize the demands placed on these forces while still conserving *Wehrmacht* divisions for crucial combat roles.

Through early summer, the forces posted along Army Group B's northern flank had little difficulty in fending off Soviet assaults. A Second Army after-action report on 21 July 1942, following the defeat of Soviet counterattacks near Voronezh, was particularly reassuring. Written at the request of the General Staff's Training Branch in Berlin and circulated throughout the German Army's higher echelons, this report allayed lingering fears caused by the Red Army's winter successes in 1941—42. "Russian infantry in the attack is even worse than before," the report began. "Much massing, greater vulnerability to artillery and mortar fire and to flanking maneuver. Scarcely any more night attacks."[81] This report brightened the prospects for successful defense along Army Group B's northern flank.

Despite this reassurance, Army Group B's left wing remained vulnerable. Hitler's own interest in this potential weakness began in early spring when he ordered that the Second Army be reinforced with several hundred antitank guns as an additional guarantee against the collapse of Blau's northern shield.[82] In anticipation of its defensive operations, Second Army also had been assigned numerous engineer detachments, labor units, and Organization Todt work parties for general construction and fortification. After its successful attack on Voronezh in early July, Second Army attempted to fortify its portion of the exposed flank using these assets throughout the remainder of the summer.[83]

To the east beyond Second Army, however, the Don flank was held by troops of the Hungarian Second Army, the Italian Eighth Army, and the Romanian Third Army. Other Romanian formations, temporarily under the command of Fourth Panzer Army, held the open flank south of Stalingrad. As expected, these forces proved to be mediocre in combat, leading German commanders to be even more uneasy about this long, exposed sector. By September, General Maximilian von Weichs, the commander of Army Group

A German 88-mm flak gun awaits attack by Soviet tanks outside Voronezh

B, regarded his northern flank to be so endangered that he ordered special German "intervention units" (*Eingreifgruppen*) rotated into reserve behind both the German- and allied-held portions of his left wing.[84]

The use of intervention units was not new to German defensive doctrine. In fact, the Elastic Defense doctrine of 1917 and 1918 had required that intervention divisions be used to reinforce deliberate counterattacks against particularly stubborn enemy penetrations. In 1942, however, the role of these intervention units went beyond counterattack. They could also provide advance reinforcement—"corsetting"—to threatened sectors since, according to Weichs' explanation, the Russians "seldom were able to conceal preparations for attack." Thus, the intervention units could support faltering allied contingents, hopefully steeling their resistance until additional help could arrive.

In October, General Zeitzler, the new chief of the Army General Staff, began to echo Weichs' concerns. In a lengthy presentation to Hitler, Zeitzler argued that the allied lines between Voronezh and Stalingrad constituted "the most perilous sector of the Eastern Front," a situation that posed "an enormous danger which must be eliminated." Although Hitler made sympathetic noises, he refused to accept Zeitzler's conclusions and ordered no major changes to German deployments or missions.[85]

Even though the Führer rejected Zeitzler's recommendation that German forces withdraw from Stalingrad, he did authorize minor actions to help shore up the allied armies. One of these measures was the interspersing of additional German units (primarily antitank battalions) among the allied divisions. In accordance with Hitler's published defensive instructions, if the allied units were overrun, these few German units were to "stand fast and limit the enemy's penetration or breakthrough. By holding out in this way, they should create more favorable conditions for our counterattack."[86] Another protective

A drawing of German sentries on the Don River

measure was the repositioning of a combined German-Romanian panzer corps behind the Romanian Third Army. This unit, the XLVIII Panzer Corps, consisted of only an untried Romanian armored division and a battle-worn, poorly equipped German panzer division. Weak as it was, this corps was not placed under the control of the Romanians or even Weichs. Rather, it was designated as a special Führer Reserve under the personal direction of Hitler and therefore could not be committed to combat without first obtaining his release.[87] Finally, from October onward, German signal teams were placed throughout the allied armies so the German High Command could independently monitor the day-to-day performance of those forces without having to rely on reports from the allies themselves. These and other measures were not executed without some friction, however: the Italians, for example, huffily rejected German suggestions for improving their defensive positions.[88]

The allied units were not the only soft spots on the defensive flank. By autumn, several newly raised German divisions, hastily consigned to Army Group B in June in order to flesh out its order of battle, were also causing some concern. For example, barely days before its preliminary June attack on Voronezh to secure the German flank, Second Army had received six brand-new German divisions. Though game enough in their initial attacks, these units quickly began to unravel due to poor training and inexperienced leadership. In one case, the 385th Infantry Division reportedly suffered "unnecessarily high losses," including half of its company commanders and five of six battalion commanders in just six weeks, due to deficient training. This fiery baptism ruined these divisions for later defensive use. The loss of so many personnel in such a short period of time left permanent scars, traumatizing the divisions before time and battle experience could produce new leaders and heal the units' psychological wounds. Second Army assessed the situation on 1 October 1942 and informed Army Group B that these once-new divisions were no longer fully reliable even for limited defensive purposes and that heavy defensive fighting might well stampede them. Unless they could be pulled out of the line for rest and rehabilitation, these divisions, which accounted for nearly half of Second Army's total infantry strength, could only be trusted in the defense of small, quiet sectors.[89]

The German southern offensive thus trusted its long northern flank to a conglomeration of listless allied and battle-weary German units. Like the forces farther north on the defensive front of Army Groups Center and North, these armies were stretched taut, manning thin lines with few reserves beyond insubstantial local forces. Barely strong enough to hold small probing attacks at bay during the summer and early fall, these armies lacked the strength to meet a major Russian offensive without substantial reinforcement (see map 10).

Shielded by this doubtful defensive umbrella, Operation Blau made good initial progress. In fierce house-to-house fighting, General Friedrich Paulus' Sixth Army gnawed its way into Stalingrad, the projected eastern terminus of Army Group B's defensive barrier. Despite nagging shortages of fuel and other supplies, as well as Hitler's confused switching of forces and missions, Army Group A had cleared Rostov and penetrated the northern reaches of the Caucasus Mountains by late August.

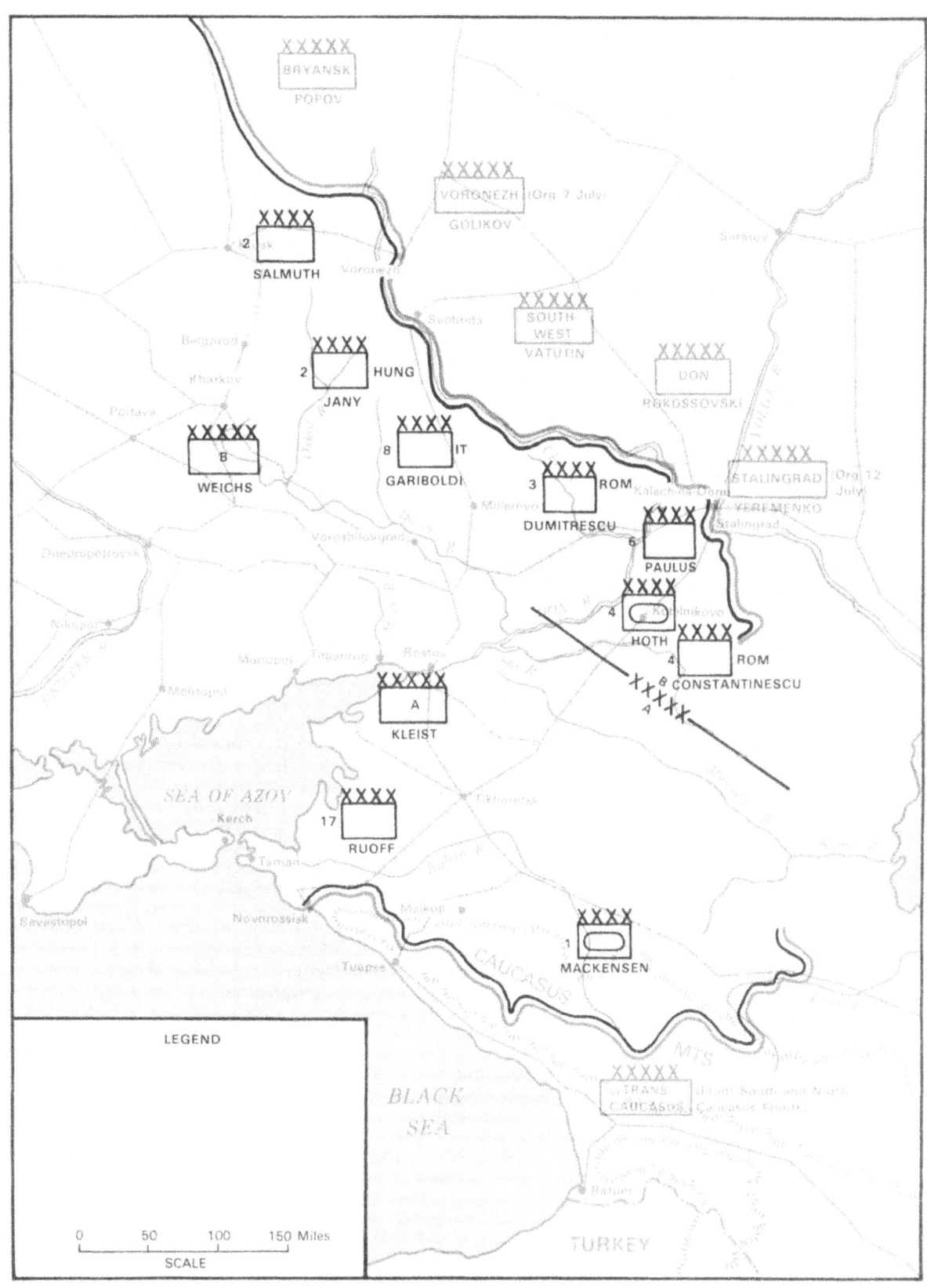

Map 10. Southern portion of Russian Front, 1 November 1942

German propaganda photograph entitled "Storming the last bastions in Stalingrad, 9 November 1942"

At this point, the German campaign lost whatever coherence it might have possessed earlier. Forgetting that Army Group B's mission was but secondary to that of the advance toward the oil fields, Hitler became obsessed with capturing Stalingrad. Ordering not only Sixth Army but even the cream of Fourth Panzer Army into the city, Hitler committed the German forces to a prolonged battle of attrition for control of Stalingrad's rubbled streets and factories. By late autumn, Operation Blau had degenerated into a test of military manhood between Hitler and Stalin on the Volga.

Whatever the outcome of the battle for possession of Stalingrad, by October it was clear that another winter defensive campaign was imminent. As described earlier, Hitler's Operations Order 1 ordered winter defensive preparations on all parts of the front, though in that same directive he bade the Stalingrad fighting continue. Yet even the Sixth Army in and around Stalingrad began to take preliminary steps for a winter defense. After discussions with Sixth Army staff members, an Army High Command liaison officer dispatched a memorandum to Berlin in mid-October assessing the feasibility of fortifying a miniature "east wall" on the Volga steppes and recommending the transfer of additional engineer units to Paulus' command for that purpose.[90]

The German defensive arrangements along the Don River held together only until 19 November, when a Red Army offensive flattened the Romanian Third Army northwest of Stalingrad and knifed southward toward the rear of the German Sixth and Fourth Panzer Armies (see map 11). A day later,

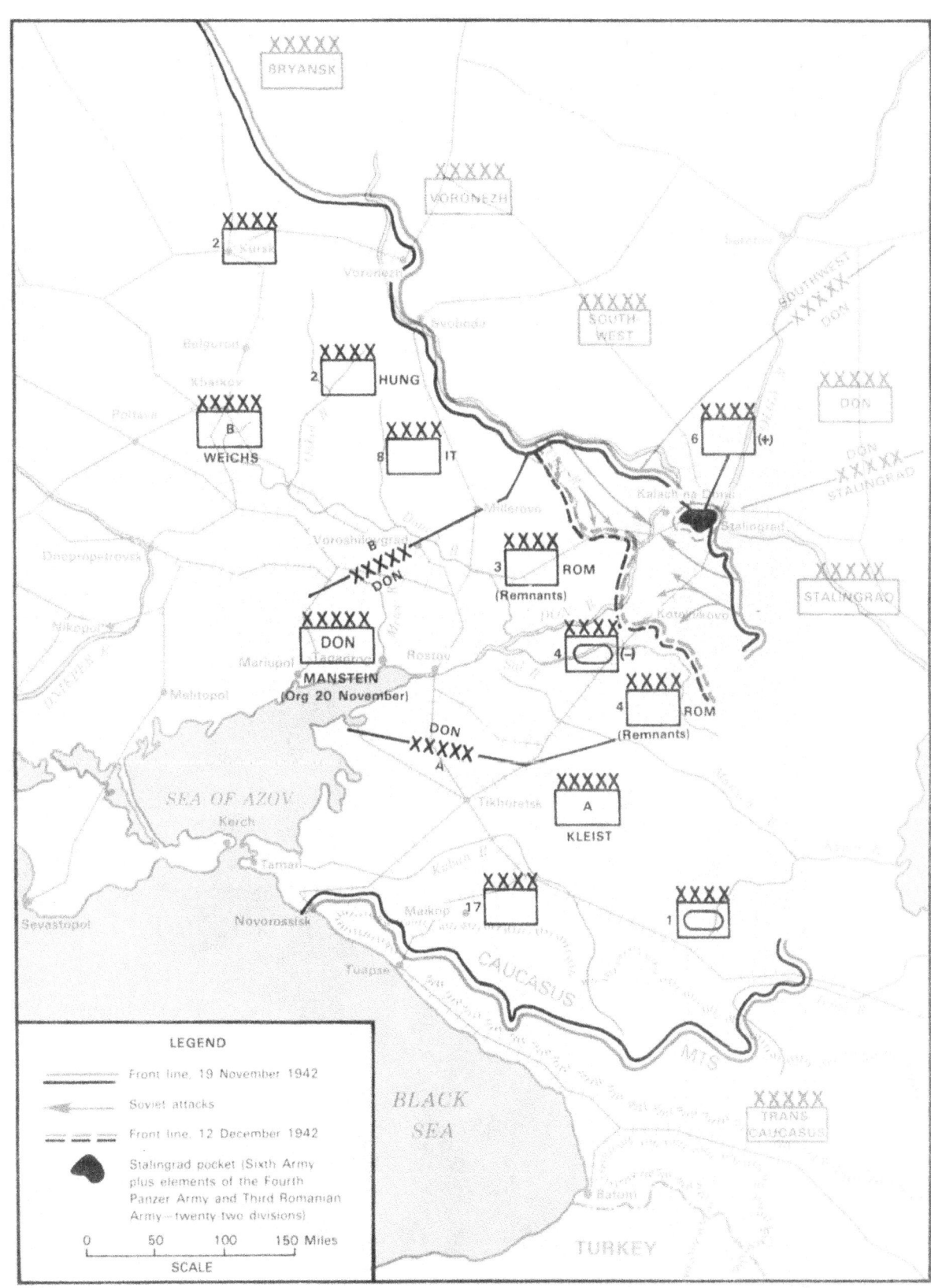

Map 11. Soviet winter counteroffensive, 19 November—12 December 1942

another Soviet attack burst through the Romanian lines south of Stalingrad. On 23 November, these pincers met near Kalach, severing Sixth Army's land supply routes. The collapse of the Axis defenses along the Don River and the encirclement of Sixth Army transformed the situation of the southern front, casting the *Wehrmacht* forces there into a desperate struggle for their very survival.

The ensuing winter defensive battles in southern Russia can be divided into three separate phases. In the first phase, lasting from 19 November until 23 December 1942, the Germans scrambled to hold an advanced defensive line near the confluence of the Don and Chir Rivers from which they could support relief operations toward Stalingrad. Once the attacks to relieve Sixth Army were irretrievably repulsed, the focus of German defensive efforts

German troops move forward to attack tractor factory in Stalingrad

German troops in hasty defensive positions overlooking the Volga River on the northern outskirts of Stalingrad

shifted. During the second phase, lasting from the last week of December 1942 to mid-February 1943, German divisions fought to block another huge Soviet envelopment, this one aimed at the rear of the entire German southern wing near Rostov. Finally, from mid-February until the spring thaw, the third phase of the winter battles saw the restabilization of the front south of Kursk.

German defensive operations differed in each phase, and these differences reflected variations in the mission, the strength and composition of German forces, and the actions of the enemy. In no case, however, were these chaotic defensive actions conducted along doctrinal lines. Instead, from the initial collapse of the Romanian armies in November 1942 to the stabilization of the front in March 1943, German defensive operations were once again almost completely extemporaneous.

The first phase of fighting focused on the fate of the beleaguered German Sixth Army in Stalingrad. Ordered to stand fast and repeatedly assured by Hitler that Sixth Army would be relieved, General Paulus swiftly put his forces into a giant hedgehog defensive posture.

Establishing an effective defensive perimeter at Stalingrad was doubly difficult due to a desperate shortage of infantrymen (the bulk of whom had fallen in the earlier street fighting) and the lack of prepared positions. On the eastern face of the Stalingrad pocket, German troops continued to occupy the defensive positions built up during previous fighting for the city. However, the southern and western portions of the perimeter lay almost completely on shelterless steppes, and the hasty defenses there never amounted to more than a few bunkers and shallow connecting trenches. (Because the steppes were almost treeless, no lumber was available for building fires for heat or for constructing covered defensive positions.) Significantly, the subsequent Soviet attacks to liquidate the surrounded Sixth Army came almost exclusively from the south and west against the least well-established portions of the German defenses. On 23 November, well-built positions to the north of Stalingrad were rashly abandoned without orders by the German LI Corps commander, General Walter von Seydlitz-Kurzbach, who had hoped thereby to provoke an immediate breakout order from Paulus. This hasty action sacrificed the 94th Infantry Division, which was overrun and annihilated by Red Army forces during the movement to the rear, and also gave up virtually the only well-constructed defensive positions within the Stalingrad *Kessel*.[91]

Sixth Army had difficulty in defending itself because of insufficient resources. Lack of fuel prevented the use of Paulus' three panzer and three motorized divisions as mobile reserves. Hoarding its meager fuel supplies for a possible breakout attempt, Sixth Army wound up employing most of its tanks and assault guns in static roles. Likewise, shortages of artillery ammunition and fortification materials hindered the German defense. The *Luftwaffe*'s heroic attempts to airlift supplies into Stalingrad were hopelessly inadequate: since daily deliveries never exceeded consumption, the overall supply problem grew steadily worse in all areas. In some ways, the aerial resupply effort was counterproductive. Scores of medium bombers were diverted from ground support and interdiction missions to serve as additional cargo carriers, a move that emptied the skies of much-needed German combat air power at an extremely critical period.[92]

For both tactical and logistical reasons, then, what the Nazi press dramatically called "Fortress Stalingrad" was, in reality, no fortress at all. Surrounded by no less than seven Soviet armies, Sixth Army was marooned on poor defensive ground without adequate forces, prepared positions, or stockpiles of essential supplies. Forbidden by Hitler to cut its way out of the encirclement, Sixth Army's eventual destruction was a foregone conclusion unless a relief attack could reestablish contact.

In response to this crisis, Hitler created Army Group Don under Field Marshal von Manstein on 20 November. Manstein was to restore order on the shattered southern front and, even more important in the short term, to direct a relief offensive to save Sixth Army. To accomplish this, Hitler promised Manstein six fresh infantry divisions, four panzer divisions, a *Luftwaffe* field division, and various other contingents.

Sixth Army's temporary aerial supply and eventual relief required the Germans to hold a forward defensive line along the Chir River, where the most advanced positions were only about forty miles from the Stalingrad perimeter. This line also covered the main departure airfields for the airlift and could serve as an excellent jumping-off point for a counterattack to link up with Sixth Army.

While Manstein worked out his plan for a relief attack, the Chir River line was held by whatever forces could be scraped together. Initially, these forces consisted of mixed combat units swept aside by the Russian offensive,

Field Marshal Friedrich Paulus, commander of the German Sixth Army trapped in Stalingrad without adequate forces or supplies

Field Marshal Erich von Manstein, commander of Army Group Don during desperate winter battles in 1942—43

alarm units called out from various support units, service troops, rear area security forces, convalescents, and casual personnel on leave. All these were formed into ad hoc battle groups and plugged into an improvised strongpoint defense along the Chir "like pieces of mosaic."[93]

That this rabble managed to hold the Chir line—and even some bridgeheads on the eastern bank—was due as much to Soviet indifference as to German improvisation. Through early December, the Soviet High Command was content to tighten its coils around Stalingrad and made little effort to exploit the German disarray farther west. In so doing, the Soviets were avoiding their great strategic mistake of the previous winter, when Stalin's failure to concentrate forces on major objectives frittered away excellent opportunities to no decisive gain.

In mid-December, however, the fighting on the Chir front accelerated, with both sides committing substantial forces to this crucial area. On 12 December, Manstein began his relief attack toward Stalingrad. Intending to pin down German forces and to prevent reinforcement of the rescue effort, Soviet forces hurled themselves against the Chir line at several points. Meanwhile, the Germans reinforced the ragtag elements along the Chir with fresh units, most notably the reconstituted XLVIII Panzer Corps (11th Panzer Division, 336th

Infantry Division, and 7th *Luftwaffe* Field Division). These mid-December defensive battles demonstrated both the capabilities and the limitations of German defenders during this phase (see map 12).

The XLVIII Panzer Corps intended to hold its sector of the Chir front with two infantry divisions forward and a panzer division in reserve. The 336th Division was an excellent, full-strength unit that had recently arrived on the Russian Front from occupation duty in France. Even though reinforced somewhat with *Luftwaffe* flak and ground combat units, the division could only man its wide front by putting all its assets forward, holding only a handful of infantry, engineers, and mobile flak guns in reserve. Even so, the 336th Division formed "the pivot and shield" of the German defense.[94] The 7th *Luftwaffe* Field Division, though well equipped and fully manned, was poorly trained and lacked leaders experienced in ground combat. Behind the infantry, General Hermann Balck's 11th Panzer Division, which had recently been transferred from Army Group Center after fighting in several tough defensive battles, assembled for duty as a mobile counterattack force. Although its infantry strength was fairly high, it (like other weakened divisions from the northern defensive front) had only a single battalion of Panzer Mark IVs in its entire tank regiment.[95]

On 7 December, even as the Germans were still settling into position, Soviet tank forces penetrated the left flank of the 336th Division. The Germans had not yet had time to lay mines or erect antitank obstacles, and their few *Paks* could not be used effectively. (Though relatively flat, the steppes were crisscrossed by deep ravines that provided excellent covered approaches into the German positions.) Facilitated by the weakness of the German antiarmor defenses, Russian tanks forced their way through the thin infantry defenses, overran part of the division's artillery, and thrust some fifteen kilometers into the division rear. In a three-day running battle, the 11th Panzer Division carved up this Russian tank force with repeated counterattacks against its flanks and rear. Despite the heady successes enjoyed by Balck's panzers and mechanized infantry (reports claimed seventy-five destroyed Russian tanks), the fighting was not all one-sided. For example, between 7 and 10 December, Russian tanks overran one infantry battalion of the 336th Division three different times.[96]

Even tougher fighting followed. Beginning on 11 December, fresh Russian attacks charged against the Chir front, forcing several local penetrations. Though eventually broken by counterattacks and the fire of the 336th Division's artillery, these Soviet probes threatened to erode the German defenders by attrition. In one case, a German battle group holding a bridgehead south of the Don-Chir confluence lost 18 officers and 750 men in ten days of combat.[97] Breakthroughs in the 336th Division's front between 13 and 15 December produced an extremely confused situation, with groups of enemy and friendly troops finally so intermixed that German artillery could not be used effectively for fear of firing on its own forces.[98] Moreover, Soviet tanks again broke through as far as the German artillery positions, overrunning some guns and knocking out others by direct fire.[99] By nightfall on 15 December, the situation of the 336th Division had become so grave that, according to one staff officer, the division's continued survival depended "exclusively on outside help."[100]

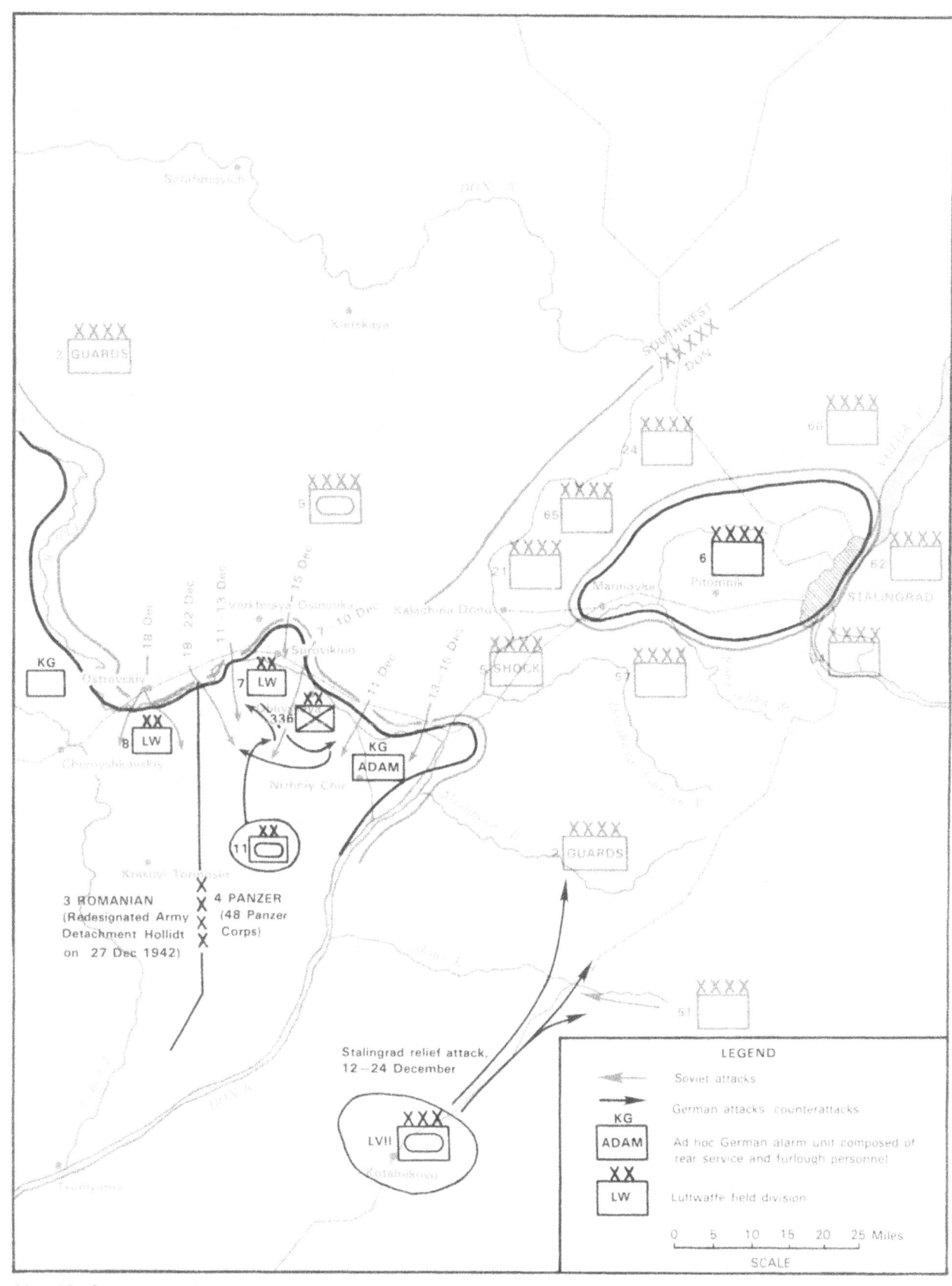

Map 12. German attack to relieve Stalingrad and defensive battles of the XLVIII Panzer Corps on the Chir River, 7—24 December 1942

Again, the 11th Panzer Division saved the German position on the Chir. Harkening to desperate appeals from the 336th Division for additional antitank support, the 11th diverted three of its precious tanks to buttress the flagging infantry, while the balance of the German armor hammered the Soviet flanks. By 22 December, the Chir front was quiet as both sides slumped into exhaustion.[101]

The battles on the Chir River had been a masterpiece of tactical improvisation by the Germans. Although regular combat troops were gradually brought into the fighting through reinforcement, the initial German defense had been conducted almost entirely by hastily organized contingents of service troops. While the performance of these units in no way matched that of regular combat veterans, their gritty stand fully vindicated the German Army's policies of training, organizing, and exercising rear-echelon alarm units on a regular basis.

Doctrinally, the committed German infantry forces in the XLVIII Panzer Corps' sector lacked the manpower and local reserves to conduct a competent defense in depth. Additionally, the German defense was throttled by Hitler's standing orders against tactical retreat, leaving the forward divisions little choice but to hold on to their initial positions even when penetrated or overrun. Short of antitank weapons, the German infantry forces were almost powerless against the Soviet armor. Had it not been for the availability of the 11th Panzer Division as a "fire brigade" counterattack force, the German defenders would almost certainly have been doomed to eventual annihilation in their positions clustered along the Chir.

The deft counterattacks by 11th Panzer Division repeatedly exploited speed, surprise, and shock action to destroy or scatter numerically superior Soviet forces. The generally open terrain provided a nearly ideal battlefield for mobile warfare, and the tank-versus-tank engagements almost resembled clashes in the North African desert more than they did other battles in Russia.

The Germans used simple command and control measures to conduct this fluid combat. According to General Balck's postwar accounts, command within the 11th Panzer Division was exercised almost entirely by daily verbal orders, amended as necessary on the spot by the division commander at critical points in the fighting.[102] Liaison between the panzer units and the forward infantry divisions also was managed largely on a face-to-face basis.[103] These casual arrangements were made possible in part by the rather simple coordination procedures that developed during the Chir fighting. The positions of the forward German infantry were well known and, due to Hitler's insistence, seldom changed. The broad sectors and relatively low force densities on both sides tended to leave units conveniently spaced. Balck's well-trained and experienced forces seldom operated in more than two or three maneuver elements. General Balck was thus able to truncate normal staff procedures largely because there were very few moving parts in the German machine, and even those were comfortably separated. However, the rude German control methods sacrificed many of the benefits of synchronization and close coordination. By General Balck's own admission, for example, little effort was made to integrate indirect fire with the German maneuver forces.[104]

The German defensive efforts benefited from other favorable circumstances. The Soviet attacks on the Chir front were not conducted in overwhelming strength and were intended primarily as diversions to pin down German forces and to prevent reinforcement of the Stalingrad relief expedition. Also, the Russian assaults were piecemealed in time and space. Instead of a single, powerful attack in one sector, the Red Army forces jabbed at the Chir line for nearly two weeks with several smaller blows. As a result, the Germans were able to make the most of their limited armored reserves.[105] Equally beneficial was the poor Soviet combined arms coordination in these battles. The Russian attacks were conducted mainly by tank forces, and the Soviet infantry played only a minor accompanying role. Therefore, the Germans concentrated their panzers solely on the destruction of the enemy armor and paid scarcely any attention to the enemy riflemen.[106] This also greatly magnified German combat power, placing a premium on the superior tactical skill of the German tank crews while allowing the weaker German infantry to remain huddled in dugouts. Furthermore, the Red Army artillery remained amazingly silent throughout the battles, which left the Russian tank forces to fight without the benefit of suppressive fires. Soviet air power likewise was ineffective.[107]

The German defensive successes on the Chir River were victories of a limited sort. First, despite their tactical virtuosity, even the German panzers were unable to wrest the operational initiative from the Soviets. Throughout the December actions, the Germans were compelled to respond to the uncoordinated Red Army blows by fighting a series of attritional engagements. The Russians retained complete freedom of maneuver and, in all likelihood, could have crushed the German resistance if they had been more skillful in massing or in coordinating their efforts. Second, even though the Germans inflicted serious losses on their enemies, they also suffered substantial casualties of their own. The hapless 7th *Luftwaffe* Field Division disintegrated during the Chir battles, and by mid-January, its ragged remnants had been amalgamated into other formations. The 11th Panzer Division, whose bold exploits saved the Chir position on several occasions, saw its combat power diminished by half from the beginning of December. Third, though driving back Soviet attacks, neither the 11th Panzer Division nor the balance of the XLVIII Panzer Corps was able to hold the ground that it won by counterattack. To defend terrain required infantry, and neither the panzer formations nor the overextended German infantry divisions had sufficient riflemen to conduct a positional defense.[108] Conversely, German tanks performed best in fluid combat and were notably less successful when trying to drive Red Army troops from their consolidated positions. For example, the Soviets managed to hold a few well-entrenched bridgeheads on the western bank of the Don-Chir line despite repeated German armored attacks.[109]

Although rebuffed by the skill and steadfastness of the German defenders, the Soviet attacks against the Chir River line succeeded in preventing reinforcement of Manstein's relief attack on Stalingrad. Under Manstein's concept, the XLVIII Panzer Corps was to have joined those elements of Fourth Panzer Army (LVII Panzer Corps) making the main relief attempt from farther south. However, as already seen, the XLVIII Panzer Corps had struggled just to stave off its own destruction and never entered into the offensive effort. Without that support and without even the full reinforcements that Hitler had originally promised, the German drive to open a corridor to Sixth Army had to be abandoned after 23 December. From that time on, the defensive battles in the south entered a new phase, with German defensive efforts shifting to the containment of a new major Soviet offensive attempt to sever the entire Axis southern wing (see map 13).

The new Russian offensive began by scattering the Italian Eighth Army, which was still in position on the northern Don. Driving southward toward Rostov, the Soviets aimed at cutting the communications of both Army Group Don and Army Group A. Also, this attack directly enveloped the German defensive line on the Chir, making the German position there untenable. This not only spoiled all prospects for a renewed attack to free Sixth Army, but it also resulted in the eventual loss of the forward airfields supplying Paulus' encircled divisions.[110]

In contrast to the earlier jabs against the Chir line, the new Russian advance swept forward on a broad front, brushing aside the counterattacks of the weak 27th Panzer Division (earlier posted behind the Italians as a stiffener) as if they were bee stings. Clearly, the sleight-of-hand defensive tactics used by the Germans so successfully on the Chir River were not sufficient to cope with this new threat.

Two major problems hampered German attempts to forge an effective defensive response to the ripening crisis. The first problem was the lack of fresh combat forces. The best units in the German Army, groomed in the spring of 1942 to carry out Operation Blau, were now either wintering uselessly in the Caucasus (Army Group A) or else withering away at Stalingrad or in vain attempts to relieve it (Sixth Army and Fourth Panzer Army). The various impromptu commands set up to defend the Chir and lower Don were barely adequate for that task alone and stood little chance in a set-piece battle against the massive new Soviet onslaught.

In addition, reinforcements could be shifted from other parts of the front only with difficulty. The drained units of Army Groups Center and North had been stripped of assets months earlier to provide resources for the Blau offensive and were hard-pressed to resist the Soviet attacks drumming against their own positions. Therefore, local commanders from the northern defensive front, who saw only their own pressing problems, opposed attempts to siphon reserves away from them. Only at the highest command levels could the assembly and transfer of reserves be accomplished fairly and effectively. In

Soviet infantrymen charge past a disabled German tank northwest of Stalingrad, December 1942

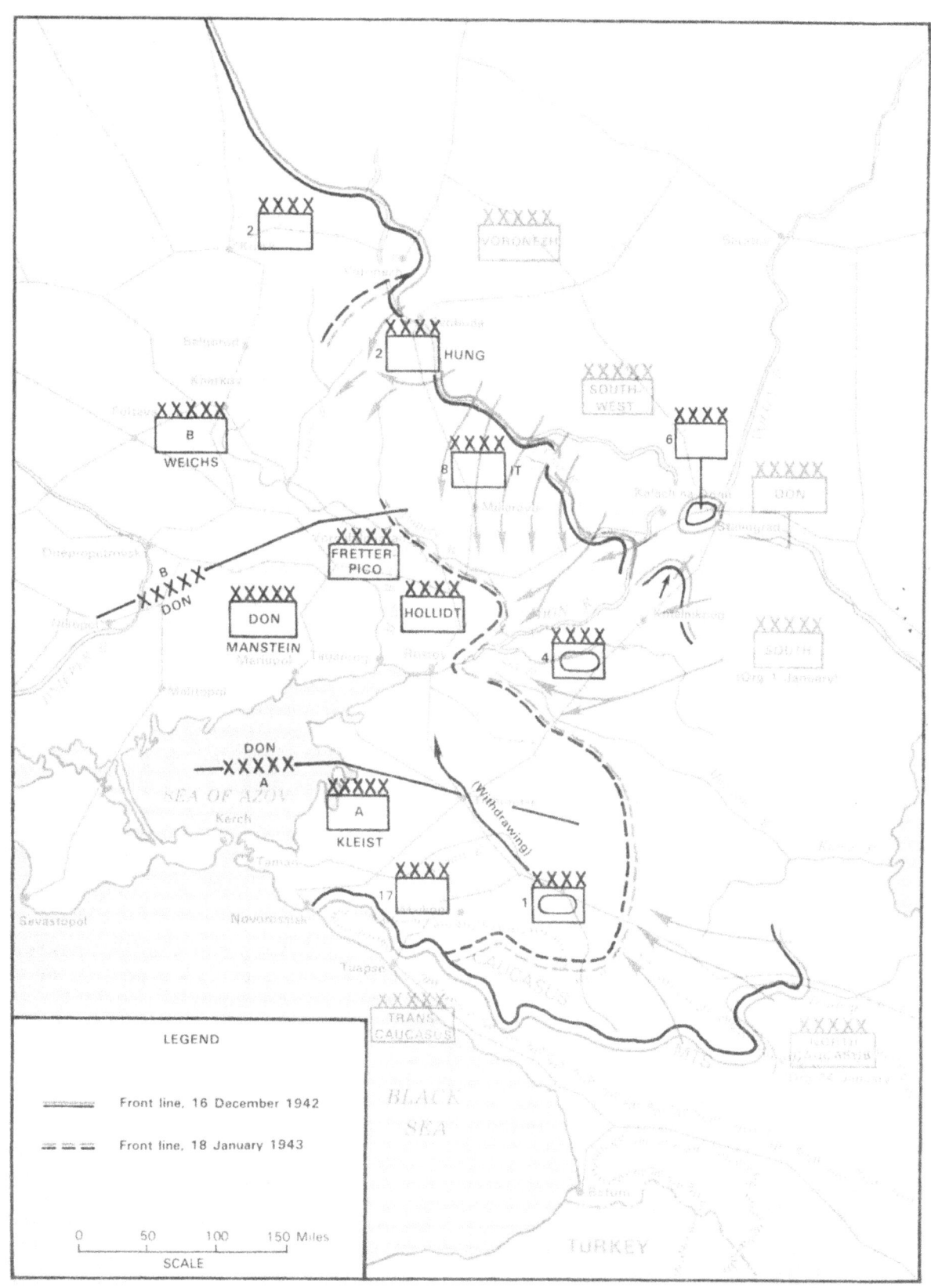

Map 13. Widening Soviet offensive and threat to German southern wing, 16 December 1942—18 January 1943

this case, however, the smooth redistribution of forces by Hitler and the Army High Command was handicapped by complex variations in the status and structure of German units.

By this point in the war, most German divisions had major discrepancies between their paper organization and their actual structure. This was due partly to unredeemed combat losses, partly to the German Army's de facto policy of propagating organizational peculiarities by constantly changing the divisional structure of newly forming units, and partly to the stripping of resources from some divisions for assignment elsewhere. Some frontline units, for example, had little or no motorized transport, substituting instead horse-drawn wagons or even bicycles for logistical and tactical mobility. Others were short their full complement of artillery or else had entire battalions fitted out exclusively with captured guns. Other divisions lacked reconnaissance units or even full infantry regiments that had been detached for anti-partisan duties.

In addition to organizational oddities, German divisions also differed greatly in combat readiness due to fluctuations in their morale, training, replacement status, combat experience, fatigue, and quality of junior leadership. These eccentricities made centralized management of German forces extremely difficult, since nearly every division deviated in some way from its normal status. Since Hitler and the Army General Staff were not always aware of these organizational peculiarities, some confusion ensued when corps and army commanders, ordered to release divisions for emergency use elsewhere on the front, sometimes forwarded units that were unsuited for the particular missions for which they had been requested. In December 1942, the Army High Command initiated a new reporting system to correct this situation, requiring corps and army commanders to submit secret subjective evaluations of their divisions' combat worthiness on a regular basis.[111] (Frontline commanders found it to be in their own interest to be as candid as possible in these assessments, since a frank statement of liabilities was considered to be some protection from having to feed additional forces into the "Stalingrad oven.") Such inventories made the paper management of the threadbare German resources more efficient, but the fundamental lack of adequate combat forces to cover the expanding Eastern Front crisis remained unresolved.

The second problem shackling German operations was the Germans' own Byzantine command arrangement. Afield in the southern portion of the Eastern Front were three autonomous army groups (Army Groups A, B, and Don). No single commander or headquarters coordinated the efforts of these army groups save for the Führer himself. From his East Prussian headquarters, Hitler continued to render his own dubious brand of command guidance. Inspired by the success of his stand-fast methods the previous winter, the Führer now balked at ordering the timely withdrawal and reassembly of the far-flung German armies, even truculently resisting the transfer of divisions from the lightly engaged Army Group A to the mortally beset Army Group Don. Hitler's opening response to the new Soviet offensive against the rear of the German southern wing was to decree a succession of meaningless halt lines, ordering the overmatched German forces to hold position after position "to the last man."[112]

Field Marshal von Manstein, whose Army Group Don was to halt the Soviet offensive, confronted both of these major problems head-on. In a series of teletype messages to Hitler, Manstein pleaded for the release of several divisions from the idle Army Group A in the Caucasus in order to put some starch into the German defense. Though relenting too late to assist the relief attack on Stalingrad, Hitler at last ordered a few divisions and then finally all of First Panzer Army to move from Army Group A to Manstein's control.[113]

Manstein also pressed Hitler about command authority. In late December, Hitler offered to place Army Group A under Manstein's operational control. However, this consolidation of authority was not consummated because, as Manstein later explained, Hitler "was unwilling to accept my conditions" that there be no "possibility of interference by Hitler or of Army Group A's invoking ... decisions in opposition to my own."[114] Less than two weeks later, furious that Hitler was still insisting on a no-retreat policy and forcing him to beg permission for each tactical withdrawal, Manstein presented the Führer with an ultimatum. On 5 January, Manstein sent a message to the chief of the Army General Staff for Hitler's consideration: "Should ... this headquarters continue to be tied down to the same extent as hitherto, I cannot see that any useful purpose will be served by my continuing as commander of Don Army Group. In the circumstances, it would appear more appropriate to replace me...."[115] Hitler chose to ignore Manstein's ultimatum, but he did at last concede a singular (though temporary) degree of autonomy and flexibility to Manstein for the conduct of defensive operations. Although Hitler's draconian stand-fast policy remained officially in effect, Manstein was allowed freedom of maneuver by means of a face-saving charade: instead of asking permission, Manstein would simply inform the Army High Command of Army Group Don's intention to take certain actions unless specifically countermanded, and Hitler by his silence would consent without actually abandoning his hold-to-the-last-man scruples.[116]

As a result of this arrangement, Manstein conducted operations from early January until mid-February largely unfettered either by Hitler's customary interference or the rigid no-retreat dictum. No other German commander was allowed to enjoy these two privileges on such a large scale for the remainder of the war. As a consequence of this independence, German defensive operations during the second phase of the southern winter battles evinced a measure of flexibility, economy, and fluid maneuver unsurpassed on the Russian Front during the entire war.

While these command arrangements were being ironed out, the operational situation continued to deteriorate. Still more Soviet attacks had routed the Hungarians and the Italians, completing the disintegration of the entire original flank defensive line along the Don River east of Voronezh. By late January, hardly any organized Axis resistance remained between the surviving units of Army Group B (Second Army) at Voronezh and the hard-pressed forces for Army Group Don along the lower Don and Donets Rivers. The German Sixth Army, now in its death throes at Stalingrad, ironically provided one source of hope: the longer Paulus' troops could hold out, the longer they would continue to tie down the powerful Russian armies encircling them, thereby delaying the reinforcement of the widening Soviet attacks farther to the west.

Manstein's overall concept of operations was to combine the withdrawal of First Panzer Army units from the Caucasus with the establishment of a defensive screen facing northward against the onrushing Soviets. One by one, the First Panzer Army divisions were pulled through the Rostov bottleneck and redeployed to the northwest, extending the makeshift German defensive line ever westward. The Soviets could still outflank this line by extending the arc of their advance to the west and, in fact, did so even while maintaining frontal pressure along the Donets (see map 14). Each of these wider envelopments, however, delayed the final decision and allowed Manstein to leapfrog more units into position. Moreover, the farther the Soviets shifted their forces to the west, the more tenuous the Russian supply lines became.[117]

This operation was exceedingly delicate. Any major Soviet breakthrough or uncontested envelopment could cut through to the rail ganglia on which both Army Groups A and Don depended for their supplies. Army Group Don thus had to accomplish three tasks simultaneously: slow the Soviet frontal advance, shift units from east to west to parry Soviet envelopments, and preserve its forces by allowing timely withdrawals to prevent encirclement or annihilation.

These tasks had to be performed under several tactical handicaps. First, even with the gradual reinforcement by First Panzer Army, Manstein's forces remained generally inferior to those of the enemy. Discounting the late arrivals, most of the divisions of Army Group Don were extremely battle worn, having been in continuous combat for over two months. Too, the preponderance of the German forces were less mobile than the Soviet tank and mechanized forces opposing them, a factor that weighed heavily against Manstein's hopes of exploiting the Germans' superiority in fluid operations.

Second, many of Manstein's forces were grouped together under impromptu command arrangements. The German order of battle included several nonstandard control headquarters identified simply by their commanders' names, such as Army Detachment Hollidt, Group Mieth, and Battle Group Adam. Even many of the divisions assigned to the various headquarters lacked normal internal cohesion. For example, by January 1942, the 17th Panzer Division was conducting defensive operations with an attached infantry regiment (156th Infantry Regiment), which possessed neither the training nor the vehicles to allow it to cooperate smoothly with the division's tanks and organic *Panzergrenadiers*.[118] Similarly, in mid-January, two infantry divisions within Army Detachment Hollidt contained substantial attachments from two shattered *Luftwaffe* field divisions, while one so-called division (403d Security Division) was actually a division headquarters controlling several thousand troops whose furloughs had been abruptly canceled.[119] These ad hoc forces generally lacked the precision that comes from habitual association and common experience, and this internal friction was magnified by the rapidly changing combat conditions confronting Army Group Don. Moreover, none of the improvised groupings were structured for sustained combat; therefore, they lacked the technical and support assets that normally would have serviced such large units.[120]

Third, though relatively fresh and well organized, the First Panzer Army divisions arriving from the Caucasus came with their own special problems. In Manstein's words, these forces suffered from the "hardening up process

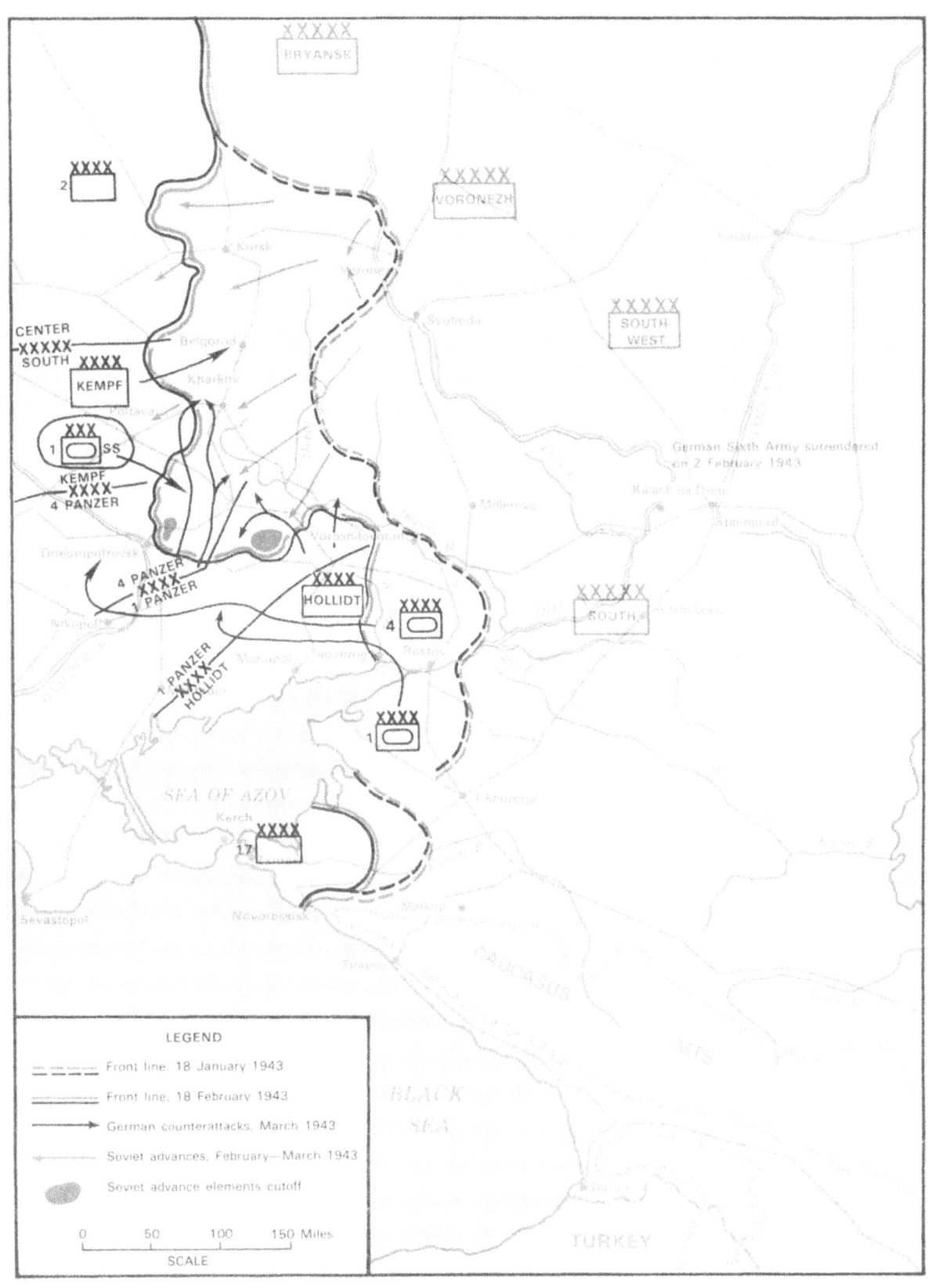

Map 14. Manstein withdraws First and Fourth Panzer Armies from southern wing and counterattacks to recapture Kharkov, January—March 1943

A German flak unit of the First Panzer Army in the Caucasus, October 1942. Manstein hurriedly withdrew these divisions and threw them into the battles to save Rostov, January—March 1943.

which inevitably sets in whenever mobile operations degenerate into static warfare." Their relatively inactive sojourn in the Caucasus from September to January had caused these "troops and formation staffs [to] lose the knack of quickly adapting themselves to the changes of situation which daily occur in a war of movement." The first symptom of this stagnation was the snail-like pace of the Caucasian disengagement. Having accumulated "weapons, equipment and stores of all kinds ... which one feels unable to do without for the rest of the war," the divisions of First Panzer Army invariably requested "a long period of grace in which to prepare for the evacuation." When finally committed to combat along the Donets, these forces maneuvered lethargically at first, their earlier snap and élan dulled by the routine of prolonged positional warfare.[121]

Finally, the Germans were plagued by the enormous mobility differential between their own infantry and panzer forces. In previous campaigns, this problem had been most evident in offensive operations, as during Barbarossa when the swift panzers had outrun their infantry support. In southern Russia in January and February of 1943, this disparity proved equally disruptive in defensive operations, vastly increasing the difficulty of orchestrating German maneuver.

Since the bulk of the German combat power consisted of infantry, of necessity the German defensive tactics were built on the less-mobile infantry forces. The infantrymen, their numbers frequently including engineers, flak units, and various alarm units, were disposed in forward defensive lines.[122] Because of the lack of heavy antitank weapons and in order to gain some protection from Russian tanks, infantry positions were preferably sited along the rivers, streams, or ravines cutting through the area. Occasionally, the defenses were laid out in continuous, entrenched lines; more often, however, infantry units deployed in strongpoints to protect their flanks and rear from armored attacks. For example, the 17th Panzer Division, a veteran of heavy fighting on the Don, Chir, and Aksai Rivers, deployed its organic infantry battalions in individual battle groups. These groups, however, were so widely separated that the divisional artillery batteries could not support them all from central locations, necessitating the temporary attachment of even heavy guns to the battle group commanders.[123] Describing the fighting along the Donets River in January (in which the 17th Panzer Division played a prominent part), Field Marshal von Manstein observed that the enemy was halted "first and foremost [by] the bravery with which the infantry divisions and all other formations and units [e.g., alarm units] helping to hold the line stood their ground against the enemy's recurrent attacks."[124]

German armored forces complemented the infantry's forward defense. The mobility of these formations allowed commanders to shuttle them about the battlefield, throwing their weight into developing crises. The scarcity of these forces prevented their employment in a general mobile defense, however. To shore up threatened sectors, counterattack remained the most common mission for the armor. Additionally, the German tanks and mechanized infantry made ideal rear guards, allowing other less-mobile units to disengage or to regroup when necessary.[125] Rear-guard mobility proved so crucial during the fluid battles in January and February that some regular infantry divisions even concocted their own motorized contingents by commandeering all available motor vehicles for use as troop carriers. As an example, Army Detachment Hollidt's 294th Infantry Division built such a mobile unit around several self-propelled 20-mm and 88-mm flak guns and used this composite group almost exclusively as a forward covering force or rear guard during that division's defensive battles.[126]

The panzer formations also delivered spoiling attacks on enemy assembly areas, buying time until other German forces could redeploy or dig in. In early January, for example, the 17th Panzer Division succeeded spectacularly with such an attack. Supported by one infantry regiment, General von Senger rammed his one weak tank battalion into a Soviet assault concentration, destroying twenty-one enemy tanks and twenty-five antitank guns against the loss of only three panzers before withdrawing. In undertaking such a thrust, the division commander

> resisted any temptation to distribute his tanks for the protection of his infantry, or even to husband them as a counterattacking force against Russian penetrations. In risking them in a far-flung [offensive] operation ... he not only made them unavailable for the defense of the division's threatened southern sector but also accepted the danger of their being cut off entirely.... But his danger was rewarded. By seizing the initiative, he was able to inflict heavy losses on the Russians at small cost, disrupt the Soviets' offensive preparations, and gain valuable time for his division and the entire army front.[127]

Such calculated boldness in using mobile forces was possible due to superior German training and leadership. As one German officer recalled: "The German superiority at this time lay not primarily in their equipment but in their standards of training. The training of tank crews never ceased, even in combat. In the 17th Panzer Division it was the practice to hold a critique after each engagement, in which successes and failures were discussed, just as after peacetime exercises."[128] Equally important was the aggressiveness, imagination, and flexibility of the German leaders. Commenting on the operations of its improvised mobile rear guard, the 294th Division's after-action report explained that "the choice of a leader [was] especially important" since such units "[were] not led according to field manuals or even according to any fixed scheme."[129]

Despite its aggressiveness and skillful use of mobile forces, Manstein's defense of the German southern wing was not a mobile defense in the classic sense. Army Group Don's forces could not be insensitive to the loss of territory, since to have done so would have endangered the vital rail lines leading through Rostov. Furthermore, the bulk of Manstein's formations were relatively immobile and could only be used in a succession of static defenses. Although playing an important role, the German panzer and motorized forces operated principally as intervention forces in support of the pedestrian infantry.[130]

The German defensive method was thus actually a potpourri of tactical techniques. What set these battles apart from others was Manstein's style of control. What Manstein did—and what Hitler, as a rule, did not—was to provide firm operational guidance to his subordinates and then to allow those commanders to use their forces and the terrain to maximum advantage. The hard-pressed infantry forces, often composed of hastily assembled patchwork units without any real unit training, were best employed in static defenses from prepared positions. Mobile panzer and motorized bands delivered sharp

A German soldier inspects a destroyed Soviet T-34 tank, February 1943. The tank's turret rests on the ground at right.

counterattacks to help sustain the infantry defenses and, occasionally, kept the enemy off-balance with preemptive spoiling attacks. If the infantry's main positions became engulfed, the panzers and mechanized infantry helped the slower forces to disengage. The mobile formations also fought delaying actions while subsequent main positions were being organized. Major defensive lines were designated well in advance, allowing units to make deliberate plans for their withdrawals. (This practice alone added considerable coherence to German operations. Hitler usually procrastinated about allowing retreats until, when finally ordered, the withdrawals had to be done pell-mell to avoid encirclement.) For example, in fighting its way back from the Chir to the Donets in January, a distance of roughly 100 miles, Army Detachment Hollidt occupied no less than nine intermediate defensive lines. Its movement from the Donets to the Mius in February followed the same pattern.[131]

In contrast to preferred German defensive methods, these battles were fought almost entirely without tactical depth. Indeed, the fluidity of the battles in southern Russia stemmed, in large measure, from the German inability to absorb the Soviet attacks within successive defensive zones. Lacking the forces to establish a deeply echeloned defense, the Germans instead combined maneuver—including both lightning attack and withdrawal—with stubborn positional defense to give artificial depth to the battlefield. In this way, the Germans were able to brake major Soviet attacks, preventing catastrophic breakthroughs while still preserving the integrity and freedom of action of their own forces.

As with the XLVIII Panzer Corps' December battles on the Chir River, these tactics—like the traditional Elastic Defense—were essentially attritional. Russian attacks were contained or worn down one by one, and even though German units occasionally seized the tactical initiative by some aggressive riposte, the operational initiative remained with the Soviets. However often single German panzer divisions sallied in preemptive spoiling attacks, the Red Army's major maneuver units were never in danger of sudden annihilation.

This situation existed because the scarcity of German forces and the great distances in southern Russia kept German units dispersed. In blocking the Soviets' relentless broad-front advance, the Germans operated completely from hand to mouth and were therefore unable to engineer any operational massing of their own. Significantly, from the time of the cancellation in late December of the three-division Stalingrad relief attack until the conclusion of the winter battles' second phase in late February, all the German panzer divisions on the southern front were employed piecemeal to relieve local emergencies. No two panzer divisions ever combined their meager assets to make a concerted blow. For instance, Army Detachment Hollidt, which in mid-January fielded four panzer divisions, retained only one division under its own control and assigned the other three to its individual subordinate commands for "fire brigade" use in support of their infantry divisions. While effective in stemming local Russian attacks, this task organization made it impossible to concentrate powerful mobile forces for larger-scale operations.[132]

Manstein appreciated this fact and, from mid-February, began laying the groundwork for a different employment of the German armor. The fresh *SS Panzer Corps*, just off-loading near Kharkov with two crack *Waffen SS* panzer divisions, together with other reinforcements formed the nucleus of an operational *masse de manoeuvre*. Convinced that casualties, mechanical breakdowns, and lengthening supply lines must have taken their toll of the Russians, Manstein foresaw an opportunity to seize the operational initiative with a counteroffensive of his own. Manstein's target was the Soviet armored spearheads, then still careening southwestward between Kharkov and Stalino.[133]

The third phase of the winter campaign saw the restabilization of the southern front. The centerpiece of this phase was a strong German counterstroke by five panzer divisions against the Soviet flank south of Kharkov. Manstein's 22 February riposte completely surprised the Russians and, within days, had shattered the Soviet First Guards Army as well as several independent armored groups. As trophies, the Germans counted 615 destroyed enemy tanks and over 1,000 captured guns. The haul in prisoners, however, was disappointingly low: as always, the infantry-poor German panzer formations were unable to seal off the battlefield, and thousands of Soviet troops casually marched out of the German trap.[134]

Despite its success, Hitler took little satisfaction in Manstein's Kharkov counteroffensive. As Hitler had admitted in his Führer Defense Order of September 1942, his defensive ideas were of a pre-1917 vintage. Consequently, Hitler's own preference, first and last, was for a rigid no-retreat defense. He had been uncomfortable enough with Manstein's parry-and-thrust tactics in January and early February, but for all of its tactical dash, that style of defense had still been operationally conservative and had remained focused

German motorized infantry on the outskirts of Kharkov, 14 March 1943

German *SS* troops inside Kharkov

on denying the Russians access to certain critical areas. What rankled Hitler most was the purposeful relinquishing of terrain on an operational scale. When Manstein continued to give up ground—even after the Soviet drive showed signs of stalling on its own—while building up his reserve striking force, Hitler's nervousness increased. In the end, Manstein barely saved his counteroffensive plan from Hitler's shrill demands that the new reserves be thrown into battle piecemeal to prevent further territorial losses. And yet this very strategem finally provided the basis for Manstein's counteroffensive, as the Russian advance eventually overextended itself and lay vulnerable to the hoarded German reserves. Hitler prized the holding of ground even over the annihilation of sizable enemy forces, however spectacular.

Bought breathing space by Manstein's successful counteroffensive near Kharkov, the other tattered German forces managed to patch together a continuous defensive line on the southern front. Army Detachment Hollidt, withdrawing by bounds from the Donets, moved into Army Group South's old defensive lines on the Mius River. Except for a series of salients north of Kharkov, the German southern armies in late March held again nearly the same positions from which the Blau offensive had begun the previous spring.

This line could easily have been forced at almost any point prior to the spring thaw at the end of March 1943. For example, the XXIV Panzer

Corps—which, in fact, had no panzer units whatsoever—held the extreme southern portion of the German line with one infantry and two patchwork security divisions. These forces, whose sector ran for nearly 125 kilometers (including a stretch of Azov coastline), amounted to only fourteen understrength infantry battalions. A XXIV Panzer Corps after-action report noted that the two security divisions' organization, cohesion, and weaponry were so uneven that little could be expected from them. Fortunately, these units occupied old defensive works along most of their front and also were able to retrain and rehabilitate their forces due to the lack of renewed offensive action by the tired Soviets.[135]

The German Kharkov counteroffensive and the tenuous restabilization of the southern front ended the winter campaign's third phase. As the crisis subsided, Manstein's independence from Hitler's close control also evaporated. Hitler's patience with Manstein had actually begun to wane in early February. Then, alarmed by the enormous swatches of territory being surrendered by Manstein's forces, Hitler reasserted his personal authority over Army Group Don on 12 February 1943 with Operations Order 4, which ordered Manstein to reestablish a solid, stand-fast front on the Mius-Donets line. In fact, only Manstein's promise to Hitler to recover much of the lost ground with the Kharkov counterstroke, together with the awkwardness of switching field commanders in the midst of such a confusing battle, probably saved Manstein from being relieved.[136]

With the dissipation of Manstein's autonomy came a reassertion of all Hitler's defensive nostrums, and the fragile German defenses taking shape along the southern front reflected this. Once again, the standard defensive guidance became "no retreat; hold to the last man!" (see map 15).

General Walther Nehring, supervising the improvement of his XXIV Panzer Corps positions, displayed the uncomfortable blend of traditional defense and Hitlerian caveat that had become doctrinal practice. In an 18 March 1943 defensive order to his units, Nehring directed the improvement of positions in depth, the careful coordination of artillery fire support, and the siting of clusters of antitank weapons behind the main positions in perfect accord with the Elastic Defense system in *Truppenführung*. However, Nehring's instructions also ordered compliance with Hitler's benumbing provisos: "Penetrating enemy elements are *instantly* to be thrown back by immediate counterattack and the HKL [main line of resistance] regained. Evasive maneuver before the enemy or evacuation of a position without my [Nehring's] special order is forbidden."[137]

German defensive practice therefore had gained little from the lessons of the previous year. Despite the strained battles on the northern defensive front, the disaster at Stalingrad, the desperate fights between the Volga and the Mius Rivers, and finally Manstein's brilliant operational riposte at Kharkov, the German armies on the Eastern Front looked forward to future defensive fighting still handicapped by Hitler's rigid constraints. Even so, German Army units continued to review their own tactical methods and to suggest modifications to defensive doctrine within the limits established by the Führer's guidance.

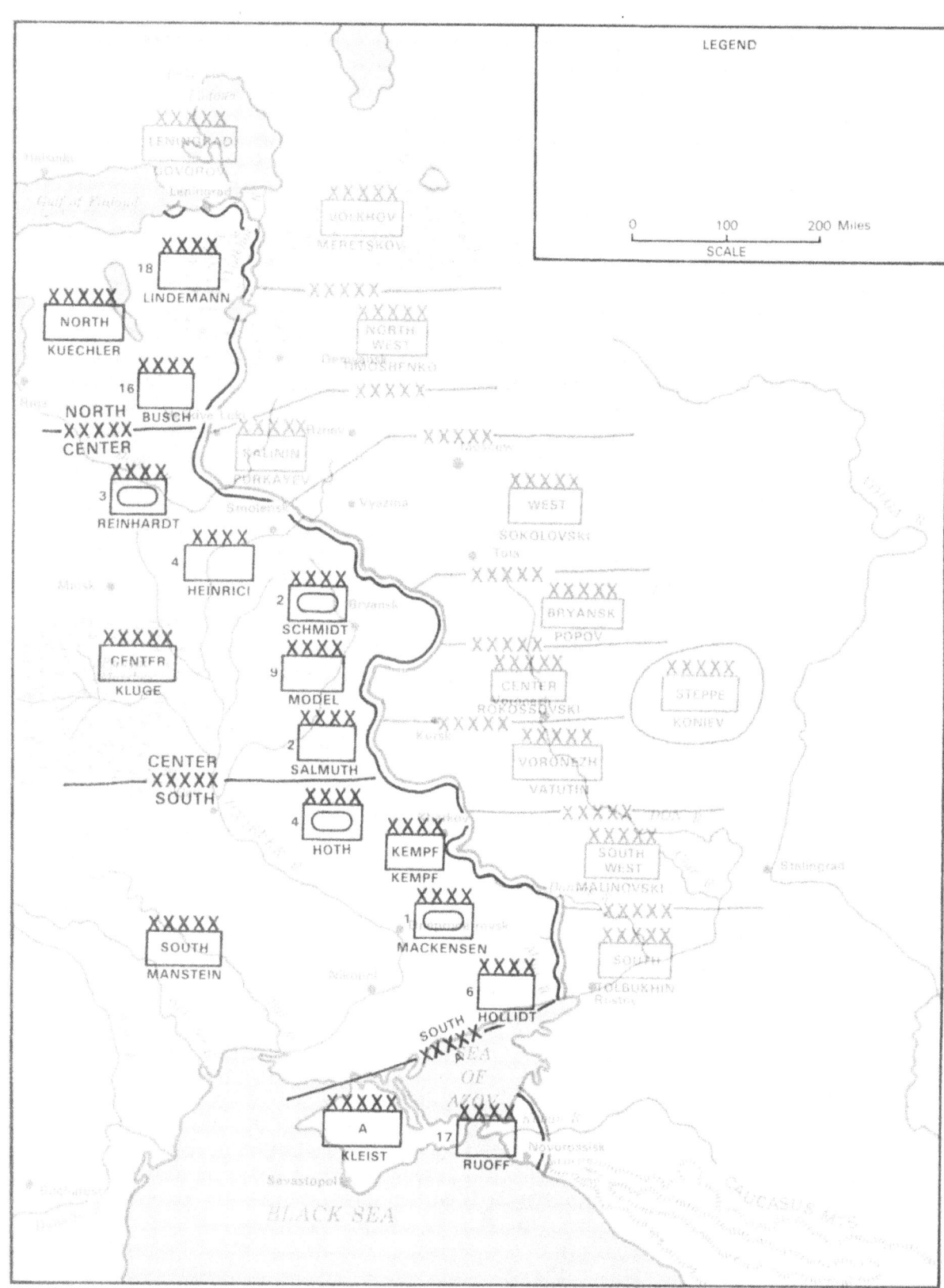

Map 15. Situation, spring 1943

German Doctrinal Assessments

In late 1942, various German units along the Russian Front prepared routine after-action reports summarizing their experiences. These reports dealt primarily with activities along the defensive fronts of Army Groups Center and North. The confusion and turmoil in the south prevented a careful assessment of those battles until the spring of 1943.

Army Group North prepared the most detailed critique of German defensive methods. On 20 September 1942, Army Group North tasked its subordinate units to prepare reports on "Experiences From Fighting on a Fixed Front" and listed sixteen major discussion topics. These items included the accuracy of German Army doctrinal manuals, methods for organizing defensive positions, location and use of major weapons, intelligence indicators of impending enemy attacks, and general training suggestions.[138]

By and large, units endorsed the basic applicability of existing doctrinal publications. "Our manuals," wrote the 21st Infantry Division's operations officer, "have generally proven themselves with respect to the selection and construction of positions."[139] However, several units complained that the German field manuals did not address the peculiar problems inherent in defending excessively wide sectors with inadequate forces. These reports noted that doctrinal guidance was deficient in explaining how standard Elastic Defense methods should be adapted to these all-too-common circumstances. The Eighteenth Army, for example, took the most extreme line in its report to Army Group North: "The principles of our field manuals... have only limited validity in the East because in practice they are seldom possible."[140]

In the same vein, several units were cautiously critical of Hitler's obsessive insistence on holding even the forwardmost trenchlines. According to one divisional report, this practice robbed the German defenses of essential depth. With so many troops and heavy weapons committed within the forward main line of resistance, only the slenderest of local reserves remained to occupy positions in depth. When enemy break-ins occurred, this immediately thrust much of the responsibility for resistance in depth on the few troops manning German command posts, artillery positions, and rear services strongpoints. Consequently, as the complaints revealed, the entire German defensive concept seemed to have degenerated to the costly retention of the main line of resistance at the expense of a legitimate defense in depth.[141]

Another criticism of German doctrinal manuals cited the lack of advice on how to defend under special conditions, such as in swamps and forests, or during periods of limited visibility. The 22d Fusilier Regiment insisted that battles fought under these circumstances required special techniques beyond those given in the German Army's training manuals. The 58th Infantry Division confirmed this, citing as an example the erroneous tendency of some leaders to deploy defensive forces along the edge of wooded areas. Once the Soviets discovered this habit, it was simple for Red Army artillery to paste the occupied woodlines since they made such well-defined targets. Experienced German commanders placed their troops in camouflaged positions forward of the woods or else had them dig in at some irregular distance 25 to 100 meters inside the treeline. (This latter method was preferred: enemy troops attacking the woods could not place accurate small-arms or indirect fire on the entrenched defenders until the enemy had advanced through the German artillery barrage and entered into the defenders' close-in killing zones. Yet the thin wooded apron forward of the defensive positions was too shallow to shelter any large body of enemy troops.)[142]

Such techniques demonstrated not only the extent to which German tactics were tailored to minimize casualties, but also the continuing desire of German commanders to avoid tactical schemes that placed unnecessary psychological strain on their soldiers. The Russian climate, periodic supply shortages, close combat antitank methods, and lack of rest—not to mention the enemy's apparent numerical superiority and reputed savagery—all imposed heavy demands on German morale and discipline. Therefore, after-action reports were full of suggestions for avoiding the wasteful depletion of German moral energies. For example, since the defense of an entire sector might well depend on the skill and aggressiveness of local reserves, many units emphasized the desirability of selecting the best leaders and most reliable men for reserve roles. Ideally, these local shock troops were kept razor sharp by constant training and alarm drills and were spared excessive fatigue details such as trench construction. Another psychological ploy suggested by General Heinrici, the Fourth Army commander, was the blind firing of German artillery at presumed Red Army attack concentrations just prior to enemy assaults. Such fire, whatever its real effect on the Russians, was of inestimable value in "giving at a minimum a moral boost to our infantry in the moment of danger."[143] Other units emphasized the extreme importance of regular training on such particularly fearsome subjects as hand-to-hand fighting and being overrun by enemy tanks. Most important to defensive morale, reported the 1st Infantry Division, was that "each soldier in the defense must be convinced of the superiority of his own training and his own weapons."[144]

Except for Hitler's command interference and crippling no-retreat strategy, the most contentious doctrinal issue to emerge during 1942 and early 1943 concerned the proper defensive role of German armor. Prewar German manuals had consigned the panzers to a counterattack role commensurate with their "inherently offensive nature." While none would deny that panzers made ideal mobile reserves and counterattack forces, a considerable doctrinal din arose about the apportionment and control of those forces.

On one side stood the panzer officers themselves. Since the 1930s, Guderian and the other high priests of armored warfare had taught their flock a simple, unremitting catechism: panzers should be employed only en masse and should never be split up or parceled out in infantry support roles. The rectitude of this view had been demonstrated most clearly in the 1940 campaign in France. There, the numerically superior French and British armor had been foolishly deployed in "penny packets" and had justly gone down to fiery perdition at the hands of the German armored forces. By late 1942, the need to employ armor en masse had become an absolute article of faith among the armored forces.

As a corollary to this, German armor commanders were reluctant to see their panzers placed under even the temporary command of nonarmor officers for fear that they might commit some sacrilege by splitting up the tanks into support roles. Discussing the proper task organization of reserves for counterattacks, for example, General Heinrich Eberbach of the 4th Panzer Division made his own feelings clear in a memorandum on 30 September 1942: "Do not subordinate a tank battalion to an infantry regiment; rather attach to it [tank battalion] an infantry battalion, an engineer company, an artillery detachment, and a self-propelled antitank company, and give to this battle group a clear mission."[145] General Hermann Hoth, whose Fourth Panzer Army was ripped apart by the Soviet November 1942 counteroffensive, had also argued against assigning small panzer detachments to infantry forces. In a 21 September 1942 memorandum to the Army High Command, Hoth declaimed that "the Panzer Arm achieves its success by *massing* [italics in original]." While conceding that small groups of tanks had played a major role in salvaging the German position during the winter of 1941—42, Hoth stated that "this should not therefore lead to single tanks as a universal solution [for strengthening defensive resistance]...." On the contrary, argued Hoth, examples in the late summer of 1942 showed that real defensive success came from "the determined will-to-attack of infantry and panzer divisions." Against "the fallacious call of the infantry divisions for 'solitary panzers,'" Hoth spluttered that such dispersion of tanks not only would compromise the armored troops as a decisive battlefield force, but also would fatally corrupt the infantry forces' "will to attack" by making them unduly dependent on armored support.[146]

In opposition to this chorus stood those German officers—primarily, but not exclusively, infantrymen—whose troops were actually holding the forward defensive lines. These officers had no argument with the massing of tanks in theory but cited several cogent reasons why German defensive interests could be better served in practice by a greater dispersion of the limited armored resources. In countless battles against Russian attacks, these officers had developed a doctrinal creed of their own, namely, that under the prevailing conditions of weakness and constraint, the best way to defeat a Soviet penetration was by immediate counterattack. While not new, this conviction grew stronger as defensive experience accumulated. On 14 October 1942, General Heinrici wrote that immediate counterattack, led by energetic leaders and striking the enemy's troops while they were still disorganized, could achieve "full success in every case."[147] This sentiment was echoed by many units who regarded speed far more important than numerical strength or firepower in dislodging Russian forces.[148] To implement their counterattacks as quickly as possible, these frontline commanders were therefore willing to sacrifice even mass in order to hit penetrating Soviets before they could consolidate.

What the infantry commanders preferred was that tanks in company or platoon strength be doled out to support their own tactical reserves. With this low-level task organizing, panzers would have to be placed under the command of local infantry commanders. Furthermore, in exceptional cases (as it was for the hard-pressed 336th Infantry Division on the Chir River in December 1942), German infantrymen would also want some tanks placed at their disposal to act as mobile antitank guns in support of their static positions. As expected, German panzer officers vigorously denounced all these ideas.

This dispute was so heated because there was little possibility for compromise. Given the width of the Russian Front and the scarcity of German

General Hermann Hoth, commander of Fourth Panzer Army

panzer forces, it was impossible to provide concentrated armored reserves to all sectors—the only solution that might have satisfied everybody.

If, as the panzer commanders desired, the German armor was kept concentrated in rearward assembly areas, then the tank forces could not arrive at the scene of local crises until hours—or even days—after the Soviet penetrations had occurred. Infantry commanders considered such belated assistance to be of little value. They reckoned that such delays would allow the Russians time either to expand their penetrations, causing the possible collapse or annihilation of the defensive line altogether, or else to have so fortified their newly won ground as to make its recovery extremely costly. Also, the infantrymen were not impressed by the occasional successes of concentrated armor in annihilating Russian breakthrough forces. They knew that these victorious panzer battles—such as those of Balck's 11th Panzer Division on the Chir River—too often came only after the forward German infantry had been all but wiped out. Cynical German infantrymen might have noted that, while the panzer officers toasted their glorious victories, the infantrymen were the ones consigned to burying their excessively numerous dead.

On the other hand, if the German tanks were parceled out by platoons to support every infantry battalion or regiment whose sector was threatened by attack, it would be impossible to reassemble the panzers in time to deal with any massive Soviet breakthrough requiring a massed German response. The 17th Panzer Division's General von Senger, whose experiences on the southern front in the winter of 1942—43 qualified him to speak with authority, wrote pointedly of his own adherence to the defensive "principle that the armor [be]

German self-propelled antitank guns support an infantry attack west of Stalingrad, January 1943

kept together in defense but [be] used offensively at the right moment. Commanders less familiar with armored tactics, and those who were conscious only of the endless front, thinly occupied and under threat from the enemy's armor, would under these conditions have been tempted to fritter away their own armor." Defending the primacy of the armored forces, Senger added: "Thus the armored divisions, originally organized as purely offensive formations, had become [by early 1943] the most effective in defensive operations."[149]

In further rebuttal, panzer officers cited their own recent experiences and indicated that dividing armor in the furtherance of limited-objective counterattacks resulted in disproportionately high tank losses. Therefore, General Eberbach suggested that the infantry be made to repulse "small break-ins" with available forces, saving the massed panzers for those penetrations that exceeded five kilometers in depth. When actually committed, opined Eberbach, the panzer commander should take control of all available assets and should return control of the embattled sector to the infantry commander only when the tanks withdrew. Justifying this judicious use of panzers, Eberbach noted that "the life of a tank crewman is not more valuable than the life of an infantryman." However, he explained, the careful commitment of armor was in the ultimate interest of both the armored and infantry forces since, otherwise, the finite German armored forces would soon be completely extinguished and no longer of any use to anyone.[150]

Both sides in this dispute were completely correct. Every German commander, regardless of branch, wanted to see his own forces used in accordance with their peculiar strengths. No panzer leader wanted to see his precious tanks sacrificed a few at a time in what were, after all, only local emergencies. Nor did any infantry officer wish to see his own men massacred in living up to Hitler's "hold-at-all-costs, recover-all-lost-ground" policies when the assistance of a few tanks could cut his casualties dramatically.

Despite a flurry of bureaucratic activity and memorandum writing, no compromise was reached on this issue. A draft "Instructional Pamphlet on the Use of Panzers in the Defense," which circulated in both the Ninth and Fourth Armies, attempted to resolve some of the outstanding sources of armor-infantry friction. Except for a suggestion that tanks never be employed in less than company strength, however, this pamphlet failed to come to grips with the broader issues.[151]

Certainly no compromise was apparent at the Panzer Training School in Wünsdorf, where a February 1943 "Instructional Pamphlet on Cooperation Between Panzers and Infantry in the Defense" sounded a particularly militant note. This tract, for example, announced the following principles for employing tanks in the defense:

• Tanks should only be employed in counterattacks and never as part of the stationary defense.

• Tanks should be held sufficiently far behind the front so they can respond to enemy penetrations across a wide sector of responsibility.

• Tanks should always be employed en masse: the commitment of individual tanks alone is forbidden.

• The smallest unit for immediate counterattacks with infantry support is the tank battalion (minimum of forty panzers).[152]

A similar pamphlet for higher-ranking leaders added that panzers should remain under the control of either division or independent task force commanders, suggesting archly that tank "attachment to subordinate [infantry] leaders can only be allowed for limited periods and for limited missions."[153] As both of these pamphlets originated at the Wünsdorf tank school, their distribution was limited primarily to panzer officers. To a great extent, therefore, these tracts merely told German armor officers what they wanted to hear. Neither publication received general dissemination throughout the German Army, and neither had any real doctrinal impact.

This confused doctrinal chorus reflected the German Army's situation on the Eastern Front. By late spring of 1943, German defensive doctrine on the Russian Front had become a patchwork of makeshift compromises. The Elastic Defense remained the basic doctrinal framework, which had been established in prewar manuals. However, this doctrine was being increasingly distorted by several factors. The Germans lacked adequate forces to man their extended fronts with a deeply echeloned defensive network, and German divisions had been forced to use a variety of tactical half measures. Adolf Hitler had further muddled German doctrine by issuing confusing directives. Though at times the Führer had benignly endorsed the general theory of elastic defense in depth, in practice he had thundered angrily against weak-willed commanders who allowed the enemy to penetrate beyond the foremost trenchline.

The upshot of these problems had been to focus German defensive efforts on the holding of a rigid linear defense. In short, the elastic defense in depth as practiced by the Germans in early 1943 had, due to Hitler's orders, lost most of its elasticity and, due to the lack of German manpower, had abandoned most of its depth as well. Still, German units did their best to adapt themselves to these straitened circumstances. They could not do so, however, without occasional strain and squabble as the arguments over the defensive use of German armor illustrated.

Chapter 5

Observations and Conclusions

In late March 1943, spring rains and mud halted operations on the Russian Front. This seasonal intermission marked a major turning point in the Russo-German War. Although unknown at the time, the German Kharkov counteroffensive was, as Manstein later remarked, "the last German victory in the East."[1]

During the first two years of the war, the Germans had regarded defensive combat as an unpleasant corollary to their own offensive designs; however, from mid-1943 onward, the war became for the Germans a massive defensive encounter requiring entirely different strategies. Instead of pursuing victory, the Germans thereafter tried to ward off defeat. Concurrently, the development of German defensive doctrine became more deliberate as German commanders hoped to maximize their dwindling combat resources by constantly honing their doctrinal edge.

The German eastern armies began the Barbarossa campaign in June 1941 with a common textbook doctrine for defensive operations. The defensive methods that carried the Germans through the defensive battles from 1941 to early 1943 included a great deal of improvisation, as German units adapted their tactical procedures to novel Russian combat conditions. These procedures varied according to circumstance and were influenced by unforeseen problems arising from insufficient German combat strength, harsh weather, difficult terrain, Russian tactics, and Hitler's command interference.

The following remarks do not attempt to recapitulate all of the major points previously developed about the evolution of German defensive doctrine. Rather, they are some general reflections about doctrinal change in the German Army and the external factors that influenced those changes.

In practice, German defensive operations never corresponded exactly to prewar doctrine. In no single campaign or engagement did German battlefield performance on the Eastern Front between 1941 and 1943 adhere to the visions of *Truppenführung* and other prewar manuals. This is because peacetime preparations can never anticipate the exact circumstances of combat. Thus, in war, the tactical methods learned during peacetime maneuvers simply do not survive intact, and individual soldiers and whole units must quickly learn to adapt themselves to battlefield conditions. In accordance with this necessity, the German Army, like any army stepping from peacetime into wartime, was forced to alter its visions to reflect actual battlefield circumstances.

At the outset of the Russo-German War, German defensive doctrine was based on the system of elastic defense in depth adopted by the Imperial German Army in the latter part of World War I. Later in World War II, when German divisions discovered that some of their doctrinal theories did not work well under Russian battlefield conditions, widespread doctrinal improvisations followed. During the war's early years, the German Army adhered to the doctrinal principles of the Elastic Defense as detailed in the 1933 manual *Truppenführung* insofar as possible, relying on local commanders to make any necessary adjustments to suit their own circumstances. As the war continued, however, *Truppenführung*'s methodology was increasingly superseded by more widespread modifications resulting from the peculiar conditions of combat on the Russian Front. However, despite these modifications to German defensive practices, *Truppenführung* remained in effect as the standard doctrinal reference until the end of the war.

Most doctrinal change was done informally, originating at the front lines where local commanders acted on their own initiative to correct inappropriate tactical methods. Whether in the use of strongpoints during the winter of 1941—42 or in the adoption of hundreds of other tactical techniques, the constant updating of German defensive methods was highly decentralized. Units worked out new procedures that became doctrine when drilled into replacements and when passed on to other units via combat reports.

This decentralization yielded both benefits and problems. The principal benefit was that German units adapted swiftly and automatically to the harsh realities of combat in Russia. During the difficult defensive fighting through the war's first winter, for example, the defensive methods were almost completely improvised. These improvisations, which probably saved the German armies from annihilation, owed less to published doctrine than to the insight, experience, and tactical judgment of local commanders. In contrast to the greater rigidity of the Red Army, the German adaptability was particularly apparent early in the war.

Like the Germans, the Soviets also adapted their own tactical methods as the war progressed. At the beginning of the war, however, the Red Army was far less able to implement timely adjustments than the German Army. The reason for this lag was that the Soviets trusted the professional discretion of their frontline commanders far less than did the Germans, even to the point of assigning political officers to most units as ideological overseers. While promoting patriotism and fanaticism in the ranks (often at gunpoint), these commissars frequently stultified the initiative of local commanders by making it safer to follow orders and to adhere to prescribed doctrine than to dare innovation. Attempts by such senior leaders as Zhukov and even Stalin to impose hasty doctrinal innovation from above, as by their tactical manifestos during the Soviet winter counteroffensives at the beginning of 1942, were far less effective than the German system of fostering change from below.

The rigidity of Soviet military thinking early in World War II thus stemmed less from an inability to recognize the needs of actual combat at the lowest levels than from an unwillingness to depart from approved methods for fear of political censure. This rigidity gradually eased, and by mid-1943, the Soviets showed themselves to be innovative and adaptable in their own right. (Significantly, following the offensive victories at Stalingrad and elsewhere during the 1942—43 winter, Stalin authorized various reforms that explicitly rewarded and promoted the professionalism of Red Army officers. These included the wearing of distinctive insignia and gold braid, as well as a curtailment of the onerous commissar system—all signs of the new esteem in which Red Army officers were held.)

For the Germans, the major problem with decentralization was the enormous amount of doctrinal parochialism that developed as different units gradually adopted different procedures. This problem was to become especially acute later in the war, but already in 1943, units were creating their own vocabularies, control measures, and fighting techniques that were incompatible with those in use by other units on other sectors of the front. This gradually reduced the interoperability of German forces until, in the war's final years, the transfer of divisions from one army group or theater to another commonly resulted in substantial confusion over tactical methodology. The growing estrangement between the panzer forces and the infantry forces in the German Army over the use of armor in defensive operations was also a symptom of this problem, as each arm sought to perfect its own techniques and to protect its own prerogatives in the absence of centralized doctrinal guidance.

Though German defensive methods were a kaleidoscope of improvisation, certain basic principles remained constant throughout the war and formed the true heart of German doctrine. The German Army's defensive methods were derived from four basic principles: depth, maneuver, firepower, and counterattack. Through all the variations in defensive methods, these principles continued to guide German commanders in conducting their operations.

German units sought to create depth by every means possible, including the distribution of heavy weapons in depth, the construction of rearward defenses, and even the commitment of service troops to combat when necessary. As one German officer wrote after the war, "Depth of the friendly positions is always more important than density."[2]

Hitler constrained maneuver with his Führer Defense Order, pinning German forces in place regardless of the tactical situation. This eclipse outraged German commanders, who considered maneuver from the individual soldier on up as one of the essential ingredients of successful defense. Within the limits allowed by Hitler, German defensive actions remained remarkable for their small-unit maneuver, with units as small as squads and platoons scrambling about the battlefield to confront the enemy's main effort or to counterattack the Russian flanks.

Firepower, in the form of concentrated blows against critical targets, was another major principle that influenced operations. The Germans particularly relished sudden attacks by fire, whether by artillery or close-range small-arms fire from concealed positions, for their ability to shock superior attacking forces into sudden retreat.

Finally, the Germans regarded counterattack as perhaps the most potent of all the defenders' weapons. Almost all orders, training directives, and experience reports published during the entire war mentioned the "decisive" role of counterattack in restoring German defenses. German officers routinely set aside their best leaders, troops, and weapons as local reserves and, at the earliest opportunity, sent them crashing into the flank of any break-in. Speed was emphasized more than mass, and for this reason, every unit in contact with the enemy from squad level up was trained to initiate its own counterattack as soon as possible without awaiting either orders from superiors or the arrival of reserve forces. Soviet local penetrations thus were stung by a swarm of counterattacks until the Russian attack stalled in place or was thrown back.

These basic principles—depth, maneuver, firepower, and counterattack—provided the common theoretical foundation on which local commanders built their own doctrinal adaptations. Even in the absence of strong central direction and even without an updated field manual to replace the 1933 *Truppenführung*, these simple principles served the Germans well as a general guide to tactical improvisation.

Many of the most important stimuli for doctrinal change had little or nothing to do with Soviet operations. German defensive doctrine was influenced as much by nonbattle factors as by Soviet tactical methods. For example, German strongpoint tactics during the 1941—42 winter did not result from an assessment of Soviet vulnerabilities. Rather, German units were drawn to village-based strongpoints because they lacked winter equipment and the manpower for a continuous linear defense and because Hitler insisted that the beleaguered forces stand fast. It was a lucky coincidence that the strongpoint defensive system denied the Russians access to road networks. That the Soviets neglected to annihilate more of the German strongpoints was also coincidental, stemming from certain erroneous Soviet strategic decisions and awkward operational techniques.

Adolf Hitler was also a major force that affected German doctrine. In almost every significant defensive battle fought by the German Army on the Eastern Front, German doctrinal conduct was hampered to some extent by the Führer's warped sense of priorities. From December 1941 onward, Hitler corrupted the traditional German concept of *Auftragstaktik* with his overbearing interference in the affairs of subordinate commanders. Another abiding millstone was the September 1942 Führer Defense Order, which codified rigid defense without retreat and curtailed much tactical maneuver.

Another source of change was the size, composition, and battle worthiness of the German Army. As seen, defensive tactics during the 1941—42 winter were dictated in part by the lack of adequate German infantry strength to man a continuous front. Weaponry and the organization of German units also helped to shape German methods. The lack of an effective, long-range antitank gun (except for the few 88-mm antiaircraft guns) turned German antiarmor defense into a test of individual courage and inventiveness, while the reduction in strength of most infantry divisions from nine to six battalions in 1942 reduced their defensive staying power and tactical flexibility. As the training proficiency of German units eroded, their abilities to fight according to the aggressive Elastic Defense principles also faded. The poor defensive performance of many new, half-trained divisions in 1942—43, together with the surprising sluggishness of many veteran units, compelled some German commanders to compromise their defensive schemes in order to accommodate the decreased efficiency of their forces. The surprisingly good performance of various ad hoc emergency units showed the soundness of basic defensive principles but also necessitated enormous doctrinal compromises to minimize the severe organizational limitations of those units.

Soviet tactics did, of course, have some impact on German doctrinal development. German experience reports regularly updated commanders on the enemy's latest tactics and outlined possible countermeasures. The evolution of German antitank tactics is again a case in point. Before the war, German defensive doctrine considered enemy tanks to be of secondary importance; therefore, German defenses were designed primarily to arrest the momentum of an artillery-supported infantry attack. In Russia, the offensive power (and, considering the feeble German antitank weaponry, the virtual invulnerability) of Soviet armor far outweighed that of massed infantry in most cases. The winter counteroffensives in 1942—43 reflected a Russian awareness of this fact as well, as each major Soviet drive was spearheaded by a phalanx of armored units. Consequently, German commanders increasingly deployed their forces and drilled their troops to foil Soviet tank attacks as the first defensive priority, with less regard being paid to the threat of dismounted infantry.

Thus, while changes to Soviet tactics and equipment did prompt some German defensive responses, German methods were bent extensively by other factors as well. The evolution of German defensive doctrine on the Russian Front during World War II demonstrates that an army's fighting techniques are shaped not only by an awareness of "the threat," but also by its own organization, training posture, weapons, traditions, and command philosophy. Armed with a defensive doctrine that constantly changed in form but remained true to the underlying principles propounded in its doctrinal manuals, the German Army pitted its proven tactical adaptability against the growing resource weight of the Soviet Red Army from mid-1943 onward.

NOTES

Introduction

1. An example of how a few out-of-context Russian Front examples can be advanced as evidence in support of a general doctrinal theory is F. W. von Mellenthin, R. H. S. Stolfi, and E. Sobik, *NATO Under Attack* (Durham, NC: Duke University Press, 1984).

2. The best English-language history of the Eastern Front is Albert Seaton, *The Russo-German War, 1941–1945* (New York: Praeger Publishers, 1970). A good narrative account, though less rigorous in its use of original sources, is Alan Clark, *Barbarossa: The Russo-German Conflict, 1941–1945* (New York: William Morrow and Co., 1965). Earle F. Ziemke, *Stalingrad to Berlin: The German Defeat in the East*, Army Historical Series (Washington, DC: Office of the Chief of Military History, U.S. Army, 1968), is a well-documented history of the years 1943–45 but includes only a brief summary of the campaigns before Stalingrad. John Erickson's *The Road to Stalingrad* (New York: Harper and Row, 1975) and *The Road to Berlin* (Boulder, CO: Westview Press, 1983) are fairly comprehensive accounts of the war as seen from the Soviet side. For a brief commentary on the professional ignorance of U.S. Army officers concerning the Russo-German War, see Michael A. Phipps, "A Forgotten War," *Infantry* 74 (November–December 1984):38–40.

3. See Mellenthin, Stolfi, and Sobik, *NATO*, 51, 66. J. R. Alford, "Mobile Defence: The Pervasive Myth (A Historical Investigation)" (London: Department of War Studies, King's College, 1977), 104–40, discredits the view that German defensive operations on the Russian Front generally amounted to any sort of successful mobile defense.

4. Phipps, "A Forgotten War," 40.

5. Mellenthin, Stolfi, and Sobik, *NATO*, 73.

Chapter 1

1. The German publication that set forth the new doctrine did not give a specific title to the new defensive technique. "Grundsätze für die Abwehrschlacht im Stellungskriege [Principles for Defensive Combat in Positional Warfare]," 20 September 1918 ed., in *Urkunden der Obersten Heeresleitung*, 3d ed., edited by Erich von Ludendorff (Berlin: E. S. Mittler und Sohn, 1922), hereafter cited as "Grundsätze." Captain Graeme C. Wynne, a British authority on German defensive doctrine during World War I, suggests that the term "elastic defense" was used informally within the Imperial German Army. Graeme C. Wynne, *If Germany Attacks: The Battle in Depth in the West* (1940; reprint, Westport, CT: Greenwood Press, 1976), 156, 158–59. The German official history of World War I used the expression "elastic battle procedure" (*das elastische Kampfverfahren*) in its discussion of the new doctrine. Oberkommando des Heeres, *Der Weltkrieg 1914–1918* (Berlin: E. S. Mittler, 1939), 12:45. When the Oberkommando des Heeres (Army High Command) is the author of a source, it is cited as OKH. This research survey will use the term "Elastic Defense" as a title for the German technique of defense in depth.

2. Wilhelm Balck, *Development of Tactics—World War*, translated by Harry Bell (Fort Leavenworth, KS: The General Service Schools Press, 1922), 79–80.

3. The discussion of the Elastic Defense that follows in the text is from Wynne, *If Germany Attacks*, 148–64; Timothy T. Lupfer, *The Dynamics of Doctrine: The Changes in German Tactical Doctrine During the First World War*, Leavenworth Papers no. 4 (Fort Leavenworth, KS: Combat Studies Institute, U.S. Army Command and General Staff College, 1981), 11–21; "Grundsätze"; and "Allgemeines über Stellungsbau [Principles of Position Construction]," 10 August 1918 ed., in *Urkunden*, and edited by Ludendorff.

4. "Grundsätze," 607.

5. Ibid., 617. The German military vocabulary included separate doctrinal terms for each type of counterattack. A hasty local counterattack by engaged units was a *Gegenstoss in der Stellung*; one reinforced with fresh reserves was a *Gegenstoss aus der Tief*; and a deliberate, coordinated counterattack was a *Gegenangriff*. This distinctive vocabulary illustrates the careful attention the Germans paid to counterattack. No comparable terms exist in the American military lexicon.

6. Ibid., 606–15; Wynne, *If Germany Attacks*, 209–10.

7. Wilhelm, Crown Prince of Germany, *My War Experiences* (London: Hurst and Blackett, 1923), 267.

8. See, for example, "General von Maur's Memorandum on the English Tank Attack of April 11, 1917," translated by David G. Rempel and Gertrude Rendtorff, in *Fall of the German Empire, 1914–1918*, edited by Ralph Haswell Lutz (Stanford, CA: Stanford University Press, 1932), 1:625–27.

9. Erich von Ludendorff, *Ludendorff's Own Story* (New York: Harper and Brothers, 1919), 2:202–3.

10. See "Grundsätze."

11. A good critique of the German 1918 strategy is given in Gordon Craig, "Delbruck: The Military Historian," in *Makers of Modern Strategy*, edited by Edward Mead Earle (1941; reprint, New York: Atheneum, 1969), 275–82. Following World War I, an official German investigating commission examined the 1918 collapse and later presented its findings to the *Reichstag*. Extracts from the commission's reports appear as "Report of the Commission of the German Constituent Assembly and of the German Reichstag, 1919–1928," in *The Causes of the German Collapse in 1918*, edited by Ralph Haswell Lutz, translated by W. L. Campbell (Stanford, CA: Stanford University Press, 1934), hereafter cited as "Commission Report." A critical assessment of the 1918 German offensive strategy is on pages 72–90.

12. Balck, *Development of Tactics*, 87.

13. "Commission Report," 81. See also Lupfer, *Dynamics of Doctrine*, 48–49.

14. Crown Prince Wilhelm, who commanded a German Army Group in the 1918 battles, wrote after the war that, "In view of the ever-increasing weight of the attack . . . it [the Elastic Defense] was without doubt right in principle, but it was dependent upon strictly-disciplined, well-trained and skillfully-led troops. As the war progressed, these conditions became increasingly difficult to fulfill." Wilhelm, *My War Experiences*, 282–83.

15. Ludendorff, *Ludendorff's Own Story*, 2:341–42.

16. "Commission Report," 71–72; Hermann Joseph von Kuhl, *Entstehung, Durchführung und Zusammenbruch der Offensive von 1918* (Berlin: Deutsche Verlagsgesellschaft für Politik und Geschichte m.b.H., 1927), 79–86.

17. Balck, *Development of Tactics*, 289–90.

18. "Headquarters, Fifth [German] Reserve Corps: Experiences from the Fighting on the West Bank of the Meuse, 29 September 1918," in Lutz, *Fall*, 662.

19. Hans Ritter, *Kritik des Weltkrieges: das Erbe Moltkes und Schlieffen im grossen Kriege* (Leipzig: K. F. Koehler, 1920), 64. Published anonymously by "A General Staff Officer."

20. Wilhelm, *My War Experiences*, 267.

21. Balck, *Development of Tactics*, 288.

22. A particularly impassioned version of the "stab in the back" is given by Balck, who asserted that the "criminal responsible for our fall . . . should be sought in the ranks of the leaders of our political parties [who] . . . placed pursuit of their own ends above the weal and woe of Germany." These cowards, according to Balck, struck down the German Army "like Hagen of old did to the unconquerable hero, Siegfried." Ibid., 294.

23. Graeme C. Wynne, "The Legacy," *Army Quarterly* 39 (October 1939 and January 1940), 26.

24. The early rebuilding of the German Army is described in Harold J. Gordon, *The Reichswehr and the German Republic, 1919—1926* (Princeton, NJ: Princeton University Press, 1957), 169—216; and Herbert Rosinski, *The German Army*, rev. ed. (Washington, DC: Infantry Journal, 1944), 123—29.

25. The most prominent spokesman of the "trench school" was General Walter Reinhardt, who served briefly as *Chef der Heeresleitung* prior to Seeckt. Reinhardt was dismissed from this position as a result of the Kapp *Putsch* in 1920. Rosinski, *German Army*, 103.

26. Reichswehrministerium, *Führung und Gefecht der verbundenen Waffen*, 2 vols. (Berlin: Offene Worte, 1921), 223, hereafter cited as *FuG*.

27. Ibid., 223.

28. Ibid., 221—22.

29. Ibid., 206.

30. Ibid., 215—16.

31. Ibid., 192.

32. Ibid., 196.

33. Ibid., 197—201.

34. On Seeckt's personal dogmatism, see Francis L. Carsten, *The Reichswehr and Politics, 1918 to 1933* (Oxford: Oxford University Press, 1966), 106—7. On his suppression of contradictory theories, see Friedrich von Rabenau, *Seeckt: Aus seinem Leben 1918—1936* (Leipzig: Von Hasse und Koehler, 1940), 505.

35. See "Grundlegende Gedanken für den Wiederaufbau unserer Wehrmacht," in Rabenau, *Seeckt*, 474—75. This same 1921 memorandum also first set forth Seeckt's idea of the *Reichswehr* as a *Führerheer* (Leader Army), a high-quality cadre for a future expansion of the German Army.

36. Ibid., 511.

37. Ibid., 512.

38. Ibid., 509. For the strategic dimensions of Seeckt's theories, see Hans von Seeckt, *Die Reichswehr* (Leipzig: R. Kittler, 1933), 34—64; Hans von Seeckt, *Thoughts of a Soldier*, translated by Gilbert Waterhouse (London: E. Benn, 1930), 59—64; and Larry H. Addington, *The Blitzkrieg Era and the German General Staff, 1865—1941* (New Brunswick, NJ: Rutgers University Press, 1971), 28—30.

39. Ritter, *Kritik*, 47; Rosinski, *German Army*, 81—91. Rosinski flatly states that the German decision in November 1914 "against a return to the mobile strategy of the first weeks of the war . . . *must be considered to be the real turning point of the war* [italics in original]." Hans Delbruck, the prominent German military historian and critic, argued even during the war that Germany's only hope for escape from *Stellungskrieg* lay in the direction of a political settlement since a German military victory was no longer within reach. Craig, "Delbruck," 278—80.

40. The military constraints on Germany are detailed in Part V (Military, Naval and Air Clauses) of the Versailles Treaty. Article 160 limited the size and composition of the German Army; Article 171 prohibited poison gas and tanks; Article 180 prohibited fortifications along Germany's western frontiers. Table II (Armament Establishment) listed allowed types and quantities of weapons. In addition to "offensive weapons" such as tanks, aircraft, and poison gas, the Germans were also forbidden to possess such patently defensive weapons as antitank and antiaircraft guns. *The Treaty of Peace with Germany, June 28, 1919* (Washington, DC, 1920).

41. Paramilitary units such as the *Freikorps* and the *Stahlhelm* remained essential to the defense of the eastern frontiers until Germany's rearmament in the mid-1930s. Carsten, *Reichswehr*, 149—50, 231—32, 265—68, 355—56.

42. Gordon, *Reichswehr*, 254—61.

43. Albert Seaton, *The German Army, 1933—1945* (New York: St. Martin's Press, 1982), 51—71. One of the earliest rearmament measures ordered by Hitler was the construction of fortifications

along Germany's border with France—a repudiation not only of the Versailles Treaty, but also of Seeckt's doctrines of offensive maneuver. Burkhart Mueller-Hillebrand, *Das Heer 1933—1945* (Darmstadt: E. S. Mittler und Sohn, 1954), 1:38—43.

44. Philip C. F. Bankwitz, *Maxime Weygand and Civil-Military Relations in Modern France* (Cambridge, MA: Harvard University Press, 1967), 40—45. Ironically, the building of the Maginot Line was inspired in part by French fears of Seeckt's theories of preemptive offensive warfare.

45. A summary of Beck's role in the development of all facets of German doctrine during this period is in Addington, *Blitzkrieg Era*, 35—38; see also S. J. Lewis, *Forgotten Legions: German Army Infantry Policy, 1918—41* (New York: Praeger, 1985), 45—55. Beck's role in restoring the Elastic Defense is spitefully discredited by Heinz Guderian in *Panzer Leader*, translated by Constantine Fitzgibbon (New York: E. P. Dutton and Co., 1952), 31—33. Guderian, who saw Beck as an obstacle to his own pet schemes of armored warfare, characterized Beck in his memoirs as "a paralyzing element wherever he appeared." As evidence of this, Guderian cited "his [Beck's] much-boosted method of fighting which he called 'delaying defense.' . . . In the 100,000-man army this delaying defense became the cardinal principle." Guderian credits the "fine, chivalrous, clever, careful" General Freiherr von Fritsch—who coincidentally tended to support Guderian's ideas—with jettisoning the "confusing" and "unsatisfactory" delaying defense in the early 1930s. In all of this, Guderian is mistaken. The *Hinhaltendes Gefecht* was not Beck's brainchild at all, but rather part of Seeckt's schemes for defense by offensive maneuver. It was conversely through Beck's efforts in *Truppenführung* that the "delaying defense" was supplanted by the more workable Elastic Defense system. Guderian's story is repeated uncritically by Robert J. O'Neill, "Doctrine and Training in the German Army, 1919—1939," in *The Theory and Practice of War*, edited by Michael Howard (New York: Frederick A. Praeger, 1966), 153.

46. Reichswehrministerium, *Truppenführung*, Teil 1, H.Dv. 300/1, dated October 1933 (1933; reprint, Berlin, 1936), 179, hereafter cited as *TF* 1.

47. Ibid., 179—208. *Truppenführung* also made minor changes in nomenclature. The battle zone (*Grosskampfzone*), for example, was retitled the main battle position (*Hauptkampffeld*).

48. OKH, *Der Stellungskrieg*, H.Dv. 91 (1938; reprint, Berlin, 1940), 59—90; OKH, Generalstab des Heeres/Ausbildungsabteilung (II) [Training Branch of the Army General Staff], *Die Ständige Front*, Teil 1: *Die Abwehr in Ständiger Front*, H.Dv. 89/1 (Berlin, 1940), 5—24; the OKH Training Branch is hereafter cited as OKH, GSII. Techniques to be used in positional warfare were also written into various branch and training manuals as well. For example, see OKH, GSII, *Ausbildungsvorschrift für die Infanterie*, Heft 11: *Feldbefestigung der Infanterie*, H.Dv. 130/11 (Berlin, 1940), and OKH, GSII, *Pionierdienst aller Waffen*, H.Dv. 316 (Berlin, 1935).

49. See, for example, "Truppenführung Stellungskrieg, Stosstrupp-Unternehmen und Angriff mit begrenzten Ziele," *Militär-Wochenblatt*, no. 23 (2 December 1938):1508—12; and "Truppen-Kriegsgeschichte: Gegenangriff des R.I.R. 93 am 15.8.1917," *Militär-Wochenblatt*, no. 38 (18 March 1938): 2435—37, and no. 39 (25 March 1938), 2499—2500.

50. Leeb's articles were compiled into book form as *Die Abwehr* (Berlin, 1938). The cited portion is from Wilhelm Ritter von Leeb, *Defense*, translated and edited by Stefan T. Possony and Daniel Vilfroy (Harrisburg, PA: Military Service Publishing Co., 1943), 121.

51. Leeb, *Defense*, 115—19.

52. Generalmajor Klingbeil, "Das Problem 'Stellungskrieg,'" *Militär-Wochenblatt*, no. 36 (19 March 1937):2149.

53. One major exception to the general trend in German strategic thought was Colonel Hermann Foertsch's *The Art of Modern Warfare*, translated by Theodore W. Knauth (Camden, NJ: Veritas Press, 1940). Foertsch theorized that modern weapons and mobility merely increased the lethality and extended the size of the battlefield. He concluded that, therefore, "the defensive has greatly gained strength as compared with the attack . . . . The war of the future will see more defense than has been the case for the last hundred years." Ibid., 217. Foertsch was convinced that future wars would necessarily be decided by the exhaustion of one of the belligerents and urged a defense in depth to conserve military resources. Foertsch later served as an army group chief of staff and commander of an infantry division during World War II.

54. Guderian, *Panzer Leader*, 32—33; Addington, *Blitzkrieg Era*, 35—38.

55. OKH, GSII, *Truppenführung*, Teil 2, H.Dv. 300/2 (1934; reprint, Berlin, 1941), 8—10 ("Abwehr gepanzerter Kampffahrzeuge"); OKH, GSII, *Die Ständige Front*, Teil 2: *Der Kampf der Infanterie* (Berlin, 1940), 25—27.

56. OKH, *Der Stellungskrieg*, 77—78. See also the sketch in "Truppenführung. Stellungskrieg," 1509—10.

57. OKH, *Die Infanterie*, Waffenhefte des Heeres (Munich: Deutscher Volksverlag, 1938?), 7; Mueller-Hillebrand, *Das Heer*, 1:158—59. The German antitank rifles were the 7.92-mm *Panzerbüchse 38* and *Panzerbüchse 39*. Neither proved particularly effective in combat. The German crew-served antitank gun was the 37-mm *Pak*, whose armor-piercing ammunition could penetrate 1.93 inches of homogeneous armor (30-degree slope) at 400 yards. U.S. War Department, TM-E 30—451, *Handbook on German Military Forces* (Washington, DC: U.S. Government Printing Office, 1945), VII-9—VII-10, VII-31—VII-32.

58. One outspoken critic of the German antitank concept was General Ludwig Ritter von Eimannsberger, who proposed a complete overhaul of German defensive doctrine in order to place primary importance on antitank defense. Eimannsberger's ideas on this and other topics related to mechanized warfare are in his *Der Kampfwagen Krieg* (Munich: J. F. Lehmanns Verlag, 1934), typescript English translation at the U.S. Army Military History Institute, Carlisle Barracks, Pennsylvania. Antitank defense is discussed on pages 117—49 of this typescript.

59. Ludwig Ritter von Eimannsberger, "Panzertaktik," *Militär-Wochenblatt*, no. 26 (8 January 1937):1448—53.

60. Major Sieberg, untitled commentary on fighting in Spain, *Militär-Wochenblatt*, no. 33 (11 February 1938):2097. Foertsch asserted that the combination of new antitank weaponry and skillful use of elastic defense in depth meant that "such advantages as tanks enjoyed in 1917 and 1918 will hardly survive." Foertsch, *Modern Warfare*, 136—37. For examples of technical disputes on antitank tactics, see "Panzerabwehr in der Praxis," *Militär-Wochenblatt*, no. 18 (29 October 1937): 1101—3; Guderian, *Panzer Leader*, 37; and Eimannsberger, "Panzertaktik," 1452.

61. Eimannsberger, *Kampfwagen Krieg* (MHI typescript), 143.

62. At the outbreak of World War II, German tank armaments were: Panzer I, two machine guns only; Panzer II, a 20-mm cannon; Panzer III, a 37-mm cannon (same ammunition and performance characteristics as the 37-mm *Pak*); and Panzer IV, a short-barreled, low-velocity 75-mm cannon. The last three models also had machine guns of various types.

63. Compare *FuG*, 2:46; *TF* 1:195; and Foertsch, *Modern Warfare*, 155.

64. *TF* 1:195; OKH, *Der Stellungskrieg*, 77.

65. Edgar Röhricht, *Probleme der Kesselschlacht* (Karlsruhe: Condor-Verlag, 1958), xv; Hermann Metz, "Die Deutsche Infanterie," in *Die Deutsche Wehrmacht*, edited by G. Wetzel (Berlin, 1939).

66. The impact of the Polish campaign on the German Army is described in Williamson Murray, "The German Response to Victory in Poland: A Case Study in Professionalism," *Armed Forces and Society* 7 (Winter 1981).

67. Ibid., 289.

68. Der Oberbefehlshaber des Heeres, GS Ia Nr. 400/39g, dated 13 October 1939, "Ausbildung des Feldheeres," microfilm series T-312, roll 234, frame 7787781, National Archives, Washington, DC. Further references to National Archives microfilm will be cited as NAM.

69. OKH, GSII, *Richtlinien für Führung und Einsatz der Panzer-Division*, D-66, dated 3 December 1940 (Berlin, 1940). The two paragraphs on defense are on page 54.

70. Guderian, *Panzer Leader*, 143—44. Although the Panzer III's main gun was enlarged to 50-mm, the German Army Ordnance Office selected a shorter, lower-velocity gun tube than the 50-mm L60 ordered by Hitler.

71. Some units also received Czechoslovakian 37-mm antitank guns. The expansion of the German Army prior to Barbarossa caused many new German divisions to have fewer antitank guns of any type than authorized. Mueller-Hillebrand, *Das Heer*, 2:108. Despite the proliferation of new weapons, German antitank training remained based on dated manuals and training guides. See

OKH, GSII, *Die Infanterie-Panzerabwehrkompanie*, H.Dv. 130/5 (Berlin, 1938); and Edler Ritter von Peter and Kurt von Tippelskirch, *Das Panzerabwehrbuch* (Berlin: Offene Worte, 1937).

72. Joseph Prinner, "Organization, Advance and Combat of the 81st Artillery Regiment in 1941," Foreign Military Studies no. MS D-251 (Historical Division, U.S. Army, Europe, 1947), 2, hereafter cited as MS D-251.

73. Wynne, "Legacy," 29. See also Armand Mermet, *Siegfried Taktik 37* (Paris: Charles-Lavauzelle, 1939).

Chapter 2

1. "Directive Number 21, 'Operation BARBAROSSA,' 18 December 1941," in U.S. Department of the Army, Pamphlet no. 20—261a, *The German Campaign in Russia: Planning and Operations, 1940—1942*, by George E. Blau (Washington, DC: U.S. Government Printing Office, 1955), 22, hereafter cited as DA Pam 20—261a.

2. The particular merits of *Keil und Kessel* tactics in Operation Barbarossa are discussed in Hans von Greiffenberg, et al., "Battle of Moscow, 1941—1942," Foreign Military Studies no. MS T-28 (Historical Division, U.S. Army, Europe, n.d.), 91—92, hereafter cited as MS T-28. For comments on the coordination of early encirclement battles, see Franz Halder, *The Private War Journal of Generaloberst Franz Halder*, edited by Arnold Lissance (Washington, DC: Office of the Chief of Military History, 1950), 7:167, 170 (entries for 24 and 25 June 1941), and 8:1 (entry for 1 August 1941); Hermann Hoth, *Panzer-Operationen: Die Panzergruppe 3 und der operative Gedanke der deutschen Führung, Sommer 1941* (Heidelberg: Kurt Vowinckel, 1956), 62—66; and Guderian, *Panzer Leader*, 161.

3. The principle of the "strategic offensive, tactical defensive" was first established in German military art by Helmuth von Moltke, chief of the Prussian (and later German) General Staff from 1857 to 1888. See Addington, *Blitzkrieg Era*, 3—4.

4. At the beginning of Barbarossa, German panzer divisions consisted of one panzer regiment and two rifle regiments plus supporting elements. Each infantry regiment had only two infantry battalions, however, giving a panzer division a total organic infantry strength of only four battalions. (This total excludes divisional reconnaissance, antitank, and other combat support units that might perform missions as infantry on occasion. Some panzer divisions also contained an additional motorcycle infantry battalion under the division headquarters.) In comparison, regular German infantry divisions consisted of three infantry regiments, each of three battalions. Panzer divisions therefore had roughly half the infantry strength of infantry divisions and were proportionately less able to hold terrain. Mueller-Hillebrand, *Das Heer*, 2:161—83.

5. Erich von Manstein, *Lost Victories*, edited and translated by Anthony G. Powell (Chicago: Henry Regnery Co., 1958), 185.

6. Wolfgang Werthen, *Geschichte der 16. Panzer-Division 1939—1945* (Bad Nauheim: Hans-Henning Podzun, 1958), 46; U.S. Department of the Army, Pamphlet no. 20—201, *Military Improvisations During the Russian Campaign* (Washington, DC: U.S. Government Printing Office, 1951), 22, hereafter cited as DA Pam 20—201.

7. Halder, *War Journal*, 7:1 (entry for 1 August 1941).

8. On 22 June 1941, all ten of the German Army's motorized infantry divisions and four *Waffen SS* motorized divisions (*Leibstandarte Adolf Hitler*, *Das Reich*, *Totenkopf*, and *Wiking*) were deployed on the Russian Front. Of these, all were assigned to one of the four German panzer groups except for 60th Motorized Division, which was initially held in *OKH* reserve. Mueller-Hillebrand, *Das Heer*, 2:190—91. Four of the army's motorized divisions (14th, 18th, 25th, and 36th) were equipped wholly or in part with captured French materiel. Halder, *War Journal*, 6:48 (entry for 3 April 1941). In mid-May 1941, General Halder noted that the training of the 18th Motorized Division was "sketchy" with "no unit training" due to its late conversion from a regular infantry division. Ibid., 6:122 (entry for 17 May 1941). Motorized infantry divisions contained only two infantry regiments and were therefore not equal to regular infantry divisions in their ability to occupy and defend terrain. Mueller-Hillebrand, *Das Heer*, 2:179. For a description of the

difficulties encountered by the German 29th Motorized Division in containing surrounded Soviet forces on 29—30 June 1941 at the cost of "very heavy losses," see Bryan I. Fugate, *Operation Barbarossa: Strategy and Tactics on the Eastern Front, 1941* (Novato, CA: Presidio Press, 1984), 112—13.

9. For a discussion of the problems inherent to subduing a "wandering pocket," see "Das Phänomen der wandernden Kessel" in Rudolf Steiger, *Panzertaktik im Spiegel deutscher Kriegstagebücher 1939—1941* (Freiburg: Romach, 1973), 52—56; and MS T-28, 91—92.

10. An account of the tactical difficulties experienced by one panzer division in defensive combat is Werthen, *Geschichte*, 53—67. See also Guderian, *Panzer Leader*, 158—67; and Rolf Hinze, *Hitze, Frost und Pulverdampf: Der Schicksalsweg der 20. Panzer-Division* (Bochum: Heinrich Pöppinghaus Verlag, 1981), 49—56.

11. Röhricht, *Probleme*, 30; Halder, *War Journal*, 6:209 (entry for 7 July). On 29 June, Halder had already expressed surprise at the small number of prisoners taken in relation to the vast quantities of equipment seized, a sign that many enemy soldiers were escaping through the German lines. Ibid., 6:181 (entry for 28 June). This problem became more pronounced as the campaign progressed. On 25 August, for example, Halder wrote that "it appears that considerable enemy elements did manage to escape encirclement. . . . The trouble is that our panzer divisions now have such a low combat strength that they just do not have the men to seal off any sizeable areas." Ibid., 7:64 (entry for 25 August).

12. The inferiority of German tanks compared to the Soviet T-34 is discussed in Steiger, *Panzertaktik*, 103—13; and Erich Schneider, "Antitank Defense in the East," Foreign Military Studies no. MS D-253 (Historical Division, U.S. Army, Europe, 1947), 22—25, hereafter cited as MS D-253. An overview of German and Soviet tank development, including performance characteristics of specific models, is Richard M. Ogorkiewicz, *Armor: A History of Mechanized Forces* (New York: Frederick A. Praeger, 1960), 206—36.

13. Hermann Plocher, *The German Air Force Versus Russia, 1941*, edited by Harry R. Fletcher, USAF Historical Studies no. 153 (New York: Arno Press, 1968), 74—75. In one of the functional redundancies typical of Nazi Germany, the *Luftwaffe* and the army had overlapping air defense responsibilities in the field. Thus, those *Luftwaffe* flak units assigned to German combat divisions were in addition to the army flak detachments organic to every German division.

14. Halder, *War Journal*, 6:173 (entry for 26 June).

15. Friedrich Hossbach, *Infanterie im Ostfeldzug, 1941—1942* (Osterode-Harz: Giebel und Oehlschlägel, 1951), 50.

16. See *TF* 1:182—83.

17. An impression of the nearly constant fighting—both offensive and defensive—performed at the small-unit level during the German advance can be gained from Wilhelm Koehler, "Engagements Fought by the 488th Infantry Regiment at the Stryanitsa and Desna Rivers (6—29 Sep 1941)," Foreign Military Studies no. MS D-134 (Historical Division, U.S. Army, Europe, 1947); and Maximilian Fretter-Pico, *Missbrauchte Infanterie: Deutsche Infanteriedivision im osteuropäischen Grossraum 1941 bis 1944* (Frankfurt am Main: Verlag für Wehrwesen, 1957), 26.

18. "Directive 3," issued by Marshal Semën K. Timoshenko on the evening of 22 June 1941, ordered an all-out counteroffensive by Red Army forces. Although "virtually impossible to carry out from a purely military point of view, [Directive 3] in a way formulated the character of the war. The idea was to make unceasing and powerful counterblows." Amnon Sella, " 'Barbarossa': Surprise Attack and Communication," *Journal of Contemporary History*, 13 (July 1978):574. See also John Erickson, "The Soviet Response to Surprise Attack: Three Directives, 22 June 1941," *Soviet Studies* 23 (April 1972):549—53. Senior Soviet military officers recognized the futility of such an order but, for the most part, endorsed its aggressive spirit. See G. K. Zhukov, *Vospominaniya i razmyshleniya* (Moscow: Novosti Press, 1971), 240.

19. MS D-251, 6. The attachment of artillery batteries to German infantry units during marches and hasty attacks was a lesson learned from the 1939 campaign in Poland. See U.S. Department of the Army, Pamphlet no. 20—255, *The German Campaign in Poland (1939)*, by Robert M. Kennedy (Washington, DC: U.S. Government Printing Office, 1956), 134.

20. Werner Prellberg, "Employment of Flak in an Army Defense Zone," Foreign Military Studies no. MS D-050 (Historical Division, U.S. Army, Europe, 1947), 14.

21. German accounts are unanimous in confirming the ineffectiveness of the 37-mm antitank gun. The German 50-mm *Pak* was somewhat more effective at short ranges against the heavier Soviet tanks, but it was still inadequate. See MS D-253, 5, 17; I. G. Andronikow and W. D. Mostowenko, *Die Roten Panzer: Geschichte der sowjetischen Panzertruppen* (Munich: J. F. Lehmanns Verlag, 1963), 252—54; and Fugate, *Barbarossa*, 106—7.

22. The problems of using field artillery for antitank defense are described in MS D-253, 9—12, 27. For a somewhat heroic account of the exploits of German artillery against Russian tanks, see Eugen Beinhauer, ed., *Artillerie im Osten* (Berlin: Wilhelm Limpert Verlag, 1944), 44—49, 55—58, 230—39.

23. See Friedrich August von Metzsch, *Die Geschichte der 22. Infanterie-Division, 1939—1945* (Kiel: Hans-Henning Podzun, 1952), 19—20; Paul Carrell, *Hitler Moves East, 1941—1943*, translated by Ewald Osers (Boston: Little, Brown and Co., 1964), 76—78; Charles W. Sydnor, *Soldiers of Destruction: The SS Death's Head Division, 1933—1945* (Princeton, NJ: Princeton University Press, 1977), 192, including note 68; and Fretter-Pico, *Infanterie*, 49.

24. Halder, *War Journal*, 6:221 (entry for 10 July).

25. Fretter-Pico, *Infanterie*, 25; Hans Breithaupt, *Die Geschichte der 30. Infanterie-Division, 1940—1945* (Bad Nauheim: Hans-Henning Podzun, 1955), 119.

26. Fretter-Pico, *Infanterie*, 21—26. This same engagement is described from the standpoint of the German artillery in MS D-251, 6—7. German light infantry divisions contained only two infantry regiments rather than three as in regular infantry divisions. Mueller-Hillebrand, *Das Heer*, 2:174—75. For an assessment of German lessons learned in this battle, see Ernst Ott, *Jäger am Feind: Geschichte und Opfergang der 97. Jäger-Division 1940—1945* (Munich: Kameradschaft der Spielhahnjäger, 1966), 37.

27. Hossbach, *Infanterie*, 54—59.

28. See Malcolm Mackintosh, *Juggernaut: A History of the Soviet Armed Forces* (New York: Macmillan Co., 1967), 132—36; and Erickson, *Road to Stalingrad*, 60—73. For the tactical readiness of Soviet forces, see Amnon Sella, "Red Army Doctrine and Training on the Eve of the Second World War," *Soviet Studies* 27 (April 1975).

29. Halder, *War Journal*, 6:195 (entry for 3 July).

30. Ibid., 6:205 (entry for 6 July). General Eugen Ott delivered this report. Although commanding a corps at the time this observation was given, General Ott had recently served as inspector general of infantry within the German Army. Ott's observations on Soviet and Russian tactics seem to have been particularly valued by Halder. General Ott's service record is in Wolf Keilig, *Das Deutsche Heer, 1939—1945: Gliederung, Einsatz, Stellenbesetzung*, 3 vols. (Bad Nauheim: Hans-Henning Podzun, 1956), 3:243.

31. Halder, *War Journal*, 7:35 (entry for 11 August).

32. The operational problems caused by the separation of German units are discussed at length in Heinz Guderian, "Flank Defense in Far-Reaching Operations," Foreign Military Studies no. MS T-11 (Historical Division, U.S. Army, Europe, 1948).

33. Halder, *War Journal*, 6:203 (entry for 5 July).

34. Ibid., 6:255 (entry for 19 July).

35. Ibid., 6:197, 272—73 (entries for 3 and 25 July); Walter Warlimont, *Inside Hitler's Headquarters, 1939—1945*, translated by R. H. Barry (New York: Frederick A. Praeger, 1964), 183.

36. Warlimont, *Inside*, 184.

37. DA Pam 20—261a, 56.

38. The German strategic indecision is traced in Ibid., 61—70; and Warlimont, *Inside*, 180—92.

39. P. N. Pospelov, et al., eds., *Great Patriotic War of the Soviet Union, 1941—1945: A General Outline*, translated by David Skvirsky and Vic Schneierson (Moscow: Progress Publishers, 1974),

66, hereafter cited as *GPWSU*; Werner Haupt, *Heeresgruppe Nord 1941—1942* (Bad Nauheim: Hans-Henning Podzun, 1967), 78—81; Percy Ernst Schramm, ed., *Kriegstagebuch des Oberkommandos der Wehrmacht 1940—1945*, vol. 1, *1 August 1940—31 December 1941* (Frankfurt am Main: Bernard und Graefe Verlag für Wehrwesen, 1965), 465—70 (entries for 13—18 August 1941), hereafter cited as *KTB/OKW*.

40. Breithaupt, *Geschichte*, 98—110.

41. Halder, *War Journal*, 7:52 (entry for 18 August).

42. Oberkommando der Wehrmacht, WFSt/L (I Op.) Nr. 441386/41, "Anlage 36," dated 15 August 1941, in *KTB/OKW*, 1:1045; Halder, *War Journal*, 7:44 (entry for 15 August).

43. Sydnor, *Soldiers*, 175—78; Manstein, *Lost Victories*, 199—201. Manstein's account misidentifies the Soviet units participating in the engagement.

44. "Operative Gedanken des Führers und Weisungen am 21. August 1941," *KTB/OKW*, 1:1061—62; and letter from Hitler to Brauchitsch, dated 21 August 1941, *KTB/OKW*, 1:1062—63.

45. Hitler's interest in strategic objectives other than Moscow predated the beginning of the Barbarossa campaign. Brauchitsch, Halder, and other officers ignored this interest insofar as possible, hoping that events would favor their preference for a drive on Moscow. The Soviet attack near Staraya Russa in mid-August roused Hitler to action. This Russian thrust seemed to confirm Hitler's prescience about the vulnerability of the German flanks and to discredit the judgment of Halder, who as late as 15 August did not regard the situation as serious. Halder, *War Journal*, 7:44 (entry for 15 August). His judgment fortified by this incident, Hitler proceeded peremptorily to order the diverging offensives to the north and south, thereby totally rejecting the strategic reasoning of his senior military advisers. Hitler added insult to injury by bluntly criticizing the army leadership in a study dated 22 August. This criticism, together with Hitler's apparent lack of confidence in the professional skills of the Army High Command, nearly led Halder and Brauchitsch to resign. Hitler's criticism is in his signed "Studie," dated 22 August 1941, in *KTB/OKW*, 1:1063—68. Halder regarded Hitler's decision to postpone the attack on Moscow to be "the final turning point of the Eastern campaign" and admitted that the Staraya Russa attack had helped influence Hitler's decisions at this critical time. See Franz Halder, *Hitler as War Lord*, translated by Paul Findlay (London: Putnam, 1950), 44—47. See also Barry Leach, *German Strategy Against Russia, 1939—1941* (London: Oxford University Press, 1973), 209—17; Seaton, *Russo-German War*, 142—52; and Warlimont, *Inside*, 190—92.

46. Halder, *War Journal*, 7:63 (entry for 24 August). Halder's assessment is confirmed by the strength reports of forward units. On 21 August, for example, the German Sixteenth Army (Army Group North) reported that each of its divisions had suffered at least 40 percent total casualties since the beginning of the campaign. A.O.K. 16 [Armeeoberkommando 16], Ia, "Gefechtskraft der Div., An Heeresgruppe Nord," dated 21 August 1941, NAM T-312/548/8156867—8156869.

47. For an analysis of German supply problems throughout Operation Barbarossa, see "Russian Roulette," in Martin van Creveld, *Supplying War* (London: Cambridge University Press, 1977), 142—80. See also U.S. Department of the Army, Pamphlet no. 20—202, *German Tank Maintenance in World War II* (Washington, DC: U.S. Government Printing Office, 1954), 2—3, 21—23, 26.

48. On 16 August, Halder projected that German personnel replacements would be virtually exhausted by 1 October. Halder, *War Journal*, 7:49. By 1 September, Halder was weighing the possibility of disbanding twelve divisions to cover anticipated winter losses. Ibid., 7:79. See also DA Pam 20—261a, 71—72; and Seaton, *Russo-German War*, 171—75.

49. Alan S. Milward, *The German Economy at War* (New York: Oxford University Press, 1965), 39—45; Leach, *German Strategy*, 133—35, 140—45.

50. The battles around Smolensk are described in Hans Baumann, "Die Kesselschlacht von Smolensk und die Abwehrkämpfe westlich des Wop," in *Die 35. Infanterie-Division im 2. Weltkrieg, 1939—1945*, edited by Hans Baumann (Karlsruhe: Verlag G. Braun, 1964), 93—100; Hoth, *Panzer-Operationen*, 98—102; Guderian, *Panzer Leader*, 176—82; and *KTB/OKW*, 1:439—58 (entries for 22 July—8 August). According to the Soviet official history, the Russians first used their new *Katyusha* multiple rocket launchers in this fighting. P.N. Pospelov, et al., eds., *Istoriya Velikoi*

Otechestvennoi Voiny Sovetskogo Soyuza 1941—1945, 6 vols. (Moscow: Voenizdat, 1961), 2:66, hereafter cited as *Istoriya*.

51. *Istoriya*, 2:69.

52. Guderian, *Panzer Leader*, 181, 186. The figure of 450 miles given by Guderian on page 186 is presumably the distance to the nearest serviceable rebuilt railroad—probably not far from the 22 June border. On the formation of the Yelnya salient, see Fugate, *Barbarossa*, 128—33.

53. Guderian, *Panzer Leader*, 181, 182, 186; Halder, *War Journal*, 7:2 (entry for 1 August).

54. Guderian, *Panzer Leader*, 179.

55. Plocher, *German Air Force*, 107—8, 110—11.

56. Guderian, *Panzer Leader*, 185.

57. Ibid., 189.

58. Halder, *War Journal*, 7:11—12 (entry for 3 August).

59. Plocher, *German Air Force*, 116.

60. DA Pam 20—261a, 65; "Tagesmeldungen der Operations-Abteilung des GenStdH," *KTB/OKW*, 1:558, 561 (reports for 7 and 8 August). See also Fugate, *Barbarossa*, 163—67.

61. Halder, *War Journal*, 7:17 (entry for 4 August).

62. Ibid., 7:22 (entry for 6 August).

63. DA Pam 20—261a, 65; "Tagesmeldungen," *KTB/OKW*, 1:567 (report for 12 August).

64. *Istoriya*, 2:73—74.

65. Halder, *War Journal*, 7:47 (entry for 15 August).

66. Soviet air superiority is mentioned in "Tagesmeldungen," *KTB/OKW*, 1:565 (report for 11 August). The pressure on Ninth Army is discussed briefly in Fugate, *Barbarossa*, 201—2.

67. Werner Haupt, *Heeresgruppe Mitte 1941—1945* (Dorheim: Hans-Henning Podzun, 1968), 73.

68. "Tagesmeldungen," *KTB/OKW*, 1:575—89 (reports for 17—24 August); Halder, *War Journal*, 7:55, 70—71 (entries for 19 and 28 August). The unit on the 161st Division's right flank was the 7th Regiment, 28th Infantry Division. The Soviet attacks during this period are described in the 7th Regiment's unit history, Romuald Bergner, *Schlesische Infanterie: Grenadier-Regiment 7* (Bochum: Heinrich Pöppinghaus Verlag, 1980), 88—103. The 161st Division was replaced by the 14th Motorized Infantry Division. This unit became available for employment only through Bock's pleas to delay that unit's departure for the attack on Leningrad. "Tagesmeldungen," *KTB/OKW*, 1:589 (report for 24 August).

69. "Tagesmeldungen," *KTB/OKW*, 1:591 (report for 25 August).

70. Halder, *War Journal*, 7:70 (entry for 28 August). The fighting in the V Corps sector is described in Baumann, *35. Infanterie-Division*, 100—102.

71. "Tagesmeldungen," *KTB/OKW*, 1:595 (report for 27 August).

72. Halder, *War Journal*, 7:69 (entry for 27 August).

73. Ibid., 7:49 (entry for 16 August).

74. Günther Blumentritt, "Moscow," in *The Fatal Decisions*, edited by Seymour Freidin and William Richardson (New York: William Sloane Associates, 1956), 61.

75. *Das Buch der 78. Sturm Division* (Tubingen: Buchdruckerei H. Lauppir, n.d.), 59—60. The general shortage of barbed wire and mines is mentioned in Halder, *War Journal*, 7:50 (entry for 16 August).

76. *78. Sturm Division*, 60—61. Other comments on the state of Yelnya defenses are in Benignus Dippold, "Commitment of the 183rd Infantry Division," Foreign Military Studies no. MS D-223 (Historical Division, U.S. Army, Europe, 1947), 25. General Dippold's 183d Division relieved the 78th Division at Yelnya between 18 and 20 September.

77. Halder, *War Journal*, 7:43, 49 (entries for 14 and 16 August); Wilhelm Meyer-Detring, *Die 137. Infanteriedivision im Mittelabschnitt der Ostfront* (Petzenkirchen, Austria: Kameradschaft der Bergmann-Division, 1962), 62—77, 274—75.

78. "Tagesmeldungen," *KTB/OKW*, 1:584 (report for 22 August); *Istoriya*, 2:75; and Zhukov, *Vospominaniya*, 289. The Soviet Reserve *Front* facing Yelnya was Zhukov's first field command of World War II. Zhukov had previously served as chief of the Soviet General Staff, being reassigned from that post on 29 July. Zhukov observed German tanks and assault guns dug in near Yelnya at the time of his arrival there. These presumably were elements of the German XLVI Panzer Corps. If Zhukov is correct, it means that the Germans were so pressed to occupy their thin lines at Yelnya that they violated the cardinal principle of panzer operations by posting stationary armored vehicles along their perimeter instead of holding them exclusively in reserve for counterattack.

79. Zhukov, *Vospominaniya*, 290.

80. Halder, *War Journal*, 7:69 (entry for 27 August); Guderian, *Panzer Leader*, 203, 208. Guderian was a difficult subordinate and managed, at one time or another, to alienate all three field marshals under whom he served during Barbarossa (Brauchitsch, Bock, and Günther von Kluge), as well as General Halder, the chief of the General Staff. On Guderian's relations with his superiors during this period, see Guderian, *Panzer Leader*, 208—10; Halder, *War Journal*, 7:62, 68—69, 77 (entries for 24, 27, and 31 August); and Kenneth Macksey, *Guderian: Creator of the Blitzkrieg* (New York: Stein and Day, 1975), 131—33, 137—40, 148—51.

81. "Tagesmeldungen," *KTB/OKW*, 1:601, 603 (reports for 30 and 31 August).

82. Small-unit actions in the Yelnya area are described in Carrell, *Hitler*, 90—96; and *78. Sturm Division*, 62—69.

83. "Tagesmeldungen," *KTB/OKW*, 1:568—604 (reports for 13—31 August); Halder, *War Journal*, 7:77 (entry for 31 August).

84. Halder, *War Journal*, 7:80 (entry for 2 September); "Tagesmeldungen," *KTB/OKW*, 1:614 (report for 5 September). The Soviet official history claims that Red Army forces finally stormed Yelnya and overran German defenses. However, Zhukov supports the German version by noting that the Germans voluntarily withdrew. Compare *Istoriya*, 2:75; and Zhukov, *Vospominaniya*, 292. The best account of the Yelnya fighting in English is Fugate, *Barbarossa*, 167—83.

85. *Istoriya*, 2:75—76.

86. *78. Sturm Division*, 67; Haupt, *Heeresgruppe Mitte*, 78.

87. Halder, *War Journal*, 7:124 (entry for 26 September). Halder also recorded that the German armies on the Eastern Front had a net deficit of 200,000 men.

88. Klaus Reinhardt, *Die Wende vor Moskau: Das Scheitern der Strategie Hitlers im Winter 1941—1942* (Stuttgart: Deutsche Verlags-Anstalt, 1972), 315; Blumentritt, "Moscow," 61.

89. Quoted in Albert Seaton, *The Battle for Moscow, 1941—1942* (London: Rupert Hart-Davis, 1971), 300.

90. Halder noted on 11 September that Army Group Center had managed to accumulate only one ammunition issue in its stockpiles. Halder, *War Journal*, 7:91. Even this paltry ammunition buildup was apparently accomplished at the expense of fuel and ration deliveries. See Van Creveld, *Supplying War*, 168—71.

91. Sydnor, *Soldiers*, 170—86; Haupt, *Heeresgruppe Nord*, 67—86.

92. Leon Goure, *The Siege of Leningrad* (Stanford, CA: Stanford University Press, 1962), 83—85; DA Pam 20—261a, 73—75.

93. "Tagesmeldungen," *KTB/OKW*, 1:661 (report for 26 September).

94. Halder, *War Journal*, 7:106. See also Guderian, *Panzer Leader*, 202—25; and Werthen, *Geschichte*, 63—67.

95. "Weisung Nr. 35," in Walter Hubatsch, ed., *Hitlers Weisungen für die Kriegführungen 1939—1945: Dokumente des Oberkommandos der Wehrmacht* (Frankfurt am Main: Bernard und Graefe Verlag für Wehrwesen, 1962), 150—53; DA Pam 20—261a, 75—76.

96. Halder, *War Journal*, 7:84 (entry for 5 September).

97. Alan F. Wilt, "Hitler's Late Summer Pause in 1941," *Military Affairs* 45 (December 1981):189.

98. Seaton, *Russo-German War*, 177—78; Hoth, *Panzer-Operationen*, 130—31.

99. The *Totenkopf* Division was holding an extremely wide sector—approximately fifteen miles—at the time of these Russian attacks. Even so, the *Waffen SS* officers and soldiers seem to have been somewhat lax in preparing their defensive positions. See Sydnor, *Soldiers*, 185—86, 188—97. Although *Waffen SS* tactical doctrine was nearly identical to that of the German Army in most respects, *Waffen SS* units apparently despised the elastic defense in depth as being unworthy of their courage and steadfastness. The *SS* increasingly accepted the principles of Elastic Defense as the war progressed. See Klaus Moelhoff, "Experiences with Russian Methods of Warfare and Their Utilization in Training at the Waffen SS Panzer Grenadier School," Foreign Military Studies no. MS D-154 (Historical Division, U.S. Army, Europe, 1947), 11—13. Early in the war, SS units occasionally suffered heavy casualties by putting National Socialist ardor ahead of tactical good sense. See George H. Stein, *The Waffen SS: Hitler's Elite Guard at War, 1939—1945* (Ithaca, NY: Cornell University Press, 1966), 91—92.

100. Breithaupt, *Geschichte*, 123—33.

101. Halder, *War Journal*, 7:138 (entry for 4 October).

102. Hoth, *Panzer-Operationen*, 136; "Tagesmeldungen," *KTB/OKW*, 1:702 (report for 15 October). Soviet accounts of the Vyazma-Bryansk battles are vague about Russian losses. The Vyazma pocket contained the Nineteenth, Twentieth, Twenty-Fourth, and Thirty-Second Armies, while the Bryansk *Kessel* snared major elements of the Third and Thirteenth Armies. *GPWSU*, 86—90 (including map facing page 88).

103. See, for example, Walter Kranz, "Meine Feuertaufe bei Wjasma," in Baumann, *35. Infanterie-Division*; and the account of 6th Panzer Division in "hedgehog defense" at Vyazma in DA Pam 20—201, 22—23. An analysis of the German tactics at Vyazma is in MS T-28, 89—92.

104. *Istoriya*, 2:240—44; Zhukov, *Vospominaniya*, 326—29; and Erickson, *Road to Stalingrad*, 216—19.

105. Halder, *War Journal*, 7:147 (entry for 8 October); Otto Dietrich quoted in Alan Bullock, *Hitler: A Study in Tyranny*, rev. ed. (New York: Harper and Row, 1962), 654.

106. Seaton, *Russo-German War*, 197.

107. See Eberhard von Mackensen, *Vom Bug zum Kaukasus: Das III. Panzerkorps im Feldzug gegen Sowjetrussland 1941/42* (Neckargemuend: Scharnhorst Buchkameradschaft, 1967), 41—42; and also the comments of Ewald von Kleist in Basil H. Liddell Hart, *The Other Side of the Hill*, 2d ed. (London: Cassell, 1973), 281—82.

108. Halder, *War Journal*, 7:187—89 (entries for 28 and 29 November). See also Rundstedt's remarks in Liddell Hart, *The Other Side*, 282.

109. Halder, *War Journal*, 7:193, 195 (entries for 30 November and 1 December); Seaton, *Russo-German War*, 197; Warlimont, *Inside*, 194.

110. Halder, *War Journal*, 7:196 (entry for 1 December); "Tagesmeldungen," *KTB/OKW*, 1:786—87 (report for 1 December).

111. Plocher, *German Air Force*, 222.

112. Seaton, *Russo-German War*, 194.

113. Mackensen, *Bug*, 44.

114. Halder, *War Journal*, 7:173 (entry for 21 November).

115. Werthen, *Geschichte*, 76.

116. Halder, *War Journal*, 7:195 (entry for 1 December).

117. A secret General Staff memorandum dated 6 November 1941 calculated the effective strength of the 136 German divisions deployed in Russia to be that of only 83 full-strength divisions. Infantry divisions averaged 65 percent of full combat strength, while motorized infantry divisions and panzer divisions were rated at 60 percent and 35 percent respectively. "Beurteilung der Kampfkraft des Ostheeres," *KTB/OKW*, 1:1074—75.

118. For accounts of Operation Taifun's final phase, see Reinhardt, *Die Wende*, 162—71; Seaton, *Battle for Moscow*, 152—69; Alfred Turney, *Disaster at Moscow: Von Bock's Campaigns, 1941—1942* (London: Cassell and Co., 1971), 136—51; Bergner, *Schlesische Infanterie*, 119—33; and MS T-28, 61—73.

119. Halder, *War Journal*, 7:170, 178, 190 (entries for 19, 23, and 29 November).

120. "Weisung Nr. 39," in Hubatsch, *Hitlers*, 171—74. The army's implementing directive, "Weisung für die Aufgaben des Ostheeres im Winter 1941/42," is in *KTB/OKW*, 1:1076—82.

Chapter 3

1. "Anlage 1 zu OKH, GenStdH, Op.Abt.(Ia) Nr. 1693141," in *KTB/OKW*, 1:1075—76. See also DA Pam 20—261a, 91; Reinhardt, *Die Wende*, 202—4; and MS T-28, 134—36.

2. Guderian, *Panzer Leader*, 260.

3. Army Group Center War Diary, quoted in Reinhardt, *Die Wende*, 214; Halder, *War Journal*, 7:209 (entry for 8 December).

4. Halder, *War Journal*, 7:206 (entry for 7 December).

5. *Istoriya*, 2:280—81; Halder, *War Journal*, 7:206, 211 (entries for 7 and 10 December); and Guderian, *Panzer Leader*, 261—62. The fighting withdrawal of the 10th Motorized Division from its positions east of Tula is described in August Schmidt, *Geschichte der 10. Division, 1933—1945* (Bad Nauheim: Podzun Verlag, 1963), 117—19. Retreats by the 10th Motorized Division and by the 269th Infantry Division both opened critical gaps in the German front that could not immediately be closed. See Hossbach, *Infanterie*, 170—71; and Halder, *War Journal*, 7:215 (entry for 12 December).

6. *Istoriya*, 2:281; Halder, *War Journal*, 7:212—15 (entries for 10 and 12 December); Guderian, *Panzer Leader*, 262; and MS T-28, 33.

7. Halder, *War Journal*, 7:225 (entry for 15 December).

8. Guderian argues that some of the intermediate positions occupied by the Germans in October during the advance on Moscow had been partially fortified and constituted rearward positions of a sort. This is probably an exaggeration. At best, these positions would have consisted of hastily prepared bunkers and trenches without minefields or other obstacles. All would probably have been buried by the intervening snowfall. Field Marshal von Bock, Guderian's superior, discounted the value of any such positions. Compare Guderian, *Panzer Leader*, 259, 262; and Seaton, *Battle for Moscow*, 181.

9. See comments by General Günther Blumentritt and General Kurt von Tippelskirch described in Liddell Hart, *The Other Side*, 284, 289; and MS T-28, 58—59. One particularly eerie reminder of the 1812 campaign was the Kutusov Monument at Borodino, commemorating the Russian field marshal's victorious efforts to repel Napoleon's invasion. Several German divisions passed by that site during their own winter retreats, an omen that did not go unremarked. See Meyer-Detring, *137. Infanteriedivision*, 100; and Martin Gareis, *Kampf und Ende der Frankisch-Sudetendeutschen 98. Infanterie-Division* (Bad Nauheim: Hans-Henning Podzun, 1956), picture facing page 176, 177.

10. Guderian, *Panzer Leader*, 259; Halder, *War Journal*, 7:221—22 (entry for 14 December).

11. Halder, *War Journal*, 7:224 (entry for 15 December); Reinhardt, *Die Wende*, 214; and MS T-28, 119.

12. Seaton, *Battle for Moscow*, 181; Seaton, *Russo-German War*, 227 (entry for 16 December); and "Abschrift, OpAbt (IM) Nr. 1725/41," dated 16 December 1941, in *KTB/OKW*, 1:1083.

13. Halder, *War Journal*, 7:227 (entry for 16 December). Schmundt was completely dedicated to Hitler and had made a recent visit to Army Group Center's headquarters. While Schmundt was there, Bock had incautiously confessed his own misgivings about a winter retreat. Schmundt reported these to Hitler, who used them as ammunition to refute the recommendations of Brauchitsch, Halder, and even Bock. See Seaton, *Battle for Moscow*, 180—81.

14. Seaton, *Battle for Moscow*, 178—79; Halder, *War Journal*, 7:227 (entry for 16 December).

15. "Fernschreiben, GenStdH, OpAbt (III) Nr. 1736/41," dated 18 December 1941, in *KTB/OKW*, 1:1084.

16. See Bullock, *Hitler*, 665—69; Walter Görlitz, *History of the German General Staff, 1657—1945*, translated by Brian Battershaw (New York: Praeger, 1953), 404—6; and Gordon Craig, *The Politics of the Prussian Army, 1640—1945* (London: Oxford University Press, 1955), 468—503. Hitler's stand-fast order was almost univerally opposed by high-level commanders, and most made no secret of their dislike of Hitler's instructions. See Reinhardt, *Die Wende*, 222.

17. Halder, *War Journal*, 7:193, 206 (entries for 30 November and 7 December).

18. Joseph Goebbels, *The Goebbels Diaries, 1942—1943*, edited, translated, and with an introduction by Louis P. Lochner (Garden City, NY: Doubleday, 1948), 135—36, hereafter cited as *Goebbels Diaries*.

19. Halder, *Hitler as War Lord*, 49.

20. Guderian, *Panzer Leader*, 263—70.

21. Halder, *War Journal*, 7:250 (entry for 8 January 1942). Not all of the sanctions against Hoepner were enforced. See Seaton, *Russo-German War*, 236. Hoepner wore his uniform on at least one later occasion—as an accomplice in the 20 July 1944 attempt to assassinate Hitler and seize control of the German government. See Gerald Reitlinger, *The SS: Alibi of a Nation, 1922—1945* (Englewood Cliffs, NJ: Prentice-Hall, 1981), 321—22.

22. Seaton, *Russo-German War*, 245; Haupt, *Heeresgruppe Nord*, 111.

23. A brief summary of major command changes, including relief dates, is in Andreas Hillgruber, "Einführung," *KTB/OKW*, 2:39—40. Görlitz counts General Karl von Stülpnagel, who was relieved from command of the Seventeenth Army in early October, as a victim of Hitler's vengeance as well. However, Stülpnagel's relief seems to have been primarily the result of criticism by Rundstedt and Brauchitsch of Stülpnagel's timid leadership. Compare Gorlitz, *History*, 403; and Halder, *War Journal*, 7:138 (entry for 4 October). See also Guderian, *Panzer Leader*, 273—74.

24. See testimony of General August Winter in *Trial of the Major War Criminals Before the International Military Tribunal, Nuremberg, 14 November 1945—October 1946* (Nuremberg: International Military Tribunal, 1948), 15:604—5. Most changes of senior commanders were publicly represented as being due to the incumbent's ill health. Poor health was a contributing factor in the replacement of some officers, several of whom were more than sixty years old. (Rundstedt, born in 1875, had actually been called out of retirement to take command of an army group in 1939.) Brauchitsch, Bock, and Strauss, to name three, were all suffering from physical ailments at the time they were relieved. However, Hitler's primary intent was to remove uncooperative senior officers, not just unhealthy ones.

25. Seaton, *Battle for Moscow*, 222—26.

26. T. N. Dupuy, *A Genius for War: The German Army and General Staff, 1807—1945* (Englewood Cliffs, NJ: Prentice-Hall, 1977), 116. See also Rudolf Hofmann, "Das XXIX A.K. in der Abwehr auf breiter Front am Nordfluegel der 6. Armee im Winter 1941/42," chapter 5 in "Selected Corps Operations on the Eastern Front," by Hellmuth Reinhardt, et al., Foreign Military Studies no. MS P-143b (Historical Division, U.S. Army, Europe, 1954), 178, hereafter cited as MS P-143b-5.

27. Halder, *War Journal*, 7:197 (entry for 3 July). Hitler had an intellectual grasp of *Auftragstaktik*, even if he found it difficult to tolerate in practice. In one of the rambling monologues that he periodically inflicted on his dinner guests, Hitler had remarked on 1 August 1941: "The

Wehrmacht gives its highest distinction to the man who, acting against orders, saves the situation by his discernment and decisiveness." Adolph Hitler, *Hitler's Table Talk, 1941—1944: His Private Conversations*, 2d ed., translated by Norman Cameron and R. H. Stevens (London: Weidenfeld and Nicholson, 1973), 19.

28. Frido von Senger und Etterlin, *Neither Fear Nor Hope*, translated by George Malcolm (New York: E. P. Dutton and Co., 1964), 219—22.

29. "197. Inf. Division Abt.Ia Nr. 264/42. Betr.: Fragebogen," dated 10 May 1942, NAM T-78/202/6145735.

30. Hossbach, *Infanterie*, 170.

31. Ibid., 171. See also the experiences of the 52d Infantry Division described in Lothar Rendulic, "Combat in Deep Snow," Foreign Military Studies no. MS D-106 (Historical Division, U.S. Army, Europe, 1947), 12—14.

32. Rudolf von Roman, "The 35th Infantry Division Between Moscow and Gzhatsk, 1941," Foreign Military Studies no. MS D-285 (Historical Division, U.S. Army, Europe, 1947), 8, hereafter cited as MS D-285.

33. Gareis, *Kampf*, 178—79.

34. MS D-285, 3—6, 22—30.

35. MS T-28, 123.

36. A discussion of the problems affecting German weapons in deep snow and severe cold is in "Anlage zu Gen.Kdo. XX.A.K. Ia Nr. 2644/42 (Erfahrungen im Winterfeldzug)," dated 16 May 1942, NAM T-78/202/6145569, 6145578—6145581, hereafter cited as "XX.A.K.—Erfahrungen"; and in "5 Panzer-Division Abt Ia Nr. 427/42. Erfahrungsbericht der 5. Panzer-Division über den Winterkrieg 1941/42 in Russland," dated 20 May 1942, NAM T-78/202/6145541—6145542. Though the German Army had previously developed a shaped-charge antitank shell, bureaucratic resistance had limited distribution of this ammunition. According to Greiffenberg, an appeal by Field Marshal von Kluge directly to Hitler helped to speed up deliveries of this ammunition, which stiffened German antitank defense somewhat. See MS T-28, 140.

37. MS T-28, 123; MS P-143b-5, 163.

38. Hossbach, *Infanterie*, 173—74.

39. MS P-143b-5, 162; MS T-28, 139. Through 5 January 1942, total German officer losses on the Eastern Front amounted to 26,775 killed, wounded, and missing. In view of the shortage of combat officers, General Halder agreed on 3 January that the "promotion of First Lieutenants and Captains must be accelerated, as nearly all are commanding battalions now." Halder, *War Journal*, 7:248 (entries for 3 and 5 January). Through the first six months of the Russian campaign, the German Army included large numbers of elderly reserve officers as regimental and even battalion commanders. Although these officers were adequate for the relatively easy campaigns in Poland and France, the arduous conditions in Russia led to the wholesale replacement of these reservists with younger, tougher officers. According to one officer with extensive Eastern Front experience, "in 1942 we had no more commanders older than 40 years except generals." Statement by Lieutenant General (Ret.) Heinz-Georg Lemm at the 1985 Art of War Symposium, reproduced in U.S. Army War College, Center for Land Warfare, *1985 Art of War Symposium: From the Dnepr to the Vistula—Soviet Offensive Operations, November 1943—August 1944, a Transcript of Proceedings* (Carlisle Barracks, PA: U.S. Army War College, August 1985), 582.

40. Hossbach, *Infanterie*, 173. See also "263. Infanterie Division. Der 1. Generalstabsoffizier (Anlage 5 zu A.O.K. 4 Ia Nr. 677/42)," dated 21 August 1942, NAM T-312/184/7730365; and "XXXXIII A.K. Der Chef der Generalstabes Ia Nr. 1391/42. Betr.: 'Stützpunkt,' 'Widerstandlinie,' " dated 22 August 1942, NAM T-312/184/7730355.

41. Meyer-Detring, *137. Infanteriedivision*, 114. The gradual adoption of strongpoint tactics in the 34th Infantry Division is traced by the commander of the 107th Infantry Regiment in "Infanterie-Regiment 107 Kommandeur. Betr., 'Stützpunkt' oder Widerstandlinie. Bericht eines Truppenkommandeurs," dated 17 August 1942, NAM T-312/184/7730359—7730360.

42. MS T-28, 283d.

43. Baumann, *35. Infanterie-Division*, 137.

44. Panzer Group 3 War Diary, 19 December 1941, quoted in Reinhardt, *Die Wende*, 207.

45. MS D-285, 9; Gerhard Dieckhoff, *Die 3. Infanterie-Division* (Göttingen: Erich Borries, 1960), 149; and Horst Grossman, *Geschichte der rheinisch-westfälischen 6. Infanterie-Division 1939—1945* (Bad Nauheim: Hans-Henning Podzun, 1958), 103. Some divisions disbanded entire infantry battalions, using those personnel as fillers for other units. The 78th Division, for example, disbanded one battalion in each of its regiments, and these disbanded battalions were never reconstituted. See *78. Sturm Division*, 151.

46. Panzer Group 3 War Diary, 19 December 1941; Panzer Group 4 War Diary, 18 December 1941; both quoted in Reinhardt, *Die Wende*, 207.

47. Allen F. Chew, *Fighting the Russians in Winter: Three Case Studies*, Leavenworth Papers no. 5 (Fort Leavenworth, KS: Combat Studies Institute, U.S. Army Command and General Staff College, 1981), 33; MS T-28, 272; and U.S. Department of the Army, Pamphlet no. 20—291, *Effects of Climate on Combat in European Russia* (Washington, DC: U.S. Government Printing Office, 1952), 3—4, hereafter cited as DA Pam 20—291.

48. On taking command of the German Army on 19 December, Hitler cited the inadequate cold-weather provisions as proof of the "mechanical," uninspired spirit of the army's officer leadership. Halder, *War Journal*, 7:233 (entry for 19 December). Concerning the winter clothing drive, see *Goebbels Diaries*, 130—31, 136. The *Sicherheitsdienst* (Security Service or *SD*), whose unsavory activities included monitoring German civilian morale, noted in a secret report on 22 January 1942: "As regards the reasons for and the implications of the wool collection [Nazi Party clothing drive], the event . . . has affected the population in the civilian sector more than any other since the beginning of the war. . . . People had seen in the dismissal of Brauchitsch an indirect reply to the many questions as to who was responsible for the failures to provide winter clothing." See Jeremy Noakes and Geoffrey Pridham, eds., *Documents on Nazism, 1919—1945* (New York: Viking Press, 1975), 661—62. See also Willi A. Boelcke, ed., *The Secret Conferences of Dr. Goebbels: The Nazi Propaganda War, 1939—1943*, translated by Ewald Osers (New York: E. P. Dutton, 1970), 196—97, 199—200, 223—24.

49. Guderian, for example, consistently blames the *OKH* (the army's leadership) for his supply problems and claims that the problem of winter clothing "would have been the easiest to avoid of all our difficulties" had senior General Staff planners only exercised sufficient forethought. Guderian absolves Hitler from responsibility by asserting that the army's quartermaster general lied to Hitler about winter clothing deliveries so that Hitler was unaware of any deficiency until informed of it by Guderian on 20 December. (Guderian also credits himself with having inspired the Nazi Party's clothing collection with his complaints. Based on entries in Goebbels' diary predating Guderian's 20 December meeting with Hitler, Guderian's claim is greatly exaggerated.) Guderian, *Panzer Leader*, 233—35, 237, 266—67. See also MS T-28, 141, where one of the German officer authors blames the winter clothing shortage on the "lack of foresight on the part of competent headquarters."

50. Halder, *War Journal*, 6:216 (entry for 9 July), 7:7, 159 (entries for 2 August and 10 November). See also Boelcke, ed., *Secret Conferences*, 191—92.

51. Mueller-Hillebrand, *Das Heer*, 3:30; and Van Creveld, *Supplying War*, 173—74.

52. MS T-28, 275—76; DA Pam 20—291, 19; and Guderian, *Panzer Leader*, 265—66.

53. Van Creveld, *Supplying War*, 174. See also Seaton, *Russo-German War*, 218—19; and MS T-28, 210.

54. German summer clothing included a long wool overcoat which, with some padding from straw or newspapers, made a passable winter outer garment. Lieutenant General (Ret.) Heinz-Georg Lemm, Interview with the author, Carlisle Barracks, PA, 2 May 1985. Lemm was a platoon leader and company commander on the Eastern Front during the winter of 1941—42. Also, many German troops removed suitable winter clothing items from Soviet corpses and, in some cases at least, probably from Russian prisoners as well. Such expedients were risky, however. A 17 December 1941 regimental order to soldiers of the 488th Infantry Regiment directed that German soldiers

in the forward lines wear only German uniform items, since German prisoners taken wearing Russian garments were being regarded by the enemy as looters and "handled accordingly" (i.e., shot). German combat troops were ordered to "exchange" any such Russian items with troops assigned to rearward units, a directive that was in all likelihood widely ignored. See "Regimentsbefehl," Anlage 16 in Meyer-Detring, *137. Infanteriedivision*, 277.

55. Hossbach, *Infanterie*, 168. See also Gareis, *Kampf*, 201; and Guderian, *Panzer Leader*, 266—67. German frostbite casualties alone during the winter of 1941—1942 exceeded 250,000, while total German losses (killed, wounded, missing, sick) from December 1941—March 1942 amounted to 723,200. See Berthold Mikat, "Die Erfrierungen bei den Soldaten der deutschen Wehrmacht in letzten Weltkrieg," appendix 8 in "Frostbite Problems in the German Army During World War II," by Alfred Toppe, Foreign Military Studies no. MS P-062 (Historical Division, U.S. Army, Europe, 1951), 2, 3; and Mueller-Hillebrand, *137. Infanteriedivision*, 3:171, 206. Seaton estimates total German casualties (including frostbite) at 900,000 for the winter period. However, as not all frostbite casualties were unfit for duty, this figure probably overestimates the actual loss of German effectives. Seaton, *Russo-German War*, 228. So severe was the danger of frostbite that most German units adopted a policy similar to that used in the 12th Infantry Division, according to which no sentry would remain outdoors longer than thirty minutes and all sentries would always be posted either in pairs or within the sight of another sentry. Lemm interview.

56. Quoted in Steiger, *Panzertaktik*, 136.

57. A medical briefing to General Halder on 9 March 1942 reported 10,204 cases of typhus, of which 1,349 had proved fatal. Halder, *War Journal*, 7:281 (entry for 9 March).

58. Baumann, *35. Infanterie-Division*, 135; Chew, *Russians in Winter*, 38. Detailed reports on problems with German equipment (radios, vehicles, etc.) during winter conditions are in "78. Inf. Division Ia/Org. Nr. 243/42. Erfahrungsbericht," dated 9 May 1942, NAM T-78/202/6145688—6145692; "XX.A.K.—Erfahrungen," NAM T-78/202/6145581—6145585; and "197. Inf. Division. Fragebogen," NAM T-78/202/6145742—6145744. One former German officer recounted how, during the night of 24 January 1942 with the outside temperature at -56°C, four out of five machine guns and nearly half of the rifles in his company would not fire. Colonel (Ret.) Arnulf von Garn, Interview with the author, Carlisle Barracks, PA, 21 May 1986.

59. A brief contemporary discussion of the reasons for adopting the strongpoint defense may be found in "Hptm. Haderecker, Kdr, I./Inf. Rgt. 20 (mot). Betr.: Erfahrungsbericht. Stützpunktsystem oder H.K.L.," dated 17 August 1942, NAM T-312/184/7730344—7730345; "10 Inf. Div. (mot) Ia (Anlage zu A.O.K. 4 Ia Nr. 4885/42). Stützpunktartige Verteidigung oder durchlaufende Verteidigungssystem," dated 20 August 1942, NAM T-312/184/7730340—7730341; and "Generalkommando LVI. Pz.Korps. Der Chef des Generalstabes. Stellungnahme zur Frage Stützpunkte oder Widerstandslinie. (Anlage zu A.O.K. 4 Ia Nr. 4885/42)," dated 1 September 1942, NAM T-312/184/7730332—7730333. The first of these documents gives the views of a battalion commander; the second, a division staff officer; and the third, a panzer corps chief of staff. Though each sees the problem from a slightly different perspective, their conclusions are similar to those given in the text.

60. "Oberkommando der Wehrmacht Nr. 442277/41 WFSt/op(H)," dated 26 December 1941, in *KTB/OKW*, 1:1086—87.

61. MS T-28, 189.

62. "A.O.K. 4 Ia Nr. 166/42. Abschrift," dated 23 January 1942, NAM T-78/202/6146773—6146775. That this document received wide circulation is evident in that the copy in the National Archives microfilm collection shows a supplementary document reference number assigned by Army Group Center ("H.Gr. Mitte, Ia Nr. 826/42") and also in that this document was found at the end of the war in a file folder of the Training Branch of the German General Staff. The combat actions on which this document was based—defense of the Roslavl-Yukhnov-Moscow *Rollbahn* supply artery—are briefly described in Schmidt, *Geschichte*, 123—27. In an enlightening aside, Schmidt notes that this *Rollbahn* was the first asphalt-paved road that the 10th Motorized Division had yet encountered in the entire Russian campaign.

63. After-action report of the 35th Infantry Division, attached as an annex to "Generalkommando IX. Armeekorps Ia Nr. 916/42. Betr.: Erfahrungsbericht aus dem Winterkrieg 1941/42," dated 3 July 1942, NAM T-78/202/6145647. This annex is untitled and undated, having only the hand-

written notation "35. Inf. Division" written across the top of the first page. It is identified as "Erfahrungsbericht der 35. I.D." on the coversheet of the IX Corps report cited above, NAM T-78/202/6145611, and hereafter is cited as "Erfahrungsbericht—35. I.D." See also "78. Inf. Division Ia/Org. Nr. 243/42. Erfahrungsbericht," dated 9 May 1942, NAM T-78/202/6145680.

64. "A.O.K. 4 Ia Nr. 166/42. Abschrift," NAM T-78/202/6146773—6146774.

65. MS T-28, 192—93.

66. "A.O.K. 4 Ia Nr. 166/42. Abschrift," NAM T-78/202/6146775.

67. "87. Inf.-Div., Ia Nr. 273/42," dated 9 May 1942, NAM T-78/202/6145707. See also "331. Infanterie Division. Der 1. Generalstabs-Offz. Betr.: Erfahrungsbericht-Widerstandlinie-Stützpunkte," dated 25 August 1942, NAM T-312/184/7730353.

68. "Erfahrungsbericht—35. I.D.," NAM T-78/202/6145647.

69. "7. Division Ia/Nr. 0479/42: Betrifft: Beanwortung des Fragebogens des Panzer-A.O.K. 4 über Wintererfahrungen," dated 11 May 1942, NAM T-78/202/6145631, hereafter cited as "7. Division—Wintererfahrungen."

70. MS T-28, 187.

71. Compare, for example, differing priorities of work developed by the 7th Infantry Division, "7. Division—Wintererfahrungen," NAM T-78/202/6145632; the 35th Infantry Division, "Erfahrungsbericht—35 I.D.," NAM T-78/202/6145647; and the 87th Infantry Division, "87. Inf.-Div.," NAM T-78/202/6145706.

72. "Erfahrungsbericht—35. I.D.," NAM T-78/202/6145649. See also Paul Schulz, "Position Warfare in Winter 1941—1942 and Experiences," Foreign Military Studies no. MS D-298 (Historical Division, U.S. Army, Europe, 1947), 4—12, hereafter cited as MS D-298.

73. "Erfahrungsbericht—35. I.D.," NAM T-78/202/6145650.

74. Willibald Utz, "Experiences of a Mountain Infantry Regiment During the Battle of the Volkhov River (Mar—May 1942)," Foreign Military Studies no. MS D-291 (Historical Division, U.S. Army, Europe, 1947), 20—23, hereafter cited as MS D-291; "A.O.K. 4 Ia Nr. 166/42. Abschrift," NAM T-78/202/6146775; and "Oberst Heine, Kommandeur des Inf. Regt. 449. Betr.: Kampferfahrungen: Stützpunkt oder Widerstandlinie," dated 17 August 1942, NAM T-312/184/7730364.

75. "Erfahrungsbericht—35. I.D.," NAM T-78/202/6145649—6145650; Garn interview; and Lemm interview.

76. "87. Inf.-Div.," NAM T-78/202/6145708. See also "Erfahrungsbericht—35. I.D.," NAM T-78/202/6145650; and Fritz Wentzell, "Combat in the East," Foreign Military Studies no. MS B-266 (Historical Division, U.S. Army, Europe, 1952), 44.

77. "Erfahrungsbericht—35. I.D.," NAM T-78/202/6145650—6145651; "87. Inf.-Div.," NAM T-78/202/6145708. The 7th Division rigged even its antitank mines with tripwires. See "7. Division—Wintererfahrungen," NAM T-78/202/6145633.

78. Gustav Hoehne, "In Snow and Mud: 31 Days of Attack Under Seydlitz During Early Spring of 1942," Foreign Military Studies no. MS C-034 (Historical Division, U.S. Army, Europe, 1953), 5; Lemm interview. Lemm's 12th Infantry Division participated in the Demyansk fighting, and he recalled that the Soviet units in this sector lacked snowshoes or skis. Forced to wade through waist-deep snow, Russian attackers were shot by defending German troops with an ease that was "truly horrible to watch."

79. "7. Division—Wintererfahrungen," NAM T-78/202/6145632; "Erfahrungsbericht—35. I.D.," NAM T-78/202/6145650; MS D-298, 9; and MS D-285, 32—33.

80. MS D-285, 33. A sketch of this type obstacle is in "197. Inf. Division. Fragebogen," NAM T-78/202/6145754.

81. "7. Division—Wintererfahrungen," NAM T-78/202/6145633.

82. "78. Inf. Division. Erfahrungsbericht," NAM T-78/202/6145683. Other divisions disputed the value of this tactic. The 6th Infantry Division, for example, reckoned that Soviet winter clothing

allowed the Russians to spend nights wherever they pleased, and the telltale smoke of burning villages seemed only to invite Russian artillery fire. Grossmann, *Geschichte,* 93.

83. Grossmann, *Geschichte,* 99.

84. "Lagebericht AOK 6 an OKH/Fremde Heere Ost, v. 27.12.41." quoted in MS P-143b-5, 65—66.

85. Otto Zeltmann, "Closing of the Large Gap in the Front Between Demidov and Velikiye Luki in 1942," Foreign Military Studies no. MS D-231 (Historical Division, U.S. Army, Europe, 1947), 9—12, hereafter cited as MS D-231.

86. "Erfahrungsbericht der 5. Panzer-Division," NAM T-78/202/6145531.

87. "87. Inf. Div.," NAM T-78/202/6145707. See also "7. Division—Wintererfahrungen," NAM T-78/202/6145631; and Oskar Munzel, "Tactical and Technical Specialties of Winter Warfare," Foreign Military Studies no. MS P-089 (Historical Division, U.S. Army, Europe, 1951), 12.

88. Patrolling techniques varied greatly between units. The 7th Division preferred to dispatch its patrols only when absolutely necessary to clarify the enemy situation and considered the half-light of dawn or early evening best suited for reconnaissance work. In contrast, the 78th Division considered daytime patrols useless and sent its scouting parties out mostly at night. Compare "7. Division—Wintererfahrungen," NAM T-78/202/6145634; and "78. Division. Erfahrungsbericht," NAM T-78/202/6145682. See also "IX. Armeekorps. Erfahrungsbericht," NAM T-78/202/6145615.

89. "331. Infanterie Division. Erfahrungsbericht," NAM T-312/184/7730353.

90. "98. Inf. Division Ia. An den Herrn Chef des Generalstabes des Gen.Kdo XII. A.K.," dated 21 August 1942, NAM T-312/184/7730379. The 98th Division preferred a continuous linear-style defensive front and considered strongpoints useful mainly in the depth of the defensive zone.

91. See MS D-231, 2; MS T-28, 75; "XXXXIII A.K.," NAM T-312/184/7730356; "263. Infanterie Division," NAM T-312/184/7730365; and "197. Inf. Division. Fragebogen," NAM T-78/202/6145735.

92. See "197. Inf. Division. Fragebogen," NAM T-78/202/6145736; "Erfahrungsbericht—35. I.D.," NAM T-78/202/6145651—6145652; "7. Division—Wintererfahrungen," NAM T-78/202/6145633; "Infanterie-Regiment 487 Kommandeur. Betr.: Kampferfahrung Stützpunkt—Widerstandlinie," dated 21 August 1942, NAM T-312/184/7730347; "Der Chef des Generalstabes der 2. Armee. 2403/42 Betr.: Stützpunkt oder Widerstandlinie," dated 8 September 1942, NAM T-312/1660/000852; and Breithaupt, *Geschichte,* 157.

93. "87. Inf Div.," NAM T-78/202/6145708.

94. "197. Inf. Division. Fragebogen," NAM T-78/202/6145736.

95. "Erfahrungsbericht—35. I.D.," NAM T-78/202/6145651. See also MS D-285, 10—11; "87. Inf. Div.," NAM T-78/202/6145708; "5 Panzer-Division—Erfahrungsbericht," NAM T-78/202/6145532; and "Hptmn. Haderecker—Erfahrungsbericht," NAM T-312/184/7730346.

96. "78. Inf. Division. Erfahrungsbericht," NAM T-78/202/6145681.

97. "Erfahrungsbericht—35. I.D.," NAM T-78/202/6145652. See also MS D-285, 31—32.

98. MS D-285, 31.

99. The composition of local reserves, together with general techniques for immediate counterattack, is discussed in "197. Inf. Division. Fragebogen," NAM T-78/202/6145736; "XX. A.K.—Erfahrungen," NAM T-78/202/6145568—6145569; and "7. Division—Wintererfahrungen," NAM T-78/202/6145633—6145634.

100. Fretter-Pico, *Infanterie,* 66.

101. Ibid., 67. The 97th Light Infantry Division's battles are described briefly on pages 63—67. This unit's remarkable success earned it the following entry in Halder's diary on 15 December: "97th Division has put up a very good fight. Good work, Fretter-Pico!" Halder, *War Journal,* 7:224.

102. Erickson, *Road to Stalingrad,* 269—70.

103. A. Yekomovskiy, "Taktika sovietskoi armii v velikoi otechestvennoi voinye," *Voyenny Vestnik*, April 1967:14.

104. Quoted in A. Ryazanskiy, "Taktika tankovikh voisk v godi velikoi otechestvennoi voinie," *Voyenny Vestnik*, May 1967:18.

105. Yekimovskiy, "Taktika," 14.

106. Ibid., 14.

107. G. K. Zhukov, "Kontrnastupleniye pod Moskvoi," *Voyenno-Istorichesky Zhurnal*, October 1966:77.

108. A case in point is that of the 78th Infantry Division of the IX Corps. After days of heavy fighting against Soviet attacks, the 78th Division learned on 13 December that a heavy Soviet blow had broken the thin strongpoint line of the neighboring 267th Infantry Division. On 14 December, the 78th Division lost all contact with other German forces and discovered that strong Russian elements had taken up blocking positions across the division's rear. Under cover of darkness on the night of 14—15 December, the 78th Division initiated a breakout through the surrounding Soviet ring. Although harassed by Russian tanks and cavalry, the 78th Division successfully picked its way past enemy units and rejoined German forces on the Ruza River on 18 December. The other divisions of the IX Corps had similar experiences. See *78. Sturm Division*, 123—41; and Bergner, *Schlesische Infanterie*, 133—47.

109. Zhukov, "Kontrnastupleniye," 71—72.

110. Mueller-Hillebrand, *Das Heer*, 3:31.

111. DA Pam 20—261a, 100—101.

112. See Martin Jenner, *Die 216./272. Niedersachsische Infanterie-Division, 1939—1945* (Bad Nauheim: Podzun Verlag, 1964), 47—53.

113. MS D-231, 4.

114. Erickson, *Road to Stalingrad*, 298.

115. Ibid., 302.

116. Ibid., 319—22, 331—32, 352—53.

117. Zhukov, *Vospominaniya*, 355—57; *Istoriya*, 2:325—32. These deep strikes were also supported by sizable airborne forces. General Halder was relieved that these Soviet thrusts lacked sufficient strength to achieve major success. On 2 February 1942, Halder wrote:

> The scenes in this battle behind the front are absolutely grotesque and testify to the degree to which this war has degenerated into a sort of slugging bout which has no resemblance whatever to any form of warfare we have known. An instance in point is the inept commitment of a group of several divisions . . . against the deep flank of Army Group Center. It is ineffectual as an operational measure and will merely serve to pin down some of our forces for a while, without producing any decisive results.

Halder, *War Journal*, 7:263. The Soviet airborne operations are discussed in David M. Glantz, *The Soviet Airborne Experience*, Research Survey no. 4 (Fort Leavenworth, KS: Combat Studies Institute, U.S. Army Command and General Staff College, November 1984), 37—56.

118. Halder, *War Journal*, 7:254. The deteriorating situation on the front of Army Group Center is discussed in detail in Reinhardt, *Die Wende*, 245—55.

119. "Führerbefehl an die H.Gr. Mitte vom 15. Januar 1942 zum Rückzug auf die 'Winterstellung,' Gen.St.d.H./Op.Abt.(I) Nr. 420021/42," in *KTB/OKW*, 2:1268—69. The new defensive line authorized by Hitler was essentially the same as that urged by Bock a month earlier.

120. Seaton, *Russo-German War*, 233. See also Hossbach, *Infanterie*, 173; Grossmann, *Geschichte*, 94; and MS T-28, 187.

121. Erickson, *Road to Stalingrad*, 299—300.

122. Zhukov, *Vospominaniya*, 357. On 1 February 1942, Zhukov was named commander of the Western Theater in addition to the Western *Front*. In this new capacity, he also exercised operational control over the Kalinin and Bryansk *Fronts*.

123. Yekimovskiy, "Taktika," 14.

124. Zhukov, *Vospominaniya*, 357—58.

125. F. Samsonov, "Artilleriya v hodie voinie," *Voyenny Vestnik*, May 1965:74.

126. Ryazanskiy, "Taktika," 18.

127. Yekimovskiy, "Taktika," 14.

128. *Istoriya*, 2:318; Samsonov, "Artilleriya," 74; Ryazanskiy, "Taktika," 18; and Erickson, *Road to Stalingrad*, 302—3.

129. *Goebbels Diaries*, 132, 135.

130. Seaton, *Battle for Moscow*, 276—80.

131. See, for example, Halder, *War Journal*, 7:260, 266 (entries for 17 January and 7 February).

132. The author was unable to locate the original tasking document. However, several unit after-action reports cite "Oberkommando der 4. Pz. Armee Ia Nr. 1712/42," dated 17 April 1942, as the source of their efforts. See, for example, "78. Division. Erfahrungsbericht," NAM T-78/202/6145679. The 78th Division's report also repeats the specific questions posed by Fourth Panzer Army that guided the unit responses. When completed, these reports were actually forwarded to Third Panzer Army since Fourth Panzer Army's headquarters had, in the meantime, been transferred to the southern portion of the front in preparation for Operation Blau.

133. "XX. A.K.—Erfahrungen," NAM T-78/202/6145569.

134. "IX. Armeekorps—Erfahrungsbericht," NAM T-78/202/6145614.

135. "Erfahrungsbericht—35. I.D.," NAM T-78/202/6145653.

136. "OKH/GenStdH. Ausb. Abtlg. (II) Nr. 1550/42. Zusammenstellung von Osterfahrungen über Bekampfung von Panzerkampfwagen und Angaben über Panzerabwehrwaffen und Munition," dated 19 May 1942, NAM T-312/1283/000203. See also "252. Inf. Division. Erfahrungsbericht über Winterfeldzug 1941/42" (undated), NAM T-78/202/6145759.

137. "Erfahrungsbericht—35. I.D.," NAM T-78/202/6145653. This report mentions a Soviet reluctance to advance single tanks very far into German defensive areas, presumably for fear of antitank gunfire or infantry close assault. On the use of heavy flak guns in an antitank role, see "12. Flakdivision (mot.) Führ. Gruppe (Ia) B.B. Nr. 2160/42 Betr.: Flakkampftrupps, Einsatz und Gliederung," dated 11 September 1942, NAM T-312/189/7736198—7736200.

138. "Erfahrungsbericht—35. I.D.," NAM T-78/202/6145653. See also "Zusammenstellung von Osterfahrungen," NAM T-312/1283/000204.

139. "Erfahrungsbericht—35. I.D.," NAM T-78/202/6145653.

140. "7. Division—Wintererfahrungen," NAM T-78/202/6145634.

141. See "Ia der 34. Division. Betr.: 'Stützpunkt' oder 'Widerstandlinie,' " dated 17 August 1942, NAM T-312/184/7730358; and "10. Inf. Div. (mot)—Stützpunktartige Verteidigung," NAM T-312/184/7730342.

142. See Ogorkiewicz, *Armor*, 215—17; and Guderian, *Panzer Leader*, 276—83.

143. "Armee-Pionier-Führer, Armee-Oberkommando 2. Merkblatt für Panzervernichtungstrupps," dated 10 February 1942, NAM T-312/1660/00941. This brief pamphlet included sketches of newer Soviet tanks, with their vulnerable points highlighted, along with instructions on tactics, equipment, and training for antitank teams.

144. Halder, *War Journal*, 7:261, 263 (entries for 29 January and 2 February). The apparent product of these discussions was a Training Branch circular to German units, "Oberkommando

des Heeres. GenStdH./Ausb. Abt. (II) Nr. 1550/42. Betr.: Kampferfahrungen, Panzerabwehr," dated 19 May 1942, NAM T-312/1283/000199. This circular included "Zusammenstellung von Osterfahrungen" (cited in note 136) as an annex.

145. The full title of the decoration was *Sonderabzeichen für das Niederkampfen von Panzer kampfwagen durch Einzelkämpfer* (Special Badge for the Single-Handed Destruction of a Tank). This badge was actually a cloth patch worn prominently on the upper right sleeve of the uniform coat. As most other German decorations were worn on the front of the coat, it may be that the particular prominence given this award was a conscious attempt to counteract the "suicidal" aura that surrounded the idea of infantry-versus-tank combat. On 26 May 1942, Hitler also authorized a special campaign medal for all German soldiers who had served in Russia during the winter campaign. This *Medaille Winterschlacht im Osten* (Medal for the Winter Battle in the East) was commonly referred to in the ranks as the "frozen flesh medal." John R. Angolia, *For Führer and Fatherland: Military Awards of the Third Reich* (San Jose, CA: R. James Bender Publishing, 1976), 69, 109.

146. "252. Inf. Division. Erfahrungsbericht," NAM T-78/202/6145757—6145758.

147. "XX. A.K.—Erfahrungen," NAM T-78/202/6145567.

148. The tasking document is cited as "Chef des Generalstabes der Heeres vom 6.8.42" in "2. Armee. Stützpunkt oder widerstandlinie," NAM T-312/1660/00852.

149. "Infanterie-Regiment 488, Ia," dated 18 August 1942, NAM T-312/184/7730391.

150. "Infanterie-Regiment 289, Kommandeur. Betr.: Kampferfahrung," dated 17 August 1942, NAM T-312/184/7730380.

151. "2. Armee. Stützpunkt oder Widerstandlinie," NAM T-312/1660/00853.

152. "331. Infanterie Division. Erfahrungsbericht," NAM T-312/184/7730352.

153. "Infanterie-Regiment 434, Kommandeur," dated 17 August 1942, NAM T-312/184/7730339.

154. "Erfahrungsbericht—35. I.D.," NAM T-78/202/6145648. See also "Erfahrungsbericht der 5. Panzer-Division," NAM T-78/202/6145531.

155. "Hptmn. Haderecker, Erfahrungsbericht," NAM T-312/184/7730345.

156. "XXXXIII. A.K. 'Stützpunkt,' " NAM T-312/184/7730355. See also "Der Chef des Generalstabes des XII. A.K. An den Herrn Chef des Generalstabes der 4. Armee," dated 21 August 1942, NAM T-312/184/7730378.

157. See "Der Chef des Generalstabes des XII. A.K.," NAM T-312/184/7730377.

Chapter 4

1. The German plan of operations was set forth in Führer Directive 41, dated 5 April 1942. Written in large part by Hitler himself, this document lacks the clarity and conciseness of other such orders drafted by General Staff officers at Hitler's behest. Directive 41 is reproduced in *Blitzkrieg to Defeat: Hitler's War Directives, 1939—1945*, edited by H. R. Trevor-Roper (New York: Holt, Rinehart, and Winston, 1964), 116—21. On the evolution of German strategy for the 1942 campaign, see DA Pam 20—261a, 109—24; and Warlimont, *Inside*, 226—33.

2. DA Pam 20—261a, 116.

3. In 1941, the Soviet Union relied on the Caucasian oil-producing centers of Maikop, Grozny, and Baku for roughly 85 percent of its petroleum. However, oil production facilities in the Urals apparently were being frantically expanded even before Operation Blau began. See Seaton, *Russo-German War*, 266—67.

4. See Halder, *War Journal*, 7:252 (entry for 12 January).

5. "The Construction of a Strategic Defense Line in the East," Foreign Military Studies no. MS D-156 (Historical Division, U.S. Army, Europe, 1947), 3—4. The author of this monograph is

unknown but seems to have been a member of Olbricht's staff. Both General Olbricht and General Fromm were conspirators in the unsuccessful 20 July 1944 attempt on Hitler's life. Both were subsequently executed on Hitler's orders.

6. Ibid., 5—9.

7. Ibid., 10.

8. "Oberkommando des Heeres, GenStdH/Op.Abt.(Ia) Nr. 420053/42. Weisung für die Kampfführung im Osten nach Abschluss des Winters," dated 12 February 1942, in *KTB/OKW*, 1:1095.

9. DA Pam 20—261a, 129. Detachments of "fortification engineers" worked on the "fortified areas" off and on for the remainder of the year. See, for example, the report on the operations of various detachments in "General der Pioniere und Festungen. Abt. L (II O) Az. 11 Nr. 1665/42. Einsatz der Fest. Pi.-Dienststellen im Osten," dated 8 December 1942, NAM T-78/343/6300839.

10. Mueller-Hillebrand, *Das Heer*, 3:62; DA Pam 20—261a, 128—29, 130, 135—36. Army Group North, for example, lost 174,330 men (killed, wounded, missing) between the beginning of April and the end of August 1942, receiving in that time only 158,400 total replacements. See Burkhart Mueller-Hillebrand, "Der Feldzug gegen die Sowjetunion im Nordabschnitt der Ostfront (Zweiter Teil: Dezember 1941—Dezember 1942)," Foreign Military Studies no. MS P-114a (Historical Division, U.S. Army, Europe, 1954), 314, hereafter cited as MS P-114a.

11. DA Pam 20—261a, 130.

12. Mueller-Hillebrand, *Das Heer*, 3:63. See also Halder, *War Journal*, 7:377 (entry for 18 August) and footnote.

13. Compare Mueller-Hillebrand, *Das Heer*, 3:63; and DA Pam 20—261a, 135—36.

14. Halder, *War Journal*, 7:258 (entry for 24 January); DA Pam 20—261a, 137.

15. Halder, *War Journal*, 7:258 (entry for 24 January). See also Mueller-Hillebrand, *Das Heer*, 3:63; and DA Pam 20—261a, 137.

16. MS D-291, 22.

17. Haupt, *Heeresgruppe Nord*, 123—31. See also Hellmuth Reinhardt, et al., "Selected Army Operations on the Eastern Front (Operational)," Foreign Military Studies no. MS P-143a (Historical Division, U.S. Army, Europe [1954]), 265—75.

18. "Generalkommando I. A.K. Abt. Ia Nr. 1819/42. Korpsbefehl Nr. 194 für die Abwehrgliederung des I. A.K.," dated 8 July 1942, NAM T-312/838/9003278. This order cites as a reference the 1938 manual H.Dv. 91 *Der Stellungskrieg* discussed in chapter 1 of this research survey.

19. "Generalkommando I. A.K. Korpsbefehl Nr. 194," NAM T-312/838/9003278, 9003280.

20. "Generalkommando I. A.K. Korpsbefehl Nr. 194," NAM T-312/838/9003279; and "Anlage 2 zu Korpsbefehl Nr. 194/I. A.K.—Ia. Einzelheiten für Artillerie," NAM T-312/838/9003284—9003286.

21. "Generalkommando I. A.K. Korpsbefehl Nr. 194," NAM T-312/838/9003281, 9003282—9003283.

22. "Bericht zur Frontreise des Hptm. Muschner in der Zeit vom 31.7—7.8.42 in den Bereich des AOK 2," dated 9 August 1942, NAM T-78/343/6300935. Though Second Army was subordinate to Army Group B, it actually formed the southern portion of the German defensive front, linking the northern army groups to Army Group B's northern defensive flank along the Don River.

23. See "21. Infanterie-Division Abt. Ia Nr. 835/42. Betr.: Erfahrungen über den Kampf an festen Fronten; hier Abwehr im Sommer," dated 27 November 1942, NAM T-312/838/9003301—9003302; and "Armee-Oberkommando 18 Abt. Ia Nr. 19140/42. Betr.: Erfahrungen über den Kampf an festen Fronten," dated 16 December 1942, NAM T-312/838/9003267—9003268.

24. "Generalkommando I. A.K. Korpsbefehl Nr. 194," NAM T-312/838/9003278.

25. "1. Division Ia Nr. 543/42. Betr.: Erfahrungen über den Kampf an festen Fronten im Sommer," dated 28 November 1942, NAM T-312/838/9003270.

26. See "21. Infanterie-Division. Erfahrungen," NAM T-312/838/9003295; "Fusilier-Regiment 22 Abt. Ia Nr. 203/42. Betr.: Erfahrungen über den Kampf an festen Fronten," dated 14 November 1942, NAM T-312/838/9003363; "58. Inf.-Div. Ia. Erfahrungen über den Kampf an festen Fronten," dated 22 November 1942, NAM T-312/838/9003386; and "A.O.K. 4 Ia Nr. 0134/42 an Heeresgruppe Mitte," dated 21 September 1942, NAM T-312/189/7736481.

27. "121. Inf.-Division Abt. Ia Nr. 600/42. Erfahrungen über den Kampf an festen Fronten (Abwehr im Sommer)," dated 15 November 1942, NAM T-312/838/9003304.

28. "58. Inf.-Div. Ia. Erfahrungen," NAM T-312/838/9003387; "Armee-Oberkommando 18. Erfahrungen," NAM T-312/838/9003259—9003260; and "21. Infanterie-Division. Erfahrungen," NAM T-312/838/9003293.

29. Antitank practices during this period remained essentially unchanged from the techniques suggested in the 1941—42 winter after-action reports discussed in chapter 3 of this research survey. See "12. Flakdivision (mot.) Flakkampftrupps, Einsatz und Gliederung," NAM T-312/189/7736198—7736200; "58. Inf. Div. Erfahrungen," NAM T-312/838/9003387—9003388; "Panzerjägerabteilung 1 Kommandeur Ia Nr. 426/42. Erfahrungen über den Kampf an festen Fronten," dated 16 November 1942, NAM T-312/838/9003377; "A.O.K. 2 Ia Nr. 2366/42. Betr.: Erfahrungsbericht über Panzerabwehrwaffen," dated 4 September 1942; "Armee-Oberkommando 2 Ia Nr. 569/42. Betr.: Panzerabwehr," dated 5 June 1942, NAM T-312/1660/000928—000929; and "Armee-Oberkommando 2 Ia Nr. 2603/42 an Oberkommando Heeresgruppe B," dated 29 September 1942, NAM T-312/1283/000142—000167. This last document is an especially lengthy discussion of Russian armor tactics and German methods as practiced by the German VII Corps during defensive battles around Voronezh in July and August 1942. An analysis of antitank tactics in the winter of 1942—43 during the fighting for Demyansk is in "A.O.K. 16 Ia Nr. 550/43. Abschrift von Abschrift," dated 7 February 1943, NAM T-312/862/9032562—9032565.

30. "Armee-Oberkommando 18. Erfahrungen," NAM T-312/838/9003259; "Fusilier-Regiment 22. Erfahrungen," NAM T-312/838/9003362, 9003363; "21. Infanterie-Division. Erfahrungen," NAM T-312/838/9003293, 9003295; and "58. Inf.-Div. Erfahrungen," NAM T-312/838/9003386—9003387, 9003391.

31. "Oberkommando des Heeres. GenStd.H/Ausb.Abt.(II) Nr. 1550/42. Betr.: Erfahrungen mit der russischen Angriffsweise im Sommer 1942," dated 3 September 1942, NAM T-312/189/7736183—7736184. See also Halder, *War Journal*, 7:388 (entry for 3 September).

32. Halder, *War Journal*, 7:367—73 (entries for 4—11 August).

33. Manstein, *Lost Victories*, 264—67; MS P-114a, 324—27. The 72d Division was detached from Manstein's command to plug yet another hole in the Army Group Center line. See Halder, *War Journal*, 7:374, 382 (entries for 14 and 24 August).

34. Halder, *War Journal*, 7:392 (entry for 10 September) and footnote. The actual order was untitled but was commonly referred to as the Führer Defense Order.

35. "Der Führer. OKH-GenStdH-Op Abt (I) Nr. 11154/42," dated 8 September 1942, NAM T-312/189/7736339, 7736341—7735246, hereafter cited as Führer Defense Order.

36. Ibid., NAM T-312/189/7736339—7736340, 7736346—7736347.

37. Ibid., NAM T-312/189/7736340—7736341.

38. Ibid., NAM T-312/189/7736343.

39. Ibid., NAM T-312/189/7736347—7736348.

40. Ibid., NAM T-312/189/7736348—7736349.

41. See "Der Oberbefehlshaber der Heeresgruppe Mitte Ia Nr. 7420/42," dated 19 September 1942, NAM T-312/189/7736420; and "Oberkommando Heeresgruppe Mitte Ia/Gen.d.Pi.-Nr. 310/42. Betr.: Stützpunktausbau," dated 18 September 1942, NAM T-312/189/7736611. The Führer Defense Order was distributed down to division level and needed little editorial comment by intermediate commanders.

42. See the minutes of 25 September 1942 meeting, "Besprechung am 25.9.42, 10.30 Uhr," NAM T-312/189/7736673. This item, one of the miscellaneous supporting documents in Fourth Army's

War Diary, includes a sketch of notional defensive positions to be built in accordance with the Führer Defense Order, NAM T-312/189/7736583—7736585.

43. "Generalkommando LVI.Pz.Korps Ia Nr. 1381/42. An A.O.K.4," dated 21 September 1942, NAM T-312/189/7736597. See also "General-Kommando XXXXIII.A.K. Abt. Ia Nr. 1622/42. Betr.: Stellungsbau," dated 21 September 1942, NAM T-312/189/7736589—7736591.

44. See "A.O.K. 4 Ia Nr. 5505/42," NAM T-312/189/7736584—7736585.

45. For example, Fourth Army's instructions to its units included the preparation of a second position, built to the same specifications as the forward lines, for emergency occupation in the event of a Soviet breakthrough. Ibid.

46. "A.O.K. 4 Ia Nr. 0134/42. An Heeresgruppe Mitte," dated 21 September 1942, NAM T-312/189/7736479—7736482.

47. See Stein, *Waffen SS*, 10—11, 34—48, 93—102. In addition to volunteers from inside Germany proper, SS officials culled ethnic German communities within occupied territories for *Volksdeutsch* recruits. These non-Reich Germans, and later non-Germanic foreigners as well, were a bountiful source of *Waffen SS* manpower since they were outside the formal administration of the draft apparatus controlled by the Armed Forces High Command. Postwar apologists for the *Waffen SS* have argued that its multinational flavor made it a "prototype NATO army" defending Western culture against Asiatic Bolshevism. In fact, the multinational character of the *Waffen SS* derived more from SS attempts to tap new sources of manpower outside army control than from any crusading zeal on the part of the various groups who fought under SS banners. See Ibid., 250—58, 287—88; and George H. Stein, "The Myth of a European Army," *Wiener Library Bulletin*, 19 (April 1965):21—22.

48. Stein, *Waffen SS*, 203.

49. Manstein, *Lost Victories*, 269; Halder, *War Journal*, 7:366 (entry for 3 August).

50. Manstein, *Lost Victories*, 268. See also Warlimont, *Inside*, 265—66; and Mueller-Hillebrand, *Das Heer*, 3:78—79.

51. Halder, *War Journal*, 7:361 (entry for 27 July) and footnote.

52. "Armee-Oberkommando 4 Abt. IIb Nr. 392/42. Betr.: Kapitulanten-Nachwuchs bei der Infanterie," dated 18 September 1942, NAM T-312/189/7736410—7736413. The memo from the chief of infantry is cited as a reference in this document. On Germany's policies for recruiting and allocating manpower for infantry service, see Hellmuth Reinhardt, et al., "Personnel and Administration Project 2b, Part I (Recruiting for the Armed Forces, Peacetime and Wartime Systems)," Foreign Military Studies no. MS P-006 (Historical Division, U.S. Army, Europe, 1948), 28—29.

53. See Halder, *War Journal*, 7:368 (entry for 5 August) and footnote. "A.O.K. 4 Ia Nr. 0134/42. An Heeresgruppe Mitte," NAM T-312/189/7736485, requests increased numbers of volunteer laborers (*Hiwis*) to carry out the contruction projects called for by Hitler's Führer Defense Order. See also "Oberkommando des Heeres. Der Chef des Generalstabes des Heeres, Org.Abt. (I) Nr. 5825/42. Grundlegender Befehl Nr. 7 (Organisation)," dated 20 November 1942, NAM T-312/1661/00070800—000709.

54. "Oberkommando des Heeres. Der Chef des Generalstabes des Heeres, Op.Abt. (I) Nr. 11548/42. Grundlegender Befehl Nr. 5 (Frontkämpfer)," dated 29 October 1942, NAM T-312/1660/000726. For a first-person account of a recruiting campaign carried out among German service troops, see Guy Sajer, *The Forgotten Soldier*, translated by Lily Emmet (New York: Harper and Row, 1971), 117—18.

55. Ziemke, *Stalingrad*, 20. Unruh's activities are described in detail in Walter von Unruh, "Combat Staff Unruh," Foreign Military Studies no. MS D-370 (Historical Division, U.S. Army, Europe, n.d.).

56. "Der Führer. Führer-Befehl Nr. 1," dated 8 October 1942, NAM T-312/1660/000745—000746.

57. "Oberkommando des Heeres. Der Chef des Generalstabes des Heeres, Org.Abt.(II) Nr. 9900/42. Grundlegender Befehl Nr. 1 (Hebung der Gefechtsstarke)," dated 8 October 1942, NAM T-312/1660/000747—000748.

58. "Grundlegender Befehl Nr. 1," NAM T-312/1660/000748—000749.

59. "Grundlegender Befehl Nr. 5," NAM T-312/1660/000724—000725. The rear support echelons of the German Army seem to have been everyone's favorite whipping boy at this time, and combat officers seldom passed up an opportunity to demand greater sacrifices from the service troops. Zeitzler's actions to cause support units to share the burden of combat should be seen in this light, as should those instructions concerning the care of front fighters. General Heinrici, the commander of Fourth Army, took it upon himself to complain to Field Marshal von Kluge about the preferential treatment given rearward personnel in the distribution of food packages. Such high-level jealousy at the eternal "soft life" of the rear echelons connotes both concern for frontline morale and frustration at repeated supply failures. See "Armee-Oberkommando 4 Abt. IIb. Betr.: Urlauberbetreuung," dated 27 September 1942, NAM T-312/189/7736350. Supply units were also mildly flogged in German military propaganda. See Sajer, *Soldier*, 76.

60. "Grundlegender Befehl Nr. 5," NAM T-312/1660/000725—000726.

61. "Grundlegender Befehl Nr. 7," NAM T-312/1660/000705.

62. Quoted in Walter Görlitz, "The Battle for Stalingrad, 1942—1943," in *Decisive Battles of World War II: The German View*, edited by H. A. Jacobsen and J. Rohwer (New York: G. P. Putnam's Sons, 1965), 231.

63. "58. Inf.-Div. Ia Nr. 1148/42. Divisionsbefehl Nr. 2," dated 17 September 1942, NAM T-312/838/9003396.

64. Führer Defense Order, NAM T-312/189/7736340.

65. "Der Führer. OKH/Gen.St.d.H./Op.Abt. (I) Nr. 420817/42. Operationsbefehl Nr. 1," dated 14 October 1942, in *KTB/OKW*, 2:1301—4.

66. *KTB/OKW*, 2:888, 890 (entry for 2 November and additional comments by General Warlimont).

67. In Operations Order 1, Hitler called for an "active defense" (*aktive Verteidigung*) throughout the winter. The "active" measures recommended by Hitler included aggressive patrolling and local spoiling attacks to keep the enemy off balance. Hitler's concept of an active defense in no way implied fluidity for the German defenses themselves.

68. DA Pam 20—291, 11.

69. Freiherr von Ulmenstein, "161st Reconnaissance Battalion (21 Jun 1941—30 Jun 1942) and 132d Bicycle Battalion (17 Oct 1942—17 May 1943): Extracts from War Diaries," Foreign Military Studies no. MS P-093 (Historical Division, U.S. Army, Europe, 1954), 10—11. (The page numbers refer to portions of manuscript dealing with *Radfahrabteilung* 132.) See also "Armee-Oberkommando 2 Ia Nr. 2448/42. Betr.: Vorbereitungen für Gliederung und Umrustung zum Winterkrieg," dated 19 October 1942, NAM T-312/1660/000736—000738; and "Oberkommando des Heeres Gen.St.d.H./Ausb.Abt. (II) Nr. /42 Verwendung von Panzerkampfwagen und Sturmgeschutzeinheiten im Winter," dated October 1942, NAM T-78/202/6146549—6146551.

70. "Fahrt des Herrn Oberbefehlshabers am 7. November 1942 zum Gen.Kdo. L.A.K. u. 2.SS-Inf. Brig.," NAM T-312/838/9002988.

71. "Fahrt des Herrn Oberbefehlshabers am Mittwoch dem 2.12.42," NAM T-312/838/9002933.

72. "Fahrt des Herrn Oberbefehlshabers am 22. und 12. Dez. 1942 zur 121. Inf. Div., 28. Jag. Div., 24. u. 154. Inf. Div.," NAM T-312/838/9002923, 9002926.

73. The winter defensive fighting in the areas of Army Groups North and Center is covered in detail in Ziemke, *Stalingrad*, 98—117.

74. The battles around Velikiye Luki are described in Ibid., 107—9; and U.S. Department of the Army, Pamphlet no. 20—234, *Operations of Encircled Forces: German Experiences in Russia* (Washington, DC: U.S. Government Printing Office, 1952), 7—14. The disruption of German plans caused by the Soviet attack and the piecemeal German relief attempts are covered in Otto Tiemann, "Closing the 40-km Gap Between Army Group North and Army Group Center (Nov 1942—Mar 1943)," Foreign Military Studies no. MS D-241 (Historical Division, U.S. Army, Europe, 1947), 7—12.

75. MS D-106, 15. A general discussion of Army Group North's combat experiences during this period is "Oberkommando Heeresgruppe Nord Ia Nr. 20/43. Betr.: Erfahrungen und Folgerungen," dated 2 January 1943, NAM T-78/202/6146492—6146507.

76. The Demyansk fighting is described in Ziemke, *Stalingrad*, 112—13; Haupt, *Heeresgruppe Nord*, 149—54; and Friedrich Sixt, "Kriegsjahr 1943," part 3 in MS P-114a, 367—83. Defensive fighting during Operation Büffel is described in Wilhelm Willemer, et al., "Selected Divisional Operations on the Eastern Front (Delaying Action at Sychevka)," Foreign Military Studies no. MS P-143c (Historical Division, U.S. Army, Europe, 1954), 154—63, hereafter cited as MS P-143c; and Bergner, *Schlesische Infanterie*, 188—203.

77. DA Pam 20—261a, 135, 138; Mueller-Hillebrand, *Das Heer*, 3:59—60. For a description of the training problems experienced by German units preparing for Operation Blau, see Felix Steiner, "Tactics of Mobile Units. Operations of the 5th SS Panzergrenadier Division 'Wiking' at Rostov and the Maikop Oilfields (Summer 1942)," Foreign Military Studies no. MS D-248 (Historical Division, U.S. Army, Europe, 1947), 6—8; and Paul Schulz, "Combat in the Caucasus Woods and Mountains During Autumn 1942," Foreign Military Studies no. MS D-254 (Historical Division, U.S. Army, Europe, 1947), 3.

78. DA Pam 20—261a, 138—39; Mueller-Hillebrand, *Das Heer*, 3:60—62.

79. DA Pam 20—261a, 131—32.

80. "Die Gliederung des deutschen Heeres, 12.8.1942," *KTB/OKW*, II2, 1378—80; Mueller-Hillebrand, *Das Heer*, 3:67—68.

81. "Armee-Oberkommando 2 Ia Nr. 1884/42. Betr.: Erfahrungen bei Angriffs-und Abwehrkampfen 28.6 bis 20.7.42," dated 21 July 1942, NAM T-312/1660/000898—000900.

82. DA Pam 20—261a, 132.

83. See Wilhelm Willemer, "Organization of the Ground for Defense on a Broad Front, as Defended by an Army or Larger Unit," Foreign Military Studies no. MS P-194 (Historical Division, U.S. Army, Europe, 1954), 8—19.

84. "Oberkommando der Heeresgruppe B Ia Nr. 2889/42. Betr.: 'Eingreifgruppen' an ständigen Fronten," dated 6 September 1942, NAM T-312/189/7736226—7736227.

85. Kurt Zeitzler, "Stalingrad," in *Fatal Decisions*, edited by Freidin and Richardson, 137—40.

86. Ibid., 142—43.

87. Seaton, *Russo-German War*, 312; Zeitzler,"Stalingrad," 147.

88. Helmuth Greiner, "Greiner Diary Notes, 12 Aug 1942—12 Mar 1943," Foreign Military Studies no. MS C-065a (Historical Division, U.S. Army, Europe, 1950), 91—93. Greiner kept the War Diary for the Armed Forces High Command during this period of the war. See also DA Pam 20—291a, 161—62.

89. "Armee-Oberkommando 2 Ia Nr. 1098/42. An Oberkommando Heeresgruppe B," dated 1 October 1942, NAM T-312/1660/000761—0007655.

90. "V.O./OKH bei AOK 6," dated 13 October 1942, NAM T-78/343/6300915—6300919.

91. Seydlitz urged Paulus to disregard Hitler's orders and begin a breakout on his (Paulus') own authority in order to save Sixth Army. Ironically, Hitler suspected that Paulus might try something of the sort and so made Seydlitz—whom the dictator considered absolutely reliable—independently responsible for holding a portion of the pocket's defensive front. This was an affront to Paulus and also a curious reward for the one man who, unknown to Hitler, was most actively lobbying for an unauthorized breakout. Taken prisoner at Stalingrad, Seydlitz became a prominent Soviet collaborator, being one of the spokesmen of the so-called Free Germany Committee that urged Germans to turn against the Nazis. See Seaton, *Russo-German War*, 320; Ziemke, *Stalingrad*, 57—58; and Walter Görlitz, *Paulus and Stalingrad*, translated by R. H. Stevens (New York: Citadel Press, 1963), 211—12.

92. In its attempts to supply Sixth Army by air, the *Luftwaffe* also lost over half of its operational Ju-52 transport aircraft fleet and a large number of valuable instructor pilots. The Stalin-

grad airlift is discussed in detail in Fritz Morzik, *German Air Force Airlift Operations*, USAF Historical Studies no. 167 (Maxwell Air Force Base, AL: USAF Historical Division, Research Studies Institute, Air University, 1961), 179—202. Sixth Army estimated its own daily supply requirements at 550 tons per day. This estimate, based on consumption rates for defensive operations only, included 75 tons of fuel for supply distribution and defensive operations by the panzers and 100 tons of ammunition. These figures did not include any stockpiling for a possible breakout. See Army Group Don message reproduced in Görlitz, *Paulus and Stalingrad*, 275—76.

93. "Vom Tschir zum Mius. Winterabwehrschlacht 1942/43. Die Kämpfe der 3. Rumänischen Armee—ab 27 Dez. Armee-Abteilung Hollidt in der Zeit vom 23. Nov. 1942 bis 28 Febr. 1943. Armee-Oberkommando 6, Juni 1943," NAM T-312/1463/000830—000831. See the detailed description of the improvised units joining in the Chir River defense by Otto von Knobelsdorff, commander of the XLVIII Panzer Corps, in Friedrich Schulz, et al., "Reverses on the Southern Wing (1942—1943); (Annex 5: The XLVIII Panzer Corps in Action Between the Don and Mius River Sectors, 5 December 1942 to 12 February 1943)," Foreign Military Studies no. MS T-15 (Historical Division, U.S. Army, Europe, 1947), 252—53, hereafter cited as MS T-15.

94. F. W. von Mellenthin, *Panzer Battles*, translated by H. Betzler (Norman: University of Oklahoma Press, 1956), 178; Heinz Schneider, "Breakthrough Attack by the V Russian Mechanized Corps on the Khir River from 10 to 16 December 1942," Appendix 3, 32, in "Small Unit Tactics—Tactics of Individual Arms (Part II)," by Burkhart Mueller-Hillebrand, Foreign Military Studies no. MS P-060f (Historical Division, U.S. Army, Europe, 1951), hereafter cited as MS P-060f. See also MS T-15, 256—57. (General von Knobelsdorff incorrectly identifies the 336th Division as the 338th Division in his account, an error apparently due in part to the similar numbering of certain infantry regiments in this battle.)

95. Mellenthin, *Panzer Battles*, 175.

96. "Vom Tschir zum Mius," NAM T-312/1463/000832—000833. The 7th *Luftwaffe* Field Division disintegrated altogether during the Chir battles. Its survivors were later incorporated into the 384th Infantry Division. See also MS T-15, 257—58.

97. "Vom Tschir zum Mius," NAM T-312/1463/000834. The 7th *Luftwaffe* Field Division was almost completely destroyed in this fighting. One measure of its lack of training was recounted by the commander of the XLVIII Panzer Corps as follows:

> The furthest advanced air force infantry battalions had been assigned their respective sectors by their division headquarters. However, the division had quite apparently neglected to inform the battalions sufficiently well on the serious nature of the situation. It had failed to give them detailed instructions and orders on how to effect an undetected night time relief. The battalions therefore drove right into the outpost lines. They rumbled along with their trains, without providing for security on the march, without reconnaissance ... until they were right in the middle of the Russians where they were duly and promptly wiped out without firing a shot. This was a terrific shock to the division—so terrific, as a matter of fact, that it was for the moment in no shape to be sent into combat as an independent unit.

See MS T-15, 261.

98. MS P-060f, 33.

99. Ibid., 12—13.

100. Ibid., 33.

101. Ibid., 21, 22. Mellenthin, citing Balck as his source, denies that single German tanks were ever left in direct support of infantry during these battles. Quoting Balck, Mellenthin concedes that "many a crisis would not have arisen had the 336th Division possessed a larger number of antitank guns." See Mellenthin, *Panzer Battles*, 183—84. General accounts of the events surrounding the Chir River fighting are in "Vom Tschir zum Mius," NAM T-312/1463/000834—000835; MS T-15, 259—67; Mellenthin, *Panzer Battles*, 172—84; presentation by Colonel David M. Glantz at the 1984 Art of War Symposium, "The Middle Don Operation, 16—28 December 1942," in U.S. Army War College, Center for Land Warfare, *1984 Art of War Symposium: From the Don to the Dnepr—Soviet Offensive Operations, December 1942—August 1943, a Transcript of Proceedings* (Carlisle Barracks, PA: U.S. Army War College, October 1985), 42—49, 51; and comments of

F. W. von Mellenthin, Ibid., 99—118. Mellenthin's symposium comments are nearly a word-for-word recitation of his earlier description in *Panzer Battles*, which is based largely on the XLVIII Panzer Corps' war diary. While providing interesting tactical insights, Mellenthin's accounts generally ignore important contextual material as well as combat actions that might tend to diminish the apparent magnitude of the German successes. For example, he does not mention the loss of the German bridgehead across the Chir River at Surovikino—a major loss under the circumstances since this bridgehead had been key to the German hopes of supporting the Stalingrad relief attack. Similarly, he gives the mistaken impression that the German successes on the Chir River constituted a major defeat for the Soviets when, from the Russian standpoint, the Chir fighting was but a minor hiccup in an otherwise widely successful general offensive. Seen in this light, the German actions on the Chir are more correctly described as a *tactical* success amid a general *operational* defeat.

102. Mellenthin, *Panzer Battles*, quoting Balck, 183—84.

103. MS P-060f, 19; Mellenthin, *Panzer Battles*, 178.

104. Mellenthin, *Panzer Battles*, quoting Balck, 184.

105. Ibid.

106. MS P-060f, 34—35.

107. Ibid., 31.

108. The inability of the German panzer divisions to hold terrain was evident not only on the Chir River, but also during the LVII Panzer Corps' attack to relieve Stalingrad. See the discussion at Hitler's headquarters on the need for infantry in the defense on 12 December 1942 in Helmut Heiber, ed., *Hitlers Lagebesprechungen: Die Protokollfragmente seiner militärischen Konferenzen, 1942—1945* (Stuttgart: Deutsche Verlags-Anstalt, 1962), 89.

109. See Clark, *Barbarossa*, 263—64; Mellenthin, *Panzer Battles*, 185—86; and MS T-15, 265. During some of the 11th Panzer Division's successful battles on the Chir, German officers noted that the Soviets were remarkably lax in consolidating their gains, leaving them unnecessarily vulnerable to German counterthrusts. See MS P-060f, 35.

110. Seaton, *Russo-German War*, 328; Morzik, *German Air Force*, 190—91. For a critique of the combat performance of the Italian and Hungarian armies in these battles, see Jurgen Forster, *Stalingrad: Risse im Bundnis 1942/43* (Freiburg: Rombach, 1975), 143—49; and MS T-15, 267—73. On the Romanian forces, see MS T-15, 282—83.

111. See "A.O.K. 2 Ia Nr. 1412/42," dated 1 December 1942, NAM T-312/1660/000694—000695; and "A.O.K. 2 an Ob.Kdo.Hgr.B, Chef des Generalstabes," dated 3 December 1942, NAM T-312/1660/000696—000702. The reporting system established four categories of divisions: category I—very good, category II—good, category III—marginal, and category IV—poor. In its report to Army Group B, Second Army on 3 December listed two of its divisions as being category I, seven category II, three category III (including its only panzer division), and two category IV. Considering that Second Army had done little fighting since late summer, this demonstrates the general erosion that had befallen all of the German armies in the East.

112. Manstein, *Lost Victories*, 384—86.

113. Ibid., 378—79.

114. Ibid., 381. See also Clark, *Barbarossa*, 280—81.

115. Manstein, *Lost Victories*, 386.

116. Ibid., 383—84.

117. Ibid., 373—74. See also the presentation by Colonel David M. Glantz, "The Donbas Operation, 29 January—6 March 1943," in *1984 Art of War Symposium*, 120—60.

118. See Willemer, "Armor in the Aggressive Defense," in MS P-143c, 144.

119. "Vom Tschir zum Mius," NAM T-312/1463/000842; Wilhelm Russwurm, "Employment of a Furlough Detachment for Rear Area Security (Don, Donets, Winter 1942—43)," Foreign Military Studies no. MS D-282 (Historical Division, U.S. Army, Europe, 1947), 1—6.

120. Army Detachment Hollidt is a case in point. According to German military terminology, an army detachment (*Armee Abteilung*) was an army-sized force that lacked the full complement of support and service units normal for a field army. This formation was initially built around General Karl Hollidt's XVII Corps and gradually grew to take control of whatever forces could be rallied.

121. Manstein, *Lost Victories*, 380. A few units that transferred to the Eastern Front from France, such as the 7th Panzer Division, also had to endure what the Germans called the "childhood diseases" of combat acclimatization. See MS T-15, 274—75.

122. See Senger und Etterlin, *Neither*, 87, 95, 101. The *Alarmeinheiten*, scraped together from disparate rear-echelon personnel, naturally had no standard organization. As a rule, these units seldom possessed any antitank guns or other heavy infantry weapons. Though *Alarmeinheiten* occasionally performed helpful defensive missions, as a rule their combat value was virtually zero. One former German officer, asked to estimate their effectiveness, remarked that they seldom lasted longer than thirty minutes in combat before disintegrating. General (Ret.) Ferdinand von Senger und Etterlin, Interview with the author, Carlisle Barracks, PA, 2 May 1985; Lieutenant General (Ret.) Gerd Niepold, Interview with the author, Carlisle Barracks, PA, 3 May 1985; Lieutenant General (Ret.) Anton-Detlev von Plato, Interview with the author, Carlisle Barracks, PA, 2 May 1985; Lemm interview. For a general discussion of the problems of *Alarmeinheiten*, see paraphrased translation of Hans Christian Treutsch, "Concerning the Organization of Ad Hoc Combat Groups" in Edward N. Luttwak, *Historical Analysis and Projection for Army 2000*, vol. 1, pt. 10, "The German Army in the Second World War: Urban-Warfare Task Forces (*Kampfgruppen*) and Emergency Ad Hoc Forces (*Alarmeinheiten*)" (Fort Monroe, VA: U.S. Army Training and Doctrine Command, 1 March 1983), 17—26.

123. Ibid., 101.

124. Manstein, *Lost Victories*, 389. For another view of this fighting, see Fretter-Pico, *Infanterie*, 100—103.

125. Senger und Etterlin, *Neither*, 98.

126. See "294 Inf. Division Ia Abschrift: Erfahrungsbericht über den Einsatz von mot. Nachtruppen beim Rückzug zwischen Donez und Mius," XVII Corps coversheet dated 18 March 1943, NAM T-312/1462/000911—000915. Reprinting this report for circulation to other headquarters, Hollidt's new Sixth Army described this expedient motorization as a demonstration that such mobile units could play an important role even in positional warfare (*Stellungskrieg*). See "Oberkommando der 6. Armee Ia Nr. 835/43. Betr.: Erfahrungsbericht," dated 25 March 1943, NAM T-312/1462/000916.

127. MS P-143c, 145—52.

128. Ibid., 151—52.

129. "294 Inf. Division: Erfahrungsbericht," NAM T-312/1462/000912.

130. See the description in "Vom Tschir zum Mius," NAM T-312/1463/000849.

131. Ibid., NAM T-312/1463/000860, 000861.

132. Ibid., NAM T-312/1463/000842.

133. Manstein, *Lost Victories*, 423—28; Seaton, *Russo-German War*, 347—48. Soviet intelligence detected heavy German convoy movements and concentrations of troop trains south of Kharkov but erroneously interpreted these activities as evidence of another major German withdrawal. Instead, Manstein was massing his force for a counterstroke. Manstein's success owed much to this important failure by Soviet intelligence analysts. See Erickson, *Road to Berlin*, 50—51; and Glantz, "Donbas Operation," 160—62.

134. Manstein, *Lost Victories*, 428—37; Mellenthin, *Panzer Battles*, 207—8; and Seaton, *Russo-German War*, 349—50.

135. "Generalkommando XXIV Pz. Korps Abt. Ia Nr. 937/43. Zusammenfassender Bericht über die Tatigkeit des Gen.Kdo.XXIV.Pz.Korps an der Tagenrog-Front in der Zeit vom 9.3.43 bis 15.4.43," dated 3 May 1943, NAM T-312/1462/000933—000938.

136. Hitler visited Manstein's headquarters on 17—19 February 1942. His apparent intention upon arrival was to remove Manstein from command; he ended up reluctantly approving Manstein's counterattack plans. See Ziemke, *Stalingrad*, 91—92; and Manstein, *Lost Victories*, 423—28.

137. "Anlage 3 zum Korpsbefehl für die Neugliederung der Verteidigung vom 18.3.43. Abt. Ia Nr. 378/43. Anweisung für die Kampfführung," NAM T-312/1462/000940; and "Zusammenfassender Bericht—XXIV Pz.Korps," NAM T-312/1462/000935—000936.

138. "H.Gr.Nord Ia Nr. 11721/42 von 20.9.1942," cited as a reference in "Armee-Oberkommando 18. Erfahrungen," NAM T-312/838/9003255.

139. "21. Infanterie-Division. Erfahrungen," NAM T-312/838/9003292.

140. "Armee-Oberkommando 18. Erfahrungen," NAM T-312/838/9003255.

141. "21. Infanterie-Division. Erfahrungen," NAM T-312/838/9003292. See also "121. Inf.-Division. Erfahrungen," NAM T-312/838/9003304; and "1. Division Erfahrungen," NAM T-312/838/9003270.

142. "Fusilier-Regiment 22. Erfahrungen," NAM T-312/838/9003362; and "58. Inf.-Div. Erfahrungen," NAM T-312/838/9003383. See also the comments of General Ortner, commander of the 69th Infantry Division, to General Lindemann during the latter's inspection tour on 2 December 1942, "Fahrt des Herrn Oberbefehlshabern am Mittwoch, dem 2.12.42 zur 69. Inf. Division," NAM T-312/838/9002932.

143. "A.O.K. 4 Ia Nr. 5245/42. Betr.: Erfahrungen bei russischen Angriffen," dated 14 September 1942, NAM T-312/289/7736217.

144. "1. Division. Erfahrungen," NAM T-312/838/9003275.

145. "4. Panzer-Division Kommandeur Nr. 1290/42. Betr.: Panzer-Einsatz in der Verteidigung," dated 30 September 1942, NAM T-78/202/6146563.

146. "Der Oberbefehlshaber der 4. Panzerarmee Ia Nr. 3121/42. Betr.: Panzer-einsatz," dated 21 September 1942, NAM T-78/202/6146563.

147. "A.O.K. 4. Erfahrungen bei russischen Angriffen," NAM T-312/189/7736218.

148. See, for example, "121. Inf. Division. Erfahrungen," NAM T-312/838/9003306, 9003310; and "58. Inf.-Div. Erfahrungen," NAM T-312/838/9003386—9003387, 9003391.

149. Senger und Etterlin, *Neither*, 95, 98. See also the comments of General von Knobelsdorff in MS T-15, 288, endorsing the concentration of armor and the autonomy of panzer commanders.

150. "4. Panzer-Division Kommandeur. Panzer-Einsatz in der Verteidigung," NAM T-78/202/6146563, 6146565. German tank commanders did not wish to engage small break-ins partly because these did not allow sufficient maneuver space for the panzers to deploy. Consequently, German armor counterattacks against smaller penetrations took on the appearance of frontal attacks regardless of the direction of attack. German commanders were also concerned about the growing tank attrition rates in counterattacks, an indirect tribute to improved Soviet training and combined arms cooperation. See, for example, "Anlage zu A.O.K. 4 Ia Nr. _____ /42 vom 18.9.42. Oberkommando der Heeresgruppe Mitte Ia Nr. 7216/42," a report on high tank losses during counterattacks around Rzhev in September 1942, NAM T-312/189/7736374—7736375.

151. A draft copy of "Merkblatt für den Einsatz von Panzern im Abwehrkampf," with marginal comments apparently by LVI Panzer Corps, is in NAM T-312/189/7736422—7736431. The interest in tank-infantry cooperation and the defensive use of tanks during this period was apparently stimulated by the announced intention of the Training Branch of the General Staff to publish a definitive manual on these subjects. See, for example, the comments in "Abteilung Feldheer Ref. III Bb. Nr. 404/43. Betr.: Zusammenarbeit zwischen Panzer und Infanterie," dated 30 April 1943, NAM T-78/202/6146475—6146476.

152. "Panzertruppenschule Wünsdorf, Merkblatt über Zusammenwirken zwischen Panzern und Infanterie in der Verteidigung für die mit der Durchführung des Panzereinsatzes verantwortlichen Truppenführer," dated February 1943, NAM T-78/202/6146516—6146521.

153. "Panzertruppenschule (Schule f.Sch.Tr., Wünsdorf). Merkblatt über Zusammenarbeit zwischen Panzern und Infanterie in der Verteidigung (für hohere Kommando-behorden)," dated February 1943, NAM T-78/202/6146522—6146523.

Chapter 5

1. Manstein's comment is quoted in Liddell Hart, *The Other Side*, 318.
2. MS P-089, 12.

BIBLIOGRAPHY

Books

Addington, Larry H. *The Blitzkrieg Era and the German General Staff, 1865–1941.* New Brunswick, NJ: Rutgers University Press, 1971.

Alford, J. R. "Mobile Defence: The Pervasive Myth (A Historical Investigation)." London: Department of War Studies, King's College, 1977.

Allmayer-Beck, Johann, and Franz Becker. *21. Infanterie-Division: Russlandfeldzug 1941.* Hamburg: Traditionsverband/Kameradenhilfswerk e.V. 21. (ostpr./westpr.) Infanterie-Division, 1960.

Andronikow, I. G., and W. D. Mostowenko. *Die Roten Panzer: Geschichte der sowjetischen Panzertruppen.* Munich: J. F. Lehmanns Verlag, 1963.

Angolia, John R. *For Führer and Fatherland: Military Awards of the Third Reich.* San Jose, CA: R. James Bender Publishing, 1976.

Balck, Wilhelm. *Development of Tactics—World War.* Translated by Harry Bell. Fort Leavenworth, KS: The General Service Schools Press, 1922.

Bankwitz, Philip C. F. *Maxime Weygand and Civil-Military Relations in Modern France.* Cambridge, MA: Harvard University Press, 1967.

Baumann, Hans, ed. *Die 35. Infanterie-Division im 2. Weltkrieg 1939–1945.* Karlsruhe: Verlag G. Braun, 1964.

Beinhauer, Eugen, ed. *Artillerie im Osten.* Berlin: W. Limpert Verlag, 1944.

Bergner, Romuald. *Schlesische Infanterie: Grenadier-Regiment 7.* Bochum: Heinrich Pöppinghaus Verlag, 1980.

Boelcke, Willi A., ed. *The Secret Conferences of Dr. Goebbels: The Nazi Propaganda War, 1939–1943.* Translated by Ewald Osers. New York: E. P. Dutton, 1970.

Breithaupt, Hans. *Die Geschichte der 30. Infanterie-Division, 1939–1945.* Bad Nauheim: Hans-Henning Podzun, 1955.

Bullock, Alan. *Hitler: A Study in Tyranny.* Rev. ed. New York: Harper and Row, 1962.

Carell, Paul [Paul Karl Schmidt]. *Hitler Moves East.* Translated by Ewald Osers. Boston: Little, Brown and Co., 1964.

Carsten, Francis L. *The Reichswehr and Politics, 1918 to 1933.* Oxford: Oxford University Press, 1966.

Chew, Allen F. *Fighting the Russians in Winter: Three Case Studies.* Leavenworth Papers no. 5. Fort Leavenworth, KS: Combat Studies Institute, U.S. Army Command and General Staff College, 1981.

Clark, Alan. *Barbarossa: The Russo-German Conflict, 1941—1945.* New York: William Morrow and Co., 1965.

Craig, Gordon. "Delbruck: The Military Historian." In *Makers of Modern Strategy*, edited by Edward Mead Earle. 1941. Reprint. New York: Atheneum, 1969.

―――――. *The Politics of the Prussian Army, 1640—1945.* London: Oxford University Press, 1955.

Das Buch der 78. Sturm Division. Tubingen: Buchdruckerei H. Lauppir, n.d.

Dieckhoff, Gerhard. *Die 3. Infanterie-Division.* Gottingen: Erich Borries, 1960.

Dupuy, T. N. *A Genius for War: The German Army and General Staff, 1801—1945.* Englewood Cliffs, NJ: Prentice-Hall, 1977.

Eimannsberger, Ludwig von. *Der Kampfwagen Krieg.* Munich: J. F. Lehmanns Verlag, 1934. Typescript English translation at U.S. Army Military History Institute, Carlisle Barracks, PA.

Erickson, John. *The Road to Berlin.* Boulder, CO: Westview Press, 1983.

―――――. *The Road to Stalingrad.* New York: Harper and Row, 1975.

Foertsch, Hermann. *The Art of Modern Warfare.* Translated by Theodore W. Knauth. Camden, NJ: Veritas Press, 1940.

Forster, Jurgen. *Stalingrad: Risse im Bundnis 1942/43.* Freiburg: Rombach, 1975.

Freidin, Seymour, and William Richardson, eds. *The Fatal Decisions.* Translated by Constantine Fitzgibbon. New York: William Sloane Associates, 1956.

Fretter-Pico, Maximilian. *Missbrauchte Infanterie: Deutsche Infanteriedivision im osteuropäischen Grossraum 1941 bis 1944.* Frankfurt am Main: Verlag für Wehrwesen, 1957.

Fugate, Bryan I. *Operation Barbarossa: Strategy and Tactics on the Eastern Front, 1941.* Novato, CA: Presidio Press, 1984.

Gareis, Martin. *Kampf und Ende der Frankisch-Sudetendeutschen 98. Infanterie-Division.* Bad Nauheim: Hans-Henning Podzun, 1956.

Glantz, David M. *The Soviet Airborne Experience.* Research Survey no. 4. Fort Leavenworth, KS: Combat Studies Institute, U.S. Army Command and General Staff College, November 1984.

Goebbels, Joseph. *The Goebbels Diaries, 1942—1943.* Edited, translated, and with an introduction by Louis P. Lochner. Garden City, NY: Doubleday, 1948.

Gordon, Harold J. *The Reichswehr and the German Republic, 1919—1926.* Princeton, NJ: Princeton University Press, 1957.

Görlitz, Walter. *History of the German General Staff, 1657—1945.* Translated by Brian Battershaw. New York: Praeger, 1953.

―――――. *Paulus and Stalingrad.* Translated by R. H. Stevens. New York: Citadel Press, 1963.

Goure, Leon. *The Siege of Leningrad.* Stanford, CA: Stanford University Press, 1962.

Greiner, Helmuth. *Die Oberste Wehrmachtführung 1939—1943*. Wiesbaden: Limes Verlag, 1951.

Grossmann, Horst. *Geschichte der rheinisch-westfälischen 6. Infanterie-Division 1939—1945*. Bad Nauheim: Hans-Henning Podzun, 1958.

Guderian, Heinz. *Panzer Leader*. Translated by Constantine Fitzgibbon. New York: E. P. Dutton and Co., 1952.

Halder, Franz. *Hitler as War Lord*. Translated by Paul Findlay. London: Putnam, 1950.

──────. *The Private War Journal of Generaloberst Franz Halder*. Edited by Arnold Lissance. 9 vols. Washington, DC: Office of the Chief of Military History, 1950.

Haupt, Werner. *Heeresgruppe Mitte 1941—1945*. Dorheim: Hans-Henning Podzun, 1968.

──────. *Heeresgruppe Nord 1941—1942*. Bad Nauheim: Hans-Henning Podzun, 1967.

Hausser, Paul. *Waffen-SS im Einsatz*. Göttingen: Plesse Verlag K. W. Schutz, 1953.

Heiber, Helmut, ed. *Hitlers Lagebesprechungen: Die Protokollfragmente seiner militärischen Konferenzen, 1942—1945*. Stuttgart: Deutsche Verlags-Anstalt, 1962.

Hermann, Carl Hans. *68 Kriegsmonate: Der Weg der 9. Panzerdivision durch den zweiten Weltkrieg*. Vienna: Kameradschaft 9. Panzer Division, 1975.

Hinze, Rolf. *Hitze, Frost und Pulverdampf: Der Schicksalsweg der 20. Panzer-Division*. Bochum: Heinrich Pöppinghaus Verlag, 1981.

Hitler, Adolph. *Hitler's Table Talk, 1941—1944: His Private Conversations*. 2d ed. Translated by Norman Cameron and R. H. Stevens. London: Weidenfeld and Nicolson, 1973.

Hoffschmidt, E. J., and W. H. Tantum. *German Tank and Antitank*. Greenwich, CT: WE, Inc., 1968.

Hossbach, Friedrich. *Infanterie im Ostfeldzug, 1941—1942*. Osterode-Harz: Giebel und Oehlschlägel, 1951.

Hoth, Hermann. *Panzer-Operationen: Die Panzergruppe 3 und der operative Gedanke der deutschen Führung, Sommer 1941*. Heidelberg: Kurt Vowinckel, 1956.

Hubatsch, Walter, ed. *Hitlers Weisungen für die Kriegführungen 1939—1945: Dokumente des Oberkommandos der Wehrmacht*. Frankfurt am Main: Bernard und Graefe Verlag für Wehrwesen, 1962.

Jacobsen, H. A., and J. Rohwer, eds. *Decisive Battles of World War II: The German View*. New York: G. P. Putnam's Sons, 1965.

Jenner, Martin. *Die 216./272. Niedersachsische Infanterie-Division, 1939—1945*. Bad Nauheim: Podzun Verlag, 1964.

Keilig, Wolf. *Das Deutsche Heer, 1939—1945: Gliederung, Einsatz, Stellenbesetzung*. 3 vols. Bad Nauheim: Hans-Henning Podzun, 1956.

Kuhl, Hermann Joseph von. *Entstehung, Durchführung und Zusammenbruch der Offensive von 1918*. Berlin: Deutsche Verlagsgesellschaft für Politik und Geschichte m.b.H., 1927.

Leach, Barry A. *German Strategy Against Russia, 1939—1941*. London: Oxford University Press, 1973.

Leeb, Wilhelm Ritter von. *Defense*. Translated and edited by Stefan T. Possony and Daniel Vilfroy. Harrisburg, PA: Military Service Publishing Co., 1943.

Lewis, S. J. *Forgotten Legions: German Army Infantry Policy, 1918—1941*. New York: Praeger, 1985.

Liddell Hart, Basil H. *The Other Side of the Hill*. 2d ed. London: Cassell and Co., 1973.

Ludendorff, Erich von. *Ludendorff's Own Story*. 2 vols. New York: Harper and Brothers, 1919.

————, ed. *Urkunden der Obersten Heeresleitung*. 3d ed. Berlin: E. S. Mittler und Sohn, 1922.

Lupfer, Timothy T. *The Dynamics of Doctrine: The Changes in German Tactical Doctrine During the First World War*. Leavenworth Papers no. 4. Fort Leavenworth, KS: Combat Studies Institute, U.S. Army Command and General Staff College, 1981.

Luttwak, Edward N. *Historical Analysis and Projection for Army 2000*. Vol. 1. Pt. 10. "The German Army in the Second World War: Urban-Warfare Task Forces (*Kampfgruppen*) and Emergency Ad Hoc Forces (*Alarmeinheiten*)." Fort Monroe, VA: U.S. Army Training and Doctrine Command, 1 March 1983.

Lutz, Ralph Haswell, ed. *Fall of the German Empire, 1914—1918*. 2 vols. Translated by David G. Rempel and Gertrude Rendtorff. Stanford, CA: Stanford University Press, 1932.

————, ed. *The Causes of the German Collapse in 1918*. Translated by W. L. Campbell. Stanford, CA: Stanford University Press, 1934.

Mackensen, Eberhard von. *Vom Bug zum Kaukasus: Das III. Panzerkorps im Feldzug gegen Sowjetrussland 1941/42*. Neckargemuend: Scharnhorst Buchkameradschaft, 1967.

Mackintosh, Malcolm. *Juggernaut: A History of the Soviet Armed Forces*. New York: Macmillan Co., 1967.

Macksey, Kenneth. *Guderian: Creator of the Blitzkrieg*. New York: Stein and Day, 1975.

Madej, W. Victor. *German Army Order of Battle, 1939—1945*. 2 vols. Allentown, PA: Game Marketing Co., 1981.

Manstein, Erich von. *Lost Victories*. Edited and translated by Anthony G. Powell. Chicago: Henry Regnery Co., 1958.

Mellenthin, F. W. von. *Panzer Battles*. Translated by H. Betzler. Norman: University of Oklahoma Press, 1956.

Mellenthin, F. W. von, R. H. S. Stolfi, and E. Sobik. *NATO Under Attack*. Durham, NC: Duke University Press, 1984.

Mermet, Armand. *Siegfried Taktik 37*. Paris: Charles-Lavauzelle, 1939.

Metzsch, Friedrich August von. *Die Geschichte der 22. Infanterie-Division 1939—1945*. Kiel: Hans-Henning Podzun, 1952.

Meyer-Detring, Wilhelm. *Die 137. Infanteriedivision im Mittelabschnitt der Ostfront*. Petzenkirchen, Austria: Kameradschaft der Bergmann-Division (137. I. D.), 1962.

Milward, Alan S. *The German Economy at War*. New York: Oxford University Press, 1965.

Morzik, Fritz. *German Air Force Airlift Operations*. USAF Historical Studies no. 167. Maxwell Air Force Base, AL: USAF Historical Division, Research Studies Institute, Air University, 1961.

Mueller-Hillebrand, Burkhart. *Das Heer 1933—1945*. 3 vols. Darmstadt: E. S. Mittler und Sohn, 1954.

Noakes, Jeremy, and Geoffrey Pridham, eds. *Documents on Nazism, 1919—1945*. New York: Viking Press, 1975.

Oberkommando des Heeres. *Der Stellungskrieg*. H.Dv. 91. 1938. Reprint. Berlin, 1940.

―――――. *Der Weltkrieg 1914—1918*. 12 vols. Berlin: E. S. Mittler, 1939.

―――――. *Die Infanterie*. Munich: Deutscher Volksverlag, 1938?

Oberkommando des Heeres. Generalstab des Heeres/Ausbildungsabteilung (II). [Training Branch of the Army General Staff]. *Ausbildungsvorschrift für die Infanterie*. Heft 11. *Feldbefestigung der Infanterie*. H.Dv. 130/11. Berlin, 1940.

―――――. *Die Infanterie-Panzerabwehrkompanie*. H.Dv. 130/5. Berlin, 1938.

―――――. *Die Ständige Front*. Teil 1. *Der Abwehr in Ständiger Front*. H.Dv. 89/1. Berlin, 1940.

―――――. *Die Ständige Front*. Teil 2. *Der Kampf der Infanterie*. H.Dv. 89/2. Berlin, 1940.

―――――. *Pionierdienst aller Waffen*. H.Dv. 316. Berlin, 1935.

―――――. *Richtlinien für Führung und Einsatz der Panzer-Division*. D-66. Berlin, 1940.

―――――. *Truppenführung*. Teil 2. H.Dv. 300/2. 1934. Reprint. Berlin, 1941.

Ogorkiewicz, Richard M. *Armor: A History of Mechanized Forces*. New York: Frederick A. Praeger, 1960.

O'Neill, Robert J. "Doctrine and Training in the German Army, 1919—1939." In *The Theory and Practice of War*, edited by Michael Howard. New York: Frederick A. Praeger, 1966.

Ott, Ernst. *Jäger am Feind. Geschichte und Opfergang der 97. Jäger-Division 1940—1945*. Munich: Kameradschaft der Spielhahnjäger, 1966.

Peter, Edler Ritter von, and Kurt von Tippelskirch. *Das Panzerabwehrbuch*. Berlin: Offene Worte, 1937.

Pitt, Barrie. *1918: The Last Act*. New York: W. W. Norton and Co., 1963.

Plocher, Hermann. *The German Air Force Versus Russia, 1941*. Edited by Harry R. Fletcher. USAF Historical Studies no. 153. New York: Arno Press, 1968.

Pospelov, P. N., et al., eds. *Great Patriotic War of the Soviet Union, 1941—1945: A General Outline*. Translated by David Skvirsky and Vic Schneierson. Moscow: Progress Publishers, 1974.

——— . *Istoriya Velikoi Otechestvennoi Voiny Sovetskogo Soyuza 1941—1945*. 6 vols. Moscow: Voenizdat, 1961.

Rabenau, Friedrich von. *Seeckt: Aus seinem Leben 1918—1936*. Leipzig: Von Hasse und Koehler, 1940.

Reichswehrministerium. *Führung und Gefecht der verbundenen Waffen*. 2 vols. Berlin: Offene Worte, 1921—23.

——— . *Truppenführung*. H.Dv. 300/1, dated October 1933. Reprint. Berlin, 1936.

Reinhardt, Klaus. *Die Wende vor Moskau: Das Scheitern der Strategie Hitlers im Winter 1941—1942*. Stuttgart: Deutsche Verlags-Anstalt, 1972.

Reitlinger, Gerald. *The SS: Alibi of a Nation, 1922—1945*. Englewood Cliffs, NJ: Prentice Hall, 1981.

Ritter, Hans. *Kritik des Weltkrieges: Das Erbe Moltkes und Schlieffen im grossen Kriege*. Leipzig: K. F. Koehler, 1920.

Röhricht, Edgar. *Probleme der Kesselschlacht*. Karlsruhe: Condor-Verlag, 1958.

Römhild, Helmut. *Die Geschichte der 269. Infanterie-Division*. Bad Nauheim: Podzun-Verlag, 1967.

Rosinski, Herbert. *The German Army*. Rev. ed. Washington, DC: Infantry Journal, 1944.

Sajer, Guy. *The Forgotten Soldier*. Translated by Lily Emmet. New York: Harper and Row, 1971.

Schmidt, August. *Geschichte der 10. Division, 1933—1945*. Bad Nauheim: Podzun Verlag, 1963.

Schramm, Percy Ernst, ed. *Kriegstagebuch des Oberkommandos der Wehrmacht 1940—1945*. 4 vols. Frankfurt am Main: Bernard und Graefe Verlag für Wehrwesen, 1965.

Seaton, Albert. *The Battle for Moscow, 1941—1942*. London: Rupert Hart-Davis, 1971.

——— . *The German Army, 1933—1945*. New York: St. Martin's Press, 1982.

——— . *The Russo-German War, 1941—1945*. New York: Praeger Publishers, 1970.

Seeckt, Hans von. *Die Reichswehr*. Leipzig: R. Kittler, 1933.

——— . *Landesverteidigung*. Berlin: Verlag für Kulturpolitik, 1930.

——— . *Thoughts of a Soldier*. Translated by Gilbert Waterhouse. London: E. Benn, 1930.

Senger und Etterlin, Frido von. *Neither Fear Nor Hope*. Translated by George Malcolm. New York: E. P. Dutton and Co., 1964.

Steiger, Rudolf. *Panzertaktik im Spiegel deutscher Kriegstagebücher 1939—1941*. Freiburg: Rombach, 1973.

Stein, George H. *The Waffen SS: Hitler's Elite Guard at War, 1939—1945*. Ithaca, NY: Cornell University Press, 1966.

Sydnor, Charles W. *Soldiers of Destruction: The SS Death's Head Division, 1933—1945*. Princeton, NJ: Princeton University Press, 1977.

The Treaty of Peace with Germany, June 28, 1919. [Versailles Treaty]. Washington, DC, 1920.

Trevor-Roper, H. R., ed. *Blitzkrieg to Defeat: Hitler's War Directives, 1939—1945*. New York: Holt, Rinehart, and Winston, 1964.

Trial of the Major War Criminals Before the International Military Tribunal, Nuremberg, 14 November 1945—1 October 1946. 42 vols. Nuremberg: International Military Tribunal, 1947—49.

Turney, Alfred. *Disaster at Moscow: Von Bock's Campaigns, 1941—1942*. London: Cassell and Co., 1971.

U.S. Army War College. Center for Land Warfare. *1985 Art of War Symposium: From the Dnepr to the Vistula—Soviet Offensive Operations, November 1943—August 1944, a Transcript of Proceedings*. Carlisle Barracks, PA: U.S. Army War College, August 1985.

———. *1984 Art of War Symposium: From the Don to the Dnepr—Soviet Offensive Operations, December 1942—August 1943, a Transcript of Proceedings*. Carlisle Barracks, PA: U.S. Army War College, October 1985.

U.S. Department of the Army. Pamphlet no. 20—201. *Military Improvisations During the Russian Campaign*. Washington, DC: U.S. Government Printing Office, 1951.

———. Pamphlet no. 20—202. *German Tank Maintenance in World War II*. Washington, DC: U.S. Government Printing Office, 1954.

———. Pamphlet no. 20—233. *German Defense Tactics Against Russian Breakthroughs*. Washington, DC: U.S. Government Printing Office, 1951.

———. Pamphlet no. 20—234. *Operations of Encircled Forces: German Experiences in Russia*. Washington, DC: U.S. Government Printing Office, 1952.

———. Pamphlet no. 20—255. *The German Campaign in Poland (1939)*. By Robert M. Kennedy. Washington, DC: U.S. Government Printing Office, 1956.

———. Pamphlet no. 20—261a. *The German Campaign in Russia: Planning and Operations, 1940—1942*. By George E. Blau. Washington, DC: U.S. Government Printing Office, 1955

———. Pamphlet no. 20—291. *Effects of Climate on Combat in European Russia*. Washington, DC: U.S. Government Printing Office, 1952.

U.S. War Department. TM-E 30—451. *Handbook on German Military Forces*. Washington, DC: U.S. Government Printing Office, 1945.

Van Creveld, Martin. *Supplying War*. London: Cambridge University Press, 1977.

Warlimont, Walter. *Inside Hitler's Headquarters, 1939—1945*. Translated by R. H. Barry. New York: Frederick A. Praeger, 1964.

Werthen, Wolfgang. *Geschichte der 16. Panzer-Division 1939—1945*. Bad Nauheim: Hans-Henning Podzun, 1958.

Wetzel, G., ed. *Die Deutsche Wehrmacht*. Berlin, 1939.

Wilhelm, Crown Prince of Germany. *My War Experiences*. London: Hurst and Blackett, 1923.

Wynne, Graeme C. *If Germany Attacks: The Battle in Depth in the West*. 1940. Reprint. Westport, CT: Greenwood Press, 1976.

Ziemke, Earl F. *Stalingrad to Berlin: The German Defeat in the East*. Army Historical Series. Washington, DC: Office of the Chief of Military History, U.S. Army, 1968.

Zhukov, G. K. *Vospominaniya i razmyshleniya*. Moscow: Novosti Press, 1971.

Periodical Articles

Eimannsberger, Ludwig von. "Panzertaktik." *Militär-Wochenblatt* no. 26 (8 January 1937).

Erickson, John. "The Soviet Response to Surprise Attack: Three Directives, 22 June 1941." *Soviet Studies* 23 (April 1972).

Klingbeil, Generalmajor. "Das Problem 'Stellungskrieg.'" *Militär-Wochenblatt* no. 36 (19 March 1937).

Murray, Williamson. "The German Response to Victory in Poland: A Case Study in Professionalism." *Armed Forces and Society* 7 (Winter 1981).

"Panzerabwehr in der Praxis." *Militär-Wochenblatt* no. 18 (29 October 1937).

Phipps, Michael A. "A Forgotten War." *Infantry* 74 (November—December 1984).

Ryazanskiy, A. "Taktika tankovikh voisk v godi velikoi otechestvennoi voinie." *Voyenny Vestnik* (May 1967).

Samsonov, F. "Artilleriya v hodie voinie." *Voyenny Vestnik* (May 1965).

Sella, Amnon. "'Barbarossa': Surprise Attack and Communication." *Journal of Contemporary History* 13 (July 1978).

―――. "Red Army Doctrine and Training on the Eve of the Second World War." *Soviet Studies* 27 (April 1975).

Sieberg, Major. Untitled commentary on fighting in Spain. *Militär-Wochenblatt* no. 33 (11 February 1938).

Stein, George H. "The Myth of a European Army." *Wiener Library Bulletin* 19 (April 1965).

"Truppenführung. Stellungskrieg, Stosstrupp-Unternehmen und Angriff mit begrenzten Ziele." *Militär-Wochenblatt* no. 23 (2 December 1938).

"Truppen-Kriegsgeschichte: Gegenangriff des R.I.R. 93 am 15.8.1917." *Militär-Wochenblatt* no. 38 (18 March 1938) and no. 39 (25 March 1938).

Wilt, Alan V. "Hitler's Late Summer Pause in 1941." *Military Affairs* 45 (December 1981).

Wynne, Graeme C. "The Legacy." *Army Quarterly* 39 (October 1939 and January 1940).

Yekimovskiy, A. "Taktika sovietskoi armii v velikoi otechestvennoi voinye." *Voyenny Vestnik* (April 1967).

Zhukov, G. K. "Kontrnastupleniye pod Moskvoi." *Voyenno-Istoricheskiy Zhurnal* (October 1966).

Foreign Military Studies, Historical Division, U.S. Army, Europe

Begun in Europe while the authors were Allied prisoners of war, the Foreign Military Studies were completed in the 1950s under the auspices of what is now the U.S. Army's Office of the Chief of Military History. Copies of the typescript manuscripts repose in the National Archives, Washington, D.C., and the U.S. Army Military History Institute, Carlisle Barracks, Pennsylvania. Other Army research libraries have copies of some but not all of the studies.

MS B-226	Wentzell, Fritz. "Combat in the East." 1952.
MS B-690	Blumentritt, Günther. "The Main Line of Resistance." 1947.
MS B-705	Blumentritt, Günther. "Advance Elements and Combat Outposts." 1947.
MS B-706	Blumentritt, Günther. "The Forward Position." 1947.
MS C-034	Hoehne, Gustav. "In Snow and Mud: 31 Days of Attack Under Seydlitz During Early Spring of 1942." 1953.
MS C-065a	Greiner, Helmuth. "Greiner Diary Notes, 12 Aug 1942—12 Mar 1943." 1950.
MS D-050	Prellberg, Werner. "Employment of Flak in an Army Defense Zone." 1947.
MS D-106	Rendulic, Lothar. "Combat in Deep Snow." 1947.
MS D-134	Koehler, Wilhelm. "Engagements Fought by the 488th Infantry Regiment at the Stryanitsa and Desna Rivers (6—29 Sep 1941)." 1947.
MS D-154	Moelhoff, Klaus. "Experiences with Russian Methods of Warfare and Their Utilization in Training at the Waffen-SS Panzer Grenadier School." 1947.
MS D-156	"The Construction of a Strategic Defense Line in the East." 1947.
MS D-223	Dippold, Benignus. "Commitment of the 183rd Infantry Division." 1947.
MS D-231	Zeltmann, Otto. "Closing of the Large Gap in the Front Between Demidov and Velikiye Luki in 1942." 1947.
MS D-241	Tiemann, Otto. "Closing the 40-km Gap Between Army Group North and Army Group Center (Nov 1942—March 1943.)" 1947.

MS D-248	Steiner, Felix. "Tactics of Mobile Units. Operations of the 5th Panzergrenadier Division 'Wiking' at Rostov and the Maikop Oilfields (Summer 1942)." 1947.
MS D-251	Prinner, Josef. "Organization, Advance and Combat of the 81st Artillery Regiment in 1941." 1947.
MS D-253	Schneider, Erich. "Antitank Defense in the East." 1947.
MS D-254	Schulz, Paul. "Combat in the Caucasus Woods and Mountains During Autumn 1942." 1947.
MS D-262	Morzik, Friedrich. "Supply by Air of the Demyansk Fortress During the Encirclement from 15 Feb to 19 May 1942." 1947.
MS D-282	Russwurm, Wilhelm. "Employment of a Furlough Detachment for Rear Area Security (Don, Donets, Winter 1942—43)." 1947.
MS D-285	Roman, Rudolf von. "The 35th Infantry Division Between Moscow and Gzhatsk, 1941." 1947.
MS D-291	Utz, Willibald. "Experiences of a Mountain Infantry Regiment During the Battle of the Volkhov River (Mar—May 1942)." 1947.
MS D-298	Schulz, Paul. "Position Warfare in Winter 1941—1942 and Experiences." 1947.
MS D-370	Unruh, Walter von. "Combat Staff Unruh." N.d.
MS P-006	Reinhardt, Hellmuth, et al. "Personnel and Administration Project 2b: Part I." 1948.
MS P-060f	Mueller-Hillebrand, Burkhart. "Small Unit Tactics—Tactics of Individual Arms (Part II)." 1951.
MS P-062	Toppe, Alfred. "Frostbite Problems in the German Army During World War II." 1951.
MS P-078	Munzel, Oskar. "Wartime Training of Panzer Troops." 1951.
MS P-089	Munzel, Oskar. "Tactical and Technical Specialties of Winter Warfare." 1951.
MS P-093	Ulmenstein, Freiherr von. "161st Reconnaissance Battalion (21 Jun 1941—30 Jun 1942) and 132d Bicycle Battalion (17 Oct 1942—17 May 1943): Extracts from War Diaries." 1954.
MS P-114a	Mueller-Hillebrand, Burkhart. "Der Feldzug gegen die Sowjetunion im Nordabschnitt der Ostfront (Zweiter Teil: Dezember 1941—Dezember 1942)." 1954.
MS P-143a	Reinhardt, Hellmuth, et al. "Selected Army Operations on the Eastern Front." [1954].
MS P-143b	Reinhardt, Hellmuth. "Selected Corps Operations on the Eastern Front." 1954.
MS P-143c	Reinhardt, Hellmuth, et al. "Selected Divisional Operations on the Eastern Front." 1954.

MS P-194	Willemer, Wilhelm. "Organization of the Ground for Defense on a Broad Front, as Defended by an Army or Larger Unit." 1954.
MS T-11	Guderian, Heinz. "Flank Defense in Far-Reaching Operations." 1948.
MS T-15	Schulz, Friedrich, et al. "Reverses on the Southern Wing (1942—1943)." 1947.
MS T-28	Greiffenberg, Hans von, et al. "Battle of Moscow, 1941—42."

Interviews

Garn, Arnulf von, Colonel (Ret.). Carlisle Barracks, PA, 21 May 1986.

Lemm, Heinz-Georg, Lieutenant General (Ret.). Carlisle Barracks, PA, 2 May 1985.

Niepold, Gerd, Lieutenant General (Ret.). Carlisle Barracks, PA, 3 May 1985.

Plato, Anton-Detlev von, Lieutenant General (Ret.). Carlisle Barracks, PA, 2 May 1985.

Senger und Etterlin, Ferdinand von, General (Ret.). Carlisle Barracks, PA, 2 May 1985.

Documents

Numerous original German documents were consulted for this paper and are listed in detail in the notes. These documents are from the National Archives Microcopy Series T-78 (Records of Headquarters, German Army High Command) and Series T-312 (Records of German Field Commands, Armies).

www.ingramcontent.com/pod-product-compliance
Lightning Source LLC
Chambersburg PA
CBHW080538170426
43195CB00016B/2604